# MANAGING SCHOOL FINANCE

*Heinemann Organization in Schools Series*
General Editor: Michael Marland

COMPREHENSIVE VALUES
P. E. Daunt

THE ENVIRONMENT OF LEARNING
Elizabeth Richardson

IN-SCHOOL EVALUATION
Marten Shipman

SCHOOL DECISION-MAKING
Cyril Poster

LEADERSHIP IN SCHOOLS
Denys John

TIMETABLE PLANNING
John Brookes

HEAD OF DEPARTMENT
Michael Marland

DEPARTMENTAL MANAGEMENT
Michael Marland and Sydney Hill

RESOURCE-BASED LEARNING
Norman Beswick

LANGUAGE ACROSS THE CURRICULUM
Michael Marland

THE CREATIVE ARTS
Malcolm Ross

PASTORAL CARE
Michael Marland

PERSPECTIVES ON PASTORAL CARE
Ron Best, Colin Jarvis and Peter Ribbins

THE TUTOR
Keith Blackburn

MIDDLE SCHOOLS
Tom Gannon and Alan Whalley

SIXTH-FORM COLLEGES
Eric Macfarlane

EDUCATION FOR THE INNER CITY
Michael Marland

THE LEICESTERSHIRE PLAN
A. N. Fairbairn

SCHOOL-FOCUSSED IN-SERVICE TRAINING
Ray Bolam

COMMUNITY EDUCATION: ITS DEVELOPMENT AND MANAGEMENT
Cyril Poster

THE PRIMARY HEAD
Patrick Whitaker

RESPONSIBILITY AND PROMOTION IN THE PRIMARY SCHOOL
Derek Waters

HEAD OF HOUSE, HEAD OF YEAR
Keith Blackburn

EDUCATION AND CARE
Ron Best, Colin Jarvis, Peter Ribbins and D. Oddy

MANAGING SCHOOL FINANCE
B. A. A. Knight

# Managing School Finance

Brian A. A. Knight
*Headmaster, Holyrood School, Chard*

HEINEMANN EDUCATIONAL BOOKS
LONDON

Heinemann Educational Books Ltd
22 Bedford Square, London WC1B 3HH
LONDON EDINBURGH MELBOURNE AUCKLAND
HONG KONG SINGAPORE KUALA LUMPUR NEW DELHI
IBADAN NAIROBI JOHANNESBURG
EXETER (NH) KINGSTON PORT OF SPAIN


First published 1983

**British Library CIP Data**

Knight, Brian
Managing school finance. – (Organization in schools)
1. Education – England – Finances
I. Title II. Series
379.1'0942 LB2901

ISBN 0 435 80480 4



Printed and bound in Great Britain by Biddles Ltd, Guildford
Phototypesetting by Georgia Origination, Liverpool

# Contents

# Foreword

Teachers are so concerned with studying the effects of the shortage of money in schools that few of them who plan and manage schools or departments have the opportunity to study the effects of their expenditure. Indeed few of those responsible for budgets within schools, whether headteachers, heads of department, or others, have the training or knowledge to make such a study. Yet it is clear that in the British educational system which allows considerable autonomy to individual schools, they have a duty, especially at times of financial stringency, to ensure that society is getting good value for money, and that educational aims are supported by the financial strategy.

Brian Knight has done education a most important service in bringing the question of school finance into discussions about school management and administration. Very little work has previously been done on school costs, and what has been available has not often been from the perspective of those who work in schools. Mr Knight has looked at finance from the viewpoint of the school.

The Heinemann Organization in School Series is a systematic and wide-ranging attempt to help those working in schools to improve the planning and thus the quality of schooling by a methodical study of the ways in which schools can be organized and administered. The books relate theory to practice in the belief that the one illuminates the other, and that the planning that takes place in schools needs to be rooted not only in a knowledge of that school, that area and those pupils, but also in an understanding of the research, ideas, and observation of others.

Brian Knight writes primarily as a practising headteacher involved in the management of a comprehensive school, but he bases his analysis on a careful study of all that has been written on the subject in this country and the United States. He has served on numerous working parties dealing with finance and has therefore had the benefit of discussions with many practitioners and academic analysts. The result is a unique book that will be useful to headteachers and their deputies in all schools, secondary school heads of departments and those with pastoral responsibility, governors, and LEA administrators.

MICHAEL MARLAND

# Preface

This book is based on three assumptions: that the study of school costs has been woefully neglected; that the repair of this neglect would ease our present problems; and that proper professional management of school finance could open new possibilities for our schools. It is therefore intended to be a practical book. It is written mainly for heads, deputies, and heads of departments; for educational administrators and bursars; for officers in treasurers' departments; for school governors and members of education committees; and for providers of in-service courses.

This book would not have been possible without help from many people. I would like to acknowledge with gratitude the encouragement I have received - particularly from Mr Barry Taylor, Chief Education Officer for Somerset, Miss Mary Ollis, Educational Research Executive, Longman Group, and Mr Tudor David, Editor of *Education*, who also kindly allowed me to use some material from articles of mine published in *Education*. I am most grateful to many officers in the Somerset Education and Treasurer's Departments who have answered my queries so patiently, and in particular to Mr Derek Esp, First Deputy Chief Education Officer, Mr Reg Brice, until recently Education Officer, long-time prophet of devolution, and to Mr Mike Pollard of the Treasurer's Department.

I am most indebted for information and advice to Mr R. H. Merrett, Headmaster of Plymouth College, Lt Cdr K. E. Williams, Bursar of Plymouth College, and to three Somerset headteacher colleagues, including Mr John Brice and Mr Chris Smith. I am also most grateful to Mr K. G. Ilett and Mr J. K. Roberts for being permitted to use their dissertations, and to Miss Helen Quigley, Head of the N U T Research Unit, for assistance. There are many others who have given assistance whom I cannot name individually but whose help I have greatly appreciated.

I would like to give particular thanks to Mr John Delany, Head of the Financial Services Division of the Department of Education and Science, who gave invaluable advice on the technical aspects of cost accounting in education; and to Dr Jim Hough, of the Education Department, Loughborough University, and Mr Joe Butterworth, Group Accountant of the Somerset County Council Treasurer's

Department, both of whom have given help and advice as well as reading through and commenting on the text.

I would also like to acknowledge the help of my teaching colleagues at Holyrood School, and in particular their patience with my fixation on the flexible use of school time; and the non-teaching staff, who have helped so often with my queries, in particular the Bursar, Mr Jim Davies.

Finally I owe a great deal to the encouragement of my family. My wife Joan typed the manuscript and helped in innumerable other ways. To her I owe more than I can say.

# PART ONE

# Analysing the Past

# 1 A Small Pinch of Theory

First, a brief excursion into some of the basic definitions and concepts necessary for cost analysis and management. Classroom practitioners should not be too impatient; the theory illuminates the more practical chapters that follow.

## *Definition of 'costs'*

We are all familiar with costs in our everyday lives. So we tend to think of costs in money terms. However, not all costs are immediately financial. For example, a new educational development may cost money. But it may also have cost implications in terms of buildings. Increased use may lead to greater maintenance, or other hidden costs; it may lead to under-use – which is an idle cost. It may have cost implications in terms of equipment. Community use of a school, for example, may lead to greater wear of its sports gear. Costs may even occur in terms of time. An innovation may cause a teacher or an administrator to spend an excessive portion of his/her time on it. The hidden cost of this may be that some of his/her other duties are less well done, or perhaps ultimately that jobs within the school or within the authority have to be restructured, and even additional staff appointed. Some of these non-financial costs can be evaluated in financial terms. For others we need to be aware of the costs, even if we cannot measure them.

*Examples of non-financial costs*

1 Teachers' time. Each teacher sets a limit on the amount of time he/she will devote to his/her job. Time spent on one activity may prevent time being spent on another.
2 Students' travel. The time of a long journey could be spent in more useful ways, and may reduce school-efficiency.
3 Students' earnings foregone – a very real cost to families with children at school over 16. This is acknowledged when local education authorities give maintenance allowances, and when labour economists regard it as investment to produce enhanced later earnings.

4 Students' nutrition. The currently fashionable cafeteria systems for school meals undoubtedly reduce a school's costs. But anyone surveying the production line of chips-with-everything must wonder at the nutritional costs! (Similarly, tuck-shops are a welcome support to capitation allowances – but at what dental cost?)
5 Packed lunches – no expense to the school, but a definite cost for parents.
6 Heating homes. The continental day could reduce school heating costs, but be replaced by a less obvious cost for parents.
7 Vandalism – a cost for the community, in time and environmental terms, as well as in rectification.

At the frontier of non-financial costs are the intangibles like the morale, health, motivation and energy of teachers and students; in the workplace, labour stability and adaptability, skills, industrial relations; in the community, social problems of many shades. But it is arguable whether these are costs, or factors influencing costs, or effects of alternative school processes.

*Example of mixed financial and non-financial costs.* The closure of a small village school is proposed. Financial costs saved include the extra teacher necessary for a small school, the costs of the premises (to be sold) – offset by some additional transport and meals costs. Non-financial costs include the effect on the community of the loss of its social centre and time spent by children travelling – offset perhaps by educational gains of children in a larger school.

Costs then cannot always be stated in money units. But those that can be are easily quantified and more easily compared.

John Fielden (1980a) put it nicely:

> Costing is the art of measuring the consumption of resources in financial terms. Contrary to most perceptions there can be a large element of subjectivity in costing exercises. There are often no easy ways of measuring resources use or of converting it into money terms, and the person carrying out the costing will therefore have to make assumptions or value judgements.

Two possible definitions of costs are: a monetary measure of the amount of resources used for some purpose, and resources sacrificed or foregone to achieve a specific objective. Neither definition is exhaustive. The former is limited to the narrower range of financial costs; the latter is broader, but depends upon our interpretation of resources. And neither clarifies which costs should be included or excluded. Textbooks and stationery, teachers' salaries and fuel oil, light bulbs and floor polish, should obviously be included in a school's costs. But what about the cost of the visiting careers officer or adviser? Of county administration? Of the local HMI? Of the professional training of teachers before they begin their careers? Should these be included? Even simple items are not necessarily so simple. If future legislation required parents to pay for transport, or for textbooks, should this change immediately delete these items from a school's costs? So, for any cost analysis the costs to be included or excluded need to be clearly defined, and assumptions made explicit.

## *Opportunity costs*

The second definition leads to another aspect - opportunity costs. Opportunity costs arise when we choose or retain a particular item and reject or ignore the next best alternative.

*Example.* A science adviser tells a head that he/she has some money in hand for the purchase of microscopes. The head accepts with gratitude, although he feels that a higher priority would be to expand the basic equipment in one of his laboratories. This is a clear example of an opportunity cost, the 'opportunity' which a particular sum of money would buy if it was not spent in this particular way.

If the opportunity foregone appears of greater value than the opportunity accepted, then the expenditure is misconceived. The education service is riddled with examples of this 'separate pocket' mentality. A greater awareness of the existence of opportunity costs would bring great benefit at every level of the service.

## *Direct and indirect costs*

Cost information is like any other data base. It needs to be organized into a pattern before significance can be read into it. The cost data of a school can be arranged in numerous different ways to bring out different features.

In industry costs are normally divided into two groups, direct costs and indirect costs. The former are costs which can be easily identified with a cost centre (a cost centre may be a factory, or more commonly a department within the factory). The latter are costs which cannot be so identified and have to be apportioned (loosely called overheads). So if a department has a separately metered electricity bill, electricity is a direct cost; if the bill relates to the factory as a whole, electricity is an indirect cost. This division is extensively used and has obvious value in controlling costs and setting prices.

*Example.* In a shoe factory, leather and the labour involved in working on the leather are a direct cost; rates for the premises, the salary of the personnel manager and publicity expenses are all examples of indirect costs.

It is tempting to take a similar approach to the costs of a school. But it should be clearly understood that the distinction between direct and indirect costs lies in the technicalities of how the account is presented. On this basis, almost all school-centred costs will be direct – salaries, purchase of books, materials, etc., rates, heating, lighting, aids to pupils, meals and transport; and most LEA-centred costs indirect – administration and inspection and numerous specialist services, such as architects, psychologists, grounds, residential centres, museum service, etc. It seems to me that this is not a very helpful distinction, and that it is much more profitable to think in terms of prime and subsidiary costs.

## *Prime and subsidiary costs*

A school's prime function is educational. Its catering, transport and administrative functions are clearly subsidiary. So, examples of

Fully prime costs ↓

Teachers' salaries and employers' contributions
Capitation allowances
Non-teaching support costs (ancillary staff salaries and employers' contributions
National cost of initial teacher training
In-service education for teachers
Interview and advertisement expenses

---

Water
Heating and light
Upkeep of premises and grounds –materials and equipment
Upkeep of premises and grounds –salaries and employers' contributions
Rates

---

School administrative costs (clerical salaries and employers' contributions, postage and telephone charges, telephone rental)
Central LEA advisory and special service costs

---

Central LEA administative costs
National DES and other administrative costs

---

Free meals, maintenance allowances
Transport costs
Meals costs

Fully subsidiary costs

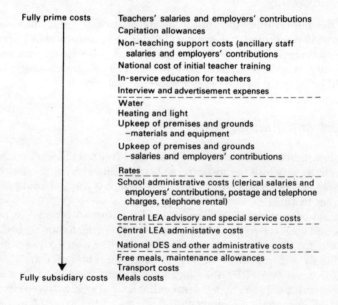

Fig. 1:1 Prime and subsidiary school costs

prime costs would be chalk, textbooks, hire of films, teachers' salaries. Examples of subsidiary costs would be school meals costs, transport costs, postage, LEA administration (to many laymen 'overheads'). However, we soon find that black-and-white theory goes through every shade of grey in practice. It is not always easy to classify items. Borderline examples would be teachers' in-service training, or the salaries of laboratory technicians, or materials for the upkeep of playing fields. It is really much more helpful to think in terms of a gradation from completely prime costs moving through intermediate stages to completely subsidiary, the grouping being judged by the distance of the items from the classroom encounter. Figure 1:1 attempts to list school costs in this way.

We have obviously moved out of the quantifiable area into the realm of value judgements. Indeed, you may well disagree with the niceties of the ranking given. However, the general concept of prime and subsidiary costs is important. Even though it cannot always be applied with precision, it does focus our attention on the relationship of the costs which are directly and closely related to the prime function of the institution and those which are not.

## *Reallocation of costs: 'Full-cost accounting'*

Using the concept of this prime/subsidiary axis of costs, it is possible to go further and reallocate some of the overhead costs among chalk-face operations. For example, almost all the central and administrative costs of an educational authority can be placed in a separate cost category, or they can be reallocated to the chalk-face. This process of reallocation may be a notional one, to provide insights and allow comparisons, or it may be an actual reallocation by 'recharging'. (See Chapter 13.) It rests upon the theory that *costs should be ultimately measured at the cost centre where they are consumed*, not at the point where they are first incurred.

Some of these central costs can be allocated easily. For example, the cost of county residential centres can be reallocated among the user schools in proportion to usage. At the other extreme, it is rather more difficult to reallocate the chief education officer's salary to the schools that he/she serves. However, even such central expenses which cannot be easily reallocated on the basis of service to the institution concerned can at least be divided on some rational basis. For example, one could divide the central administrative costs of a local authority among primary schools, secondary schools and colleges in the ratio of the total costs of those three types of centres, and then reallocate within each category to individual schools and colleges on a per capita or similar proportionate basis. Obviously reallocation of costs cannot be precise, and once again we are into the area of value judgements in deciding the basis for it. Nevertheless, it still has considerable use. In particular it does put a quantitative value upon the services provided by central and other agencies for institutions, and allows some assessment of the opportunity costs involved.

*Example*. If it was shown that the reallocated costs of the educational psychological service to a particular secondary school in one year was £1,000, and if in fact the school had received total assistance from that service amounting to a single one hour visit during that year, then several questions arise. Is the service unreasonably costly? Could it be better provided in an alternative

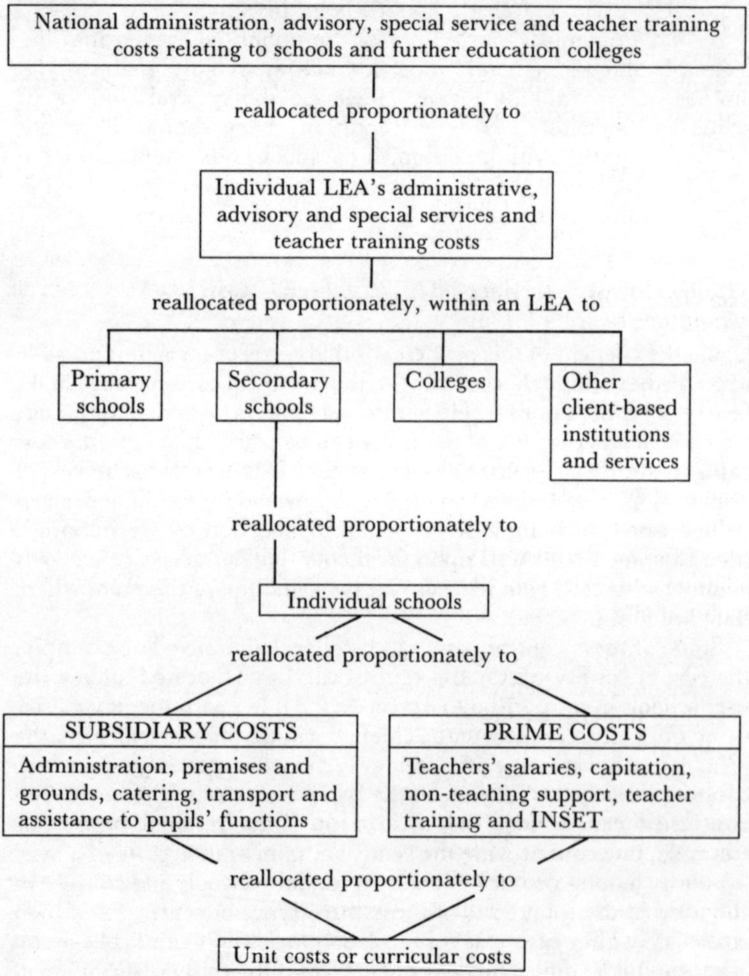


**Fig. 1:2** Reallocation of educational costs

form? Or is the school making unreasonably little use of it? Could the amount be better used elsewhere – the opportunity cost – assuming that it could actually be redeployed? Or possibly, is the basis of allocation unsound? An important point about this example is that it is only through the reallocation of costs that these questions are raised. Without it, the figure would probably not even be known to the service's users, and certainly not questioned.

One can think of this reallocation of costs rippling downwards from the highest level to the lowest, from the remotest cost centre to the chalk-face (Figure 1:2). This process is termed 'full-cost accounting'. It seeks to establish the full cost of a school's educational functions, by reallocating indirect or service costs.

Full-cost accounting may appear to be a complicated, theoretical exercise. Educational administrators tend to dismiss it. Yet it is not really that complicated. It can be developed quite simply on a formula basis from readily available data. Significantly, it is widely used in industry – because it establishes what *total* costs really are. Failure to use it masks the real costs of operating a school. Obviously the basis for reallocation will sometimes be debatable and even crude. However, it does offer insights and raise questions which would not be found in any other way.

## *Variable and fixed costs*

The distinction between variable and fixed costs is a very important one in the industrial and commercial field. Variable costs are those which change in proportion to the quantitative changes in the processes of the industry; fixed costs are those which remain unchanged for a given period of time, despite fluctuations in the volume of the activity undertaken.

*Example.* In a shoe factory, the quantities of leather, thread and glue used will be directly related to the number of shoes produced, while the rent of the factory will remain unaltered whether the factory is on overtime or short time.

In industry this distinction is of great importance. Constant watchfulness is needed to keep fixed costs as low as possible and to increase the volume of activity so that they are spread more thinly upon each item of production. Fixed costs are not, of course, fixed in the other sense. They will vary from time to time – rates and rents may go up, for example – but this variation is related to external factors, not to internal changes in the volume of production.

Schools are a different type of organization and their costs do not rapidly reflect fluctuations in volume of pupils. However, the distinction is still important. It is particularly important at a time of falling rolls, when a number of costs may remain completely or relatively fixed, even though the number of pupils may fall dramatically.

However, although the concept is important, its use in practice is more difficult. Once again black and white shades into grey. At one extreme we find costs which clearly vary in exact proportion to the number of pupils. The best example are capitation allowances for textbooks, stationery, materials and equipment, which by definition are allocated per capita to the school's population. An almost equally close relationship to pupil numbers will be found attached to examination fees, free school meals, and uniform and maintenance allowances, although these of course may be affected by other external factors as well. At the other extreme, the best example of fixed costs are debt charges and telephone rentals. However, in between we find some costs which respond broadly in line with pupil numbers but with some lag – for example, teachers' salaries; others which are considerably affected such as meals and transport costs; others which are affected to some degree such as heating and lighting, and finally others which may be affected to some extent, but probably only after a substantial change in numbers and after a considerable time-lag – for example, central administration costs, the specialized central

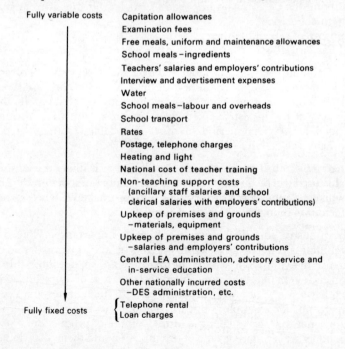

Fully variable costs ↓

- Capitation allowances
- Examination fees
- Free meals, uniform and maintenance allowances
- School meals – ingredients
- Teachers' salaries and employers' contributions
- Interview and advertisement expenses
- Water
- School meals – labour and overheads
- School transport
- Rates
- Postage, telephone charges
- Heating and light
- National cost of teacher training
- Non-teaching support costs (ancillary staff salaries and school clerical salaries with employers' contributions)
- Upkeep of premises and grounds – materials, equipment
- Upkeep of premises and grounds – salaries and employers' contributions
- Central LEA administration, advisory service and in-service education
- Other nationally incurred costs – DES administration, etc.

Fully fixed costs: Telephone rental; Loan charges

**Fig. 1:3** Variable and fixed school costs

services, in-service education, salaries of non-teaching staff, upkeep of premises.

All costs can be placed on a variable/fixed axis (see Figure 1:3). In one sense no costs are totally 'fixed'. Even loan charges, for example, are only fixed as long as that particular school building is still in use. If it is possible to amalgamate two schools and to sell one of the buildings, then at that point, they become a variable cost. It is important to appreciate that costs that appear fixed may over a longer time-scale be open to variation. This is particularly important in the school situation, because the slow annual rhythm of schools makes some costs often appear more fixed than they actually are. Part III attempts to explore some of the areas where radical changes could bring substantial variations in such fixed costs.

## *Controllable and non-controllable costs*

Who controls costs? The question is not as simple as it sounds. In accounting convention, costs are normally managed by those who hold budget responsibility for them. So a manager is responsible for all his or her budget costs except those which are completely fixed during the period in question. Budgetary responsibility is aimed at identifying the person who has the most effective cost control over the item concerned.

But in real school life the situation is not so clear. Obviously the head has virtually no control over, say, county administrative costs or transport costs. But on the other hand the central LEA administration may have little influence or control over the heating or lighting costs, even though these are clearly its budgetary responsibility. So the concept of budgetary responsibility encounters the same blurring as the two axes considered earlier. For example, the cost of the teaching salaries in a school will be influenced by the preference of the head or others responsible for the appointment of younger or older teachers. But it will also be affected by decisions of the LEA concerning staffing scales and allocation of points for responsibility allowances – and by national pay awards. In the same way, examination fees will be affected considerably by the examination entry policy of the school, but they will also be affected by LEA regulations.

Reference to Figure 1:1 shows that most of the prime costs are incurred on the site of the school. In the maintained sector almost all are controlled under current practice by the LEA, although influenced by the school staff. Even capitation, although expended by the school, is controlled in total by the LEA. In independent schools all costs are controlled at the school level. So some fundamental questions are now beginning to emerge. This realization brings its own insights. It emphasizes those costs which react most easily to control; it determines where control lies, and asks us to consider the best levels for control (this area is discussed much more fully in Chapter 13); and it stresses that control must be related to time – many changes are impossible in three months, but quite possible in three years.

## *Unit, marginal, and incremental costs*

The simplistic view is that unit costs are total costs divided by the number of units involved. This is broadly correct – but in practice unit costs come in all shapes and sizes. For example, total costs are not self-evident. It will often be a matter of contention as to exactly what component costs should be included. So currently a number of studies into school unit costs are not comparable because each takes a different cost base. Often totals should be disaggregated. For example, unit costs per pupil in two schools may be of limited value if one school has 30 per cent of its pupils over 16. So we often need to subdivide totals according to age of pupils, type of activity, etc.

Similarly, the divisor-units show equal variety. We can choose input units – £s, space, etc. – or output units – pupils, examination passes, etc. We can choose historic cost units, standard units (equivalent to the standard costs used in industry), or modelling units ('what will happen if . . .?'). Units can be pupils, or classes, or schools; meals, journeys, or courses; they can be units of time, hours, or lessons, or days; or any other useful unit. They give insight, often dramatically. Try waving two £10 notes in front of a pupil who is thoroughly idle – the cost of his week's education – and ask him if the ratepayers have had their money's-worth this week! They are also very useful for comparisons – between schools, for example, or over a period of time.

But such unit costs lack dynamism. They suggest a static total divided by a static number of units. But in real life pupil numbers rise or fall, buildings close, meals shrink and buses fill. In real life there is usually a change in the volume of units. If one unit is added at the margin the extra costs – usually referred to as the *marginal costs* – of that extra unit will be much less than the previous average unit cost. For example, an extra pupil joining a school may need extra staffing and extra capitation allowance, but his effect on the cost of heating, lighting, postage, non-teaching staff, central administrative costs, etc., will be minimal. In theory, a graph line of expenditure in schools will rise in steps as the number of pupils increases. For example, a need for an extra teacher or classroom could be triggered off by the addition of one pupil. However, in practice the graph tends to level out and unit costs tend to decline in line with rising numbers. The current charge of an extra district pupil – a pupil residing in one LEA but educated by another – is £1,004 (1981-82). This represents the approximate average national unit pupil cost, but is certainly above the marginal cost for most authorities. This means that on cost grounds these LEAs welcome immigrants but discourage emigrants!

In practice, however, we look less at the cost of one extra unit than at the group of extra units implied in any change. This is the *incremental cost* – the cost of the group of units added by growth – or for those subtracted by contraction, the *decremental cost*. John Fielden (1980 b) has put it succinctly:

> In terms of political and practical reality incremental cost (or more realistically, the reverse, realisable savings) is the key cost definition for our times, whereas total cost has less practical value, although it can help to give us pointers towards high cost areas.

## The cost-benefit approach: cost efficiency and cost effectiveness

Fundamental to any approach to school costs must be an understanding of cost-benefit analysis, and of the distinction and sometimes contradiction between cost efficiency and cost effectiveness. *Cost efficiency* lies in the relationship between inputs and outputs. *A* is more efficient than *B* because either it uses less resources for the same output or it uses equal resources to achieve greater output. *Cost effectiveness* relates outputs to longer-term objectives.

*Examples*

1 A new lending procedure to reduce losses of books from the school library would be cost efficient. If, however, this led to a severe discouragement of borrowing, this would certainly not be cost effective.

2 A local education authority rations very strictly the number of words schools can use in advertisements for teaching vacancies, and thereby reduces the amount spent on advertisements. This is cost efficiency. If, however, this process leads to a fall in the number and quality of applicants, and so to a deterioration in the quality of new staff appointed, then this is not cost effective.

The cost-benefit approach looks beyond the immediate tactics of detailed decision on choices about costs to the broader strategy relating these to the aims of the institution.

## Cost characteristics of schools

Before proceeding in the next chapter to look at actual school costs in detail, it is worth considering some of the cost characteristics of schools as institutions.

P. H. Coombs and J. Hallak in *Managing Educational Costs* (1972) drew on extensive UNESCO experience of schools world-wide. They pointed out that the behaviour of costs is strikingly similar in all educational systems, overriding differences of development or regime.

A number of features characteristic of school systems in many countries can be identified:

1 Most schools are 'non-profit' organizations. In maintained schools the profit motive is largely absent – and, more important, the profit measure. In a profit-orientated organization, profit provides a single measure of efficiency of performance; it relates benefits (expressed in income and profit); it assists comparisons of efficiency between different centres and different types of activity. Non-profit organizations, lacking the profit measure, have inherent problems in performance measurement:
   (a) There is no single objective criterion to use in measuring or comparing performance, or in assessing alternatives
   (b) There is no easy way of estimating the relationship between inputs and outputs, or judging the effect of particular expenditure
   (c) A realistic pricing policy is not necessary, nor the discipline of cost control which goes with it.

   Some independent schools are profit-orientated, making profits for their proprietors. The majority are not profit-seeking in that sense, but they do have to adopt a realistic pricing policy and avoid making a loss. They are profit conscious, although not profit orientated.

2 Schools are service organizations and perform a social as well as an economic function. This makes measurement and costing of their output difficult. We can estimate the cost of teaching pupils mastery of skills in metalwork, or the achievement of an O-level pass in physics. But it is quite impossible to cost the school's efforts in promoting good citizenship or desirable social qualities. Given the very variable nature of the human material schools deal with, it is very difficult to cost many of their 'outputs'. Measuring productivity, and improving it, is even more difficult. And services cannot be stored – another obstacle to efficient organization.

3 School cost structures are very stable. This reflects primarily the stability of educational technologies and practices. Technological change in education is very slow. It also reflects the stability of assumptions on which schools are based. Education is the only industry where all employees and all customers (parents) have had their assumptions moulded by prolonged first-hand involvement in the process. So schools are very conservative institutions.

4 Schools work within a very slow cycle. They are geared to an annual rhythm. Once the school year begins, the costs for the institution are more or less committed, apart from unforeseen

changes because of inflation, etc. Indeed, any attempt to reduce costs *during* the school year causes a lot of disruption, and often creates damage out of proportion to the savings made. Beyond that, pupils usually spend several years in a particular school, and many changes have to be introduced slowly and phased over a long period so that pupils' education is not damaged. Schools cannot be amalgamated or closed like factories without ignoring pupils' long-term needs. So introducing substantial changes in schools is a little like turning an oil-tanker – it can be done, but it takes a long time.

5 School unit costs tend to rise when education becomes more technical and science-centred, when it deals with older pupils, and when there is greater concern for quality. So in most countries of the world school unit costs are rising in real terms.

6 Schools are very labour-intensive. The Chartered Institute of Public Finance and Accountancy (CIPFA) *Education Estimates 1980/81* shows that 73 per cent of school costs comes from salaries and on-costs. Catch 22 now surfaces. The conventional labour-intensive industry invests in improved technology to reduce labour costs. Hospitals speed the turnover of patients; restaurants automate the cooking; shops convert to self-service. But if schools do this they increase the pupil–teacher ratio, and thereby increase class size, narrow the curriculum, and loosen their social control.

7 School calendars cause high costs. The traditional school day, school week and school year lead to heavy under-use of premises. Most English primary schools and many secondary schools are not used for 46 per cent of the days in the year. On the 190 to 200 days that they are open, school proper only lasts for seven hours (and only four and a half to five hours of this is 'education'). Out-of-school activities will make partial use of the school for say another two hours, but this will usually be for only a tiny proportion of the premises. Evening classes or community activities will commonly only use a fraction of the total capacity. Even if we exclude the dead hours from 10.30 p.m. to 8.30 a.m., most schools only use for 'education' about 20 per cent (*a) of their total annual premises capacity – and only about 30 per cent (*b) if we include breaks, lunches, out-of-school and community activities. For over 80 per cent of the hours in the year (*c) the

*(a) $\frac{\text{200 schooldays}}{\text{365 days}} \times \frac{\text{5 `education' hours}}{\text{14 `sociable' hours}} = 20\%$

(b) $\frac{\text{200 schooldays}}{\text{365 days}} \times \frac{\text{7 `school' hours}}{\text{14 `sociable' hours}} = \frac{27{\cdot}4\% + \text{6 hours at}}{\text{10\% capacity}} = 30\%$

(c) $\frac{\text{200 schooldays}}{\text{365 days}} \times \frac{\text{7 `school' hours}}{\text{24 hours}} = \frac{16\% + \text{some out-}}{\text{of-school use}} = \text{say } 18\%$

So a typical classroom is unused for 82 per cent of the time.

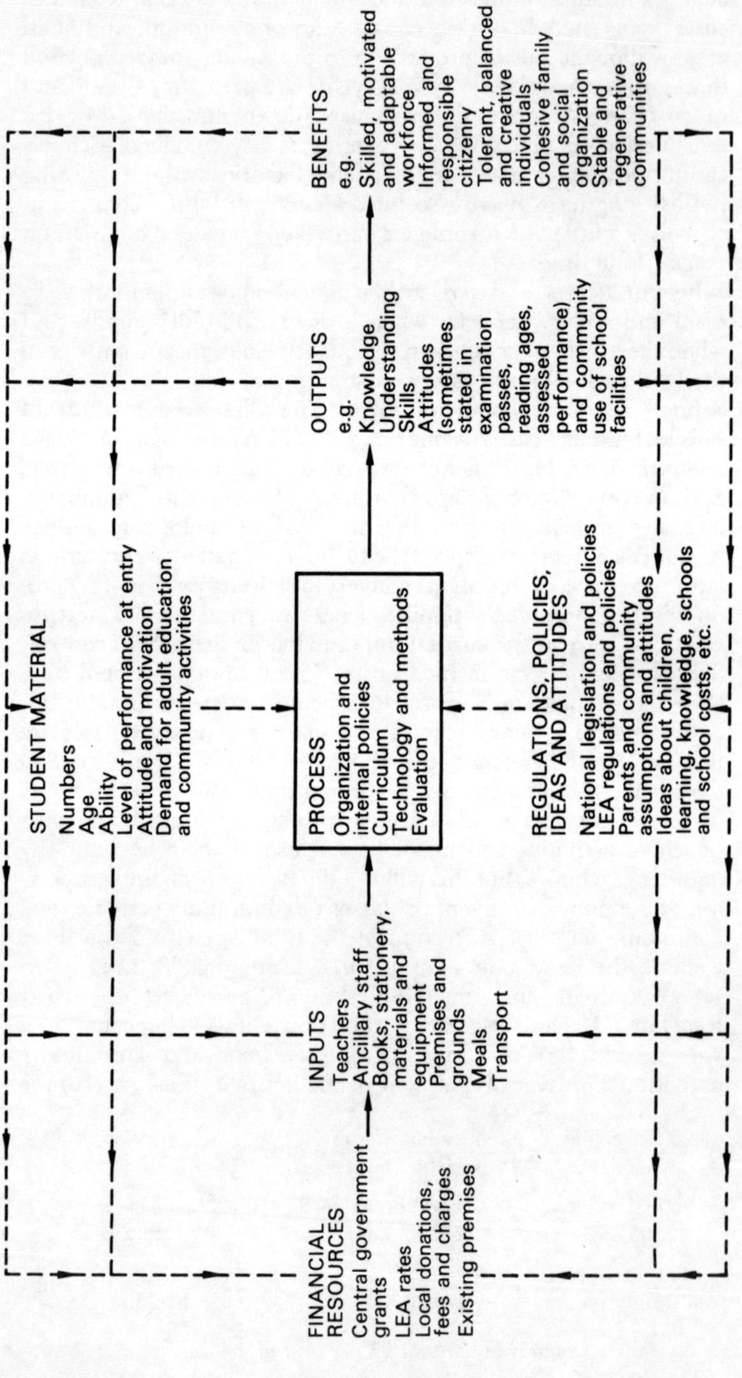


**Fig. 1:4** Education as a cost system

typical classroom lies unused and undisturbed save by the occasional cleaner or classroom ghost.

8 Schools are constrained by legislation, regulations, policies and attitudes which have often developed without consideration for costs, and yet which considerably affect them.

## *Education as a cost system*

We can gain a better understanding of school costs if we visualize education as a system where changes in one area affect cost in another (see Figure 1:4).

A school is a cost-accountant's nightmare: a labour-intensive, non-profit-making service organization, with ill-defined objectives, with uncosted and unquantifiable outputs and ill-costed inputs, in a straitjacket of constraints and with an arthritic lack of flexibility in buildings and staff.

# 2 The Running Costs of One Secondary School

Where shall we begin? It is easiest to start with one actual school – not because it is average or typical or special, but because it gives us a working example in a real context. That way, it is easier to see some of the forces at work. First, though, there are some problems to resolve.

## *Collection of data*

How accurate is the information? Much of the data came from LEA computer print-outs and school records, some by personal inquiry. Every attempt has been made to achieve accuracy, and the data is reasonably complete. However, a number of costs needed to be estimated, or allocated on certain assumptions.

## *Selection of costs*

Which costs should be included?
1 *Financial costs only* – actual expenditure and other costs on which a firm financial value can be placed. I have excluded all non-financial costs like those described in the previous chapter, on the grounds that they are difficult to quantify and that their inclusion makes comparisons between schools almost impossible.
2 *Full costs* – all expenditures from the educational budget which can be attributed to the school, including an allocation of central overheads and shared services. This rests upon the 'chalk-face principle' – that since schools exist to educate children and not primarily to feed, transport or administer them, *all costs*, including meals, transport and administration, should ultimately be allocated to the chalk-face. Every penny spent by the LEA should be attributed to its institutions (with the exception of grants to higher education students, and a tiny handful of services which can be attributed to 'school-less' children, for example, home tuition).

When I suggested this in 1977, it was criticized on the grounds that the costs it produced were unrealistic. For example, it was suggested that central costs which are not controllable by the school are not relevant to it; that total costs are a paper exercise; and that marginal costs are far more important. I feel very strongly that this view is mistaken.

(a) McNamara's 'First Law of Analysis': 'Always start looking at the grand total. Whatever problem you are studying, back off and look in the large.' (Robert McNamara, formerly U S Secretary of Defence and President of the World Bank.)
(b) We cannot just set aside LEA overheads, and almost pretend they do not exist.
*Example.* If Trust House Forte (Schools) Ltd moves into the education business, it cannot ignore or exclude the costs of its central offices when looking at the costs of its schools. It has to take all its costs into account.
(c) Including central overheads relates them to other costs of schools and colleges. Putting them both in the same bed makes us more aware of them, and alerts us to any change in relationship between them. This will be increasingly important with falling rolls when central overheads will lag behind the fall in pupil numbers.
(d) Total cost allocation is essential for inter-school comparisons. Expenses such as grounds maintenance, maintenance of premises, school library services, are sometimes incurred directly by schools, and sometimes carried by LEA central services.
(e) Total costs make it easier to assess the cost of a function.
*Example.* Schools' premises costs are grossly underestimated at present, because they are split up between central services, school-based salaries, repairs and maintenance, and loan charges.
(f) Full-cost accounting is a perfectly respectable practice, already operated by many LEAs when they divide central costs such as the chief executive's and treasurer's departments among all departments, and when they allocate a share of central education department overheads to school meals, psychological and careers service costs. So why not for schools? (Incidentally, independent schools often use it to allocate their overheads between the main school, the preparatory department, and the boarding houses.)

3 *Loan charges* are an important element of LEA overheads, close to 10 per cent on average of the total costs of maintained schools. Unfortunately, no one is quite sure what to do about them. They are a great puzzlement. In the CIPFA statistics, for example, they are initially shown separately from LEA net expenditure. The Department of Education and Science does not include them in expenditure forecasts, and so they are off ration in relation to government budget

targets. The uncertainty possibly arises because loan charges pay for capital items, and capital items are shown in a capital account. However, this is a misunderstanding. The charges themselves are quite clearly a revenue account expenditure, almost analogous to rent. They are included in LEA budgets, and allowed for when the rate is fixed! They are also included in the Grant Related Expenditure assessments which are the basis for the new Rate Support Grant.

So loan charges are clearly a cost, and should be included in any school cost analysis. The problem is how to allocate them. There are various alternatives:

(a) The historical debt charges attributable to the buildings of any one school. However, many LEAs do not keep their loan charge accounts in this way and are not able to trace the charges of a particular school. They constantly refund their total loan to suit market conditions. In any case, this would insert a differential between schools for purely historical reasons, often with little relationship to the buildings they inhabit.

(b) A percentage of the LEA's total debt charges, in the proportion of school roll to the LEA's total roll. Advantage: easy to calculate; disadvantage: linked to pupil numbers, and so to bodies and not buildings.

(c) A share of the LEA total debt charges, related to the floor area or rateable value of the school.

(d) The annual replacement cost. James Hough in *A Study of School Costs* (NFER-Nelson, 1981) refers to two such methods, by Norris (pages 34-5) and Pearson (page 144). The former calculated the current replacement cost of a building of given size, amortized over sixty years at a discount rate of 8 per cent. The latter took one-tenth of present capital construction costs per place, based on capital amortized over forty years at a discount rate of 10 per cent. Both entail a considerably greater cost element than present debt charges – Norris' method, for example, showed capital costs as 20 to 25 per cent of a school's current costs. More recently the report by Arthur Young McClelland Moores & Co. 'Costing Educational Provision for the 16-19 Age Group' (HMSO, 1981) adopted a similar approach to estimate recurrent costs implied by capital expenditure for a particular reorganization option. They used an 'equivalent annual cost' i.e. the conversion of capital expenditure into a number of fixed annual instalments (at constant prices). They suggested that with a true interest rate of 5 per cent per annum, a capital expenditure of £100,000 would be equivalent to £13,000 per annum over ten years, £9,000 per annum over fifteen years, or £8,000 per annum over twenty years (page 21, and Appendix F). This may well be a useful method for projecting future costs of alternatives, but it is not very helpful in establishing the current cost of earlier capital expenditure for existing schools.

(e) A notional rent. This is based on the assumption that since many debt charges have been paid off, and others reduced in real cost by inflation, they are not a realistic basis for the annual valuation of property. Instead it is suggested that a 'rental' should be charged, perhaps related to realistic potential rents. Such rental would be particularly useful in establishing realistic hire charges.

The last two have the merit that they offset the current under-valuation of LEA buildings. Certainly if LEAs were quoted on the stock-market, they would be gobbled up for their understated assets. And perhaps revaluing loan charges would make LEAs appreciate their assets more – and be more anxious to sell off surplus. But both (*d*) and (*e*) involve introducing paper valuations, beyond LEAs actual cash transactions. In practice loan charges have become a rolling depreciation fund for replacement of buildings, new loans being added as old loans are paid off. So it seems reasonable to base the allocation on the current charges. I have chosen the second version of (*c*), the share related to rateable value, on the grounds that it does reflect broadly the building a school occupies. It is also easy to calculate. It can be worked out as follows:

$$\text{total LEA debt charges} \times \frac{\text{rateable value of the school}}{\text{rateable value for all LEA premises}}$$

However as the rateable value is reduced when a school's numbers fall, floor area would actually be preferable. There is also the question of depreciation of capital equipment. LEAs normally make no arrangement for this. However, there is a continual process of replacement both through capitation and through central funds, so depreciation could be said to be covered by these.

4 *Costs of other departments*. What about expenditures by other departments which are not recharged to the education budget?

*Examples*

(a) a school-based social worker, paid from the social services department budget;

(b) a course provided and financed by the DES, attended by one of the school's teachers.

It seems rational to include these, grouping them for convenience with other LEA overheads. They are difficult to identify, particularly if one is examining a number of schools from a distance, but fortunately are a small element.

5 *Gross expenditure or net?* Gross expenditure is the total spent by an LEA, financed both by rates and by government grants. However, this is reduced by income paid by parents and others under LEA regulations for items such as materials for practical subjects, school meals, certain examination fees, community education fees. This reduced total is net expenditure, much more interesting to LEAs because it is this which determines the level of rate demand and dominates LEA budgets.

Unfortunately there is other income. Some of it is payments for 'unofficial' activities – those not financed by the LEA, such as the running of a school vehicle or a self-help building project – which are routed via the LEA either for convenience or more commonly to avoid paying VAT. This income does not reduce net expenditure, because although the payment increases total income, the activity it finances increases gross expenditure. Other income may have a similar effect – for example, if a school buys textbooks and sells them to parents, or if children pay for a visit to the theatre – providing the transaction passes through the LEA ledgers. Such payments are best termed donations. They are gifts which do enhance gross expenditure, but do not affect LEA net expenditure. But of course many donations do not go through the LEA at all, but are expended via school unofficial funds, parents' associations funds, etc., or even are presented in kind. Yet it will be argued below that they certainly ought to be included in complete school expenditure.

I have chosen to include only *complete net school expenditure* in Table 2:1 below – LEA net expenditure plus non-LEA net donations, on the grounds that the former is an LEA's main interest, and the latter cannot be ignored. However, it needs to be made clear that this is not the total of goods and services provided by a school. This will be the *complete gross expenditure* – LEA gross expenditure plus non-LEA gross expenditure.

6 *Donations*. Funds from a trust or charity, a PTA, an appeal, the local community, industry, sponsorship, individual donations, parents' purchases of textbooks, the school tuckshop and other unofficial school funds – the list is ever growing, in range and in importance.

It is difficult to argue that expenditure of such funds is not a cost. Some donors, of course, would splutter indignantly that these are nothing to do with the local authority. Certainly capital costs should not be included. It could be said that including donations unduly inflates the apparent cost of a school. But this revenue is now a significant factor. At times it provides essential items. It often appears within LEA accounts. An alternative and supplementary system of finance is beginning to emerge. We need to accept this, and to measure it.

However, there are difficulties with this approach. It makes inter-school comparison more difficult, and is difficult to interpret. I have, therefore, included it in a separate section.

7 *Community education.* This includes adult classes and activities, youth activities, 'dual use' of leisure facilities, hiring of school premises, etc. Conceptually it throws up difficulties. On the one hand, it can be argued that education is a seamless garment, that it is quite unreasonable to exclude community education costs, and that total costs of the institution do mean total costs of the total institution. Also it can be argued that if two schools of *X* pupils each cost £*Y* and the second school has a large community centre, then it is somewhat cheaper to run, and this should be reflected in the presentation of its costs.

However, in practice there are severe difficulties. In some schools, community education facilities may be self-contained, for example, a dual-use sports centre with split metering for electricity, and so on. However, in many cases there will be a very blurred line between school and community use. Commonly one 'subsidizes' the other.

The most rational approach seems to be an attempt to identify all community education cost elements, and to allocate these to a separate category within the total institution budget.

## *Presentation of costs*

Following the reasoning above, I have presented cost information in a matrix with three main sections:

1 LEA overheads
2 School-based costs
3 Donations

and six functional headings:

1 Teaching costs
2 Premises and grounds
3 Assistance to pupils
4 School transport
5 School meals
6 Community education

## *The running costs of Holyrood School, 1979/80*

Holyrood School is a maintained school of the Somerset LEA. Formerly a secondary modern, it was reorganized in 1970 as an 11 to 18 mixed comprehensive. It serves Chard, a town of about 10,000, and a reasonably compact rural catchment area. The school is housed in sturdy buildings built in 1959 and less solid modern extensions of 1970/71, with extensive fields. In 1979/80 the buildings had high room utilization. There were 1088 pupils on roll in September 1979 (86 of them in the sixth form).

Table 2:1 below sets out the full costs for Holyrood School in the financial year 1979–80.

## *Commentary on school's costs*

The analysis below must be treated with care. It merely describes the cost of one particular school in one year. There is some margin of error. There is much margin for argument about the inclusion or exclusion of particular items, and about their grouping. These statistics, like all statistics, will be false, treacherous and seductive. They need close scrutiny

*LEA overheads*

These are obviously determined by the existing organization of the LEA and its present policies. Somerset is an impecunious county, and in recent rounds of cuts has been forced to reduce its administrative structure considerably. It is a fairly compact county, and therefore can keep overheads down. It has worked hard to establish realistic recharging from other departments, to maximize its recoupment from other LEAs and national pools, and to minimize its own contributions to them. My impression is that, making allowance for its poverty and therefore limitations of provision, Somerset is quite an efficient authority, and therefore the LEA overheads are probably reasonable. Its administration and inspection costs as a proportion of net expenditure are somewhat below the average of non-metropolitan counties (2·1 per cent compared with 2·4 per cent).

The allocation of LEA overheads has been determined as follows. First, proportional shares of the LEA budget have been established

(a) the secondary schools' share – $\dfrac{\text{budget for secondary schools}}{\text{total LEA budget}}$

then (b) Holyrood's share – $\dfrac{\text{the number of pupils at Holyrood School}}{\text{the total number of secondary pupils in Somerset}}$

All central LEA administration and services which minister to the school directly or indirectly have been allocated in the above manner. Boarding and special education for pupils of secondary age has been excluded. Services which only cover certain age groups, such as the careers advisory service, received a revised calculation. Full details of the formulas used are given in Appendix A. The social worker (schools) is broadly equivalent to an Educational Welfare Officer in other LEAs.

**Table 2:1** The costs of one secondary school, 1979/80

| | | Sub-total (£s) | % of total costs | Costs per pupil (£s) | Teaching costs (£s) | Premises and grounds (£s) | Assistance to pupils (£s) | School transport (£s) | School meals (£s) | Community education (£s) |
|---|---|---|---|---|---|---|---|---|---|---|
| LEA OVERHEADS | | | | | | | | | | |
| Central administration and inspection | (a)* | 25,000 | 2·9 | 23·0 | 25,000 | | | | | |
| Central administration recharged to school meals | (k) | 1,800 | 0.2 | 1·7 | | | | | 1,800 | |
| ditto to grounds maintenance | (l) | 2,700 | 0.3 | 2·5 | | 2,700 | | | | |
| Library and museum service | (b) | 1,600 | 0·2 | 1·5 | 1,600 | | | | | |
| Residential centres | (c) | 300 | 0·03 | 0·3 | 300 | | | | | |
| Educational psychological service | (d) | 1,300 | 0·1 | 1·2 | 1,300 | | | | | |
| Careers service | (e) | 8,000 | 0·9 | 7·4 | 8,000 | | | | | |
| In-service training for teachers | (f) | 3,300 | 0·4 | 3·0 | 3,300 | | | | | |
| Education and resource centres | (f) | 3,000 | 0·3 | 2·8 | 3,000 | | | | | |
| Debt charges and revenue contributions to capital outlay (RCCO) | (g) | 102,700 | 11·8 | 94·4 | | 102,700 | | | | |
| Transport, central costs | (m) | 2,400 | 0·3 | 2·2 | | | | 2,400 | | |
| Community education administration | (h) | 2,000 | 0·2 | 1·8 | | | | | | 2,000 |
| Social worker (schools) | (i) | 3,000 | 0·3 | 2·8 | | | 3,000 | | | |
| Total LEA overheads | | 157,100 | 18·1 | 144·4 | 42,500 | 105,400 | 3,000 | 2,400 | 1,800 | 2,000 |
| SCHOOL-BASED COSTS | | | | | | | | | | |
| *Teaching costs* | | | | | | | | | | |
| Salaries, teaching (establishment) | | 420,020 | 48·3 | 386·0 | | | | | | |
| ditto (supply) | | 8,500 | 1·0 | 7·8 | | | | | | |
| Salaries, non-teaching support | | 48,120 | 5·5 | 44·2 | | | | | | |

| | | Sub-total (£s) | % of total costs | Costs per pupil (£s) | Teaching costs (£s) | Premises and grounds (£s) | Assistance to pupils (£s) | School transport (£s) | School meals (£s) | Community education (£s) |
|---|---|---|---|---|---|---|---|---|---|---|
| Capitation and other allowances, expenditure (books, stationery, materials, equipment, furniture) | | 39,850 | 4·6 | 36·6 | | | | | | |
| less income credited | | – 5,450 | – 0·6 | – 5·0 | | | | | | |
| Net capitation expenditure | | 34,400 | 4·0 | 31·6 | | | | | | |
| Examination fees | | 5,500 | 0·6 | 5·1 | | | | | | |
| less income received | | – 780 | – 0·1 | – 0·7 | | | | | | |
| Net expenditure, examination fees | | 4,720 | 0·5 | 4·4 | | | | | | |
| Postage and telephone | | 2,690 | 0·3 | 2·5 | | | | | | |
| Travelling expenses | | 180 | 0·02 | 0·2 | | | | | | |
| Advertisements | (j) | 500 | 0·06 | 0·5 | | | | | | |
| Interview expenses | | 850 | 1·0 | 0·8 | | | | | | |
| Total teaching costs | | 519,980 | 59·8 | 478·0 | 519,980 | | | | | |
| *Premises and grounds costs* | | | | | | | | | | |
| Salaries (caretaking, cleaning) | | 30,820 | 3·5 | 28·3 | | | | | | |
| ditto (grounds) | | 9,620 | 1·1 | 8·8 | | | | | | |
| ditto (clerical support) | (r) | 500 | 0·6 | 0·5 | | | | | | |
| Rates | | 28,560 | 3·3 | 26·2 | | | | | | |
| Maintenance of premises | | 24,700 | 2·8 | 22·7 | | | | | | |
| ditto (grounds) | | 1,590 | 0·2 | 1·5 | | | | | | |

| | | Sub-total (£s) | % of total costs | Costs per pupil (£s) | Teaching costs (£s) | Premises and grounds (£s) | Assistance to pupils (£s) | School transport (£s) | School meals (£s) | Community education (£s) |
|---|---|---|---|---|---|---|---|---|---|---|
| Heating and lighting | | | | | | | | | | |
| electricity | | 4,020 | 0·5 | 3·7 | | | | | | |
| oil | | 10,100 | 1·2 | 9·3 | | | | | | |
| gas | | 270 | 0·03 | 0·2 | | | | | | |
| Total heat and light costs | | 14,390 | 1·7 | 13·2 | | | | | | |
| Water | | 1,450 | 0·2 | 1·3 | | | | | | |
| Cleaning materials and equipment | | 2,550 | 0·3 | 2·3 | | | | | | |
| Swimming-pool | | | | | | | | | | |
| repairs | | 790 | 0·1 | 0·7 | | | | | | |
| electricity | | 130 | 0·01 | 0·1 | | | | | | |
| chemicals, others | | 140 | 0·01 | 0·1 | | | | | | |
| Total swimming-pool costs | | 1,060 | 0·1 | 1·0 | | | | | | |
| Total premises and grounds costs | | 115,240 | 13·3 | 105·9 | | 115,240 | | | | |
| *Assistance to pupils* | | | | | | | | | | |
| Salaries, clerical support | (r) | 120 | 0·01 | 0·1 | | | | | | |
| Free meals served at paying rate | | 4,510 | 0·5 | 4·1 | | | | | | |
| Uniform grants | (n) | 860 | 0·1 | 0·8 | | | | | | |
| Maintenance grants | | 2,150 | 0·2 | 2·0 | | | | | | |
| Total assistance to pupils costs | | 7,640 | 0·9 | 7·0 | | | 7,640 | | | |

| | Sub-total (£s) | % of total costs | Costs per pupil (£s) | Teaching costs (£s) | Premises and grounds (£s) | Assistance to pupils (£s) | School transport (£s) | School meals (£s) | Community education (£s) |
|---|---|---|---|---|---|---|---|---|---|
| *School transport* | | | | | | | | | |
| Salaries, clerical support | 40 | — | 0·03 | | | | | | |
| School buses, other vehicles, season tickets | 35,250 | 4·1 | 32·4 | | | | | | |
| Total school transport costs | 35,290 | 4·1 | 32·4 | | | | 35,290 | | |
| *School meals* | | | | | | | | | |
| Food | 12,080 | 1·4 | 11·1 | | | | | | |
| Salaries, supervisors | 2,260 | 0·3 | 2·1 | | | | | | |
| ditto kitchen staff | 16,010 | 1·8 | 14·7 | | | | | | |
| ditto clerical support (r) | 960 | 0·1 | 0·9 | | | | | | |
| Premises | 3,080 | 0·4 | 2·8 | | | | | | |
| Equipment | 500 | 0·1 | 0·5 | | | | | | |
| Total expenditure | 34,890 | 4·0 | 32·0 | | | | | | |
| Less income received | 7,980 | 0·9 | 7·3 | | | | | | |
| Net total school meals costs | 26,910 | 3·1 | 24·7 | | | | | 26,910 | |
| *Community education* | | | | | | | | | |
| Salaries and expenses, tutors | 4,600 | 0·5 | 4·2 | | | | | | |
| ditto, clerical | 930 | 0·1 | 0·9 | | | | | | |
| ditto, caretaking | 640 | 0·1 | 0·6 | | | | | | |
| Postage, telephone, printing | 260 | 0·03 | 0·2 | | | | | | |
| Total expenditure | 6,430 | 0·7 | 5·9 | | | | | | |
| less fees received | 3,930 | 0·5 | 3·6 | | | | | | |
| Net total, community education | 2,500 | 0·3 | 2·3 | | | | | | 2,500 |

| | | | | | | | | | | |
|---|---|---|---|---|---|---|---|---|---|---|
| DONATIONS | | | | | | | | | | |
| Parents and Friends Association | 2,940 | 0·3 | 2·7 | 2,940 | | | | | | |
| Purchases by parents of books, files, etc., and payments for school visits (p) | 1,000 | 0·1 | 0·9 | 1,000 | | | | | | |
| Swimming-pool key-holders | 260 | 0·03 | 0·2 | | 260 | | | | | |
| Total, donations | 4,200 | 0·5 | 3·8 | | | | | | | |
| Full cost totals | 868,860 | 100.0 | 798·6 | 566,420 | 220,900 | 10,640 | 37,690 | 28,710 | 4,500 |
| Functional full cost totals; as a percentage of whole school total | | | | 65·2% | 25·4% | 1·2% | 4·3% | 3·3% | 0·5% |
| Functional full cost totals; cost per pupil | | | | £520·7 | £203·0 | £9·8 | £34·6 | £26·4 | £4·1 |

*Letters (a), (b), etc., refer to Appendix A.

*Teaching costs*

Teachers' salaries
They loom out of the mist like a mountain.
The salary structure of the school was determined by decisions about reorganization in the area in the late 1960s. This altered the school's status and size and established it in the middle of group 11. In theory, Somerset aimed to place all its schools in the middle of their appropriate points score range. In practice, Holyrood in the year in question was just below the middle of its range with 67 points. Allocation of special responsibility allowances was made by the school governors on the recommendation of the head, after consultations with senior staff and advisers. In practice, the allowances were weighted towards scale 4 and lighter towards scale 2, but this probably made very little difference to the salary total. (Readers who are unversed in the mysteries of the Burnham Salary Scales can find all revealed in Appendix A of J. Hough's *A Study of School Costs*.) More important was the decision that all available allowances should be awarded and none kept in hand. The authority had the discretion to create a second deputy head (in effect a third deputy) and senior teachers. The policy for its comprehensives, however, was not to provide the former and only one of the latter.

The greatest determinant of salary costs was the authority's staffing policy. In 1979/80, the staffing scale was 1:20 below the sixth form and 1:10 in the sixth. The establishment for 1979/80 was originally set at Head + 61 and included a supplement to ease a merger with another school. As it became clear that actual numbers in September 1979 would be slightly lower, the total was revised to Head + 60·2.

Another significant factor was the age structure of the staff. Because the school had expanded rapidly in 1970 it had taken on a large number of young teachers, who tended to stay in a pleasant area. As a result, a number of staff were still on the lower incremental points of their scales, and so the school's teachers' total salary bill was somewhat lower than it might have been.

Employers' contributions to teachers' superannuation and national insurance were a very significant addition to gross salaries, adding 17·7 per cent.

Within the teaching establishment an equivalent of three teachers was made up by part-time staff. Employers' contributions were lower, but in other ways this did not affect the school's salary total.

Supply teachers' salaries
The authority's policy was that supply teachers would be employed when the third day of absence had been logged up in any half term, and earlier in special cases. Supply teachers could only be used to cover absence for illness, not for teachers on courses. The school

normally tried to use supply teachers, but a proportion of absence through illness was covered internally because of difficulties in finding them at short notice.

Salaries of non-teaching support staff

This included laboratory and workshop technicians, librarian and resource centre assistant, bursar and clerical staff. In the analysis above, an element of the bursar's and clerical salaries has been re-allocated to premises and school meals. The school's non-teaching establishment had grown with comprehensive reorganization, and for historical reasons was relatively generous.

Capitation allowances for the financial year 1979/80

In 1979/80 Somerset allowed £19.40 for each pupil aged 11 to 16, and £30 for each over 16, to provide books and stationery, equipment, furniture, materials and educational visits. There was an additional allowance based on a formula combining numbers of pupils, numbers of dinners and floor area to provide cleaning materials and equipment, protective clothing, with an additional element for swimming-pool chemicals. In April 1979 a new allowance was provided for postage and telephones. All these were treated as one combined allowance. The school was allowed to add to this any income collected, mainly from sales in the practical subjects, and from payments for visits. It was also allowed to carry forward surplus or deficit, and in fact the surplus from the previous year had been £2,654.

The authority had an efficient system for assessing capitation. It paid in April for the estimated number in September 1979, and adjusted this after September. The per capita allowances included an element for inflation of 9·3 per cent established by the county treasurer for the twelve months ending November 1978. The authority attempted to provide value for money for schools by participating in the South Western Consortium for stationery, equipment and materials, etc.

The total for the capitation, cleaning, postage and telephone allowances at the beginning of the year was £26,126. This was increased over the twelve months by an additional £15,800 in thirty-four separate grants, for various items of equipment, resources, etc. These mainly originated from advisers and to some extent reflect priorities and pressures from the school's staff. The authority had also launched a replacement programme for major items of equipment, having suddenly realized that major equipment such as lathes was depreciating fast, and schools could not afford to replace it. These allocations were made in kind. The authority screened the school's requests and itself chose and ordered the equipment. In all, the equipment and fittings supplied under this policy was approximately equivalent to £2,200.

Examination fees
Somerset's policy was that it would only normally pay for seven subject entries, and that entries beyond seven, 'double-entries', and retakes (except where candidates had failed themselves to do justice) should be paid for by parents. The school kept strictly to this policy and in fact exceeded it by requiring payment for all sixth-form retakes. The school's internal policy was to encourage pupils to take examinations. Of the fifth year of 251 pupils, 227 did in fact do so, averaging 6·9 entries per candidate (a number of these, of course, would be paid by parents). Reasonable borderline entries were accepted, but 'no hope' entries were discouraged, despite pressure from parents, and sometimes teachers. The school operated a six-box option system, and so the maximum number of subjects possible was normally nine.

The school entered mainly for the Cambridge GCE and the South-Western CSE Board, but with a few subjects taken with the AEB.

Postage
The school office stamped letters handed in for mailing. The main users were departments, and those concerned with careers education and, in the summer particularly, examinations. Expensive items were examination scripts and films.

Telephones
An extensive telephone system had been installed at the time of re-organization. It was generally felt to be invaluable, but was also expensive.

The PBX system with several external lines and a number of internal extensions had been paid for centrally by the LEA. In April 1979, a new system was introduced by which call charges were paid from the school's capitation allowance, to which an element was added. An extra element was added, equivalent to the rental charge. As it turned out, the charges for the year somewhat exceeded this allowance, and during the year steps were taken to reduce telephone expenses.

Travelling allowances
Teachers travelling to courses were paid on a lower scale. Travelling to non-in-service meetings, and transporting sick children, was paid on the casual user's scale. All these were paid centrally, and the latter logged against the school for record purposes. Travelling expenses to staff meetings and parents meetings could be paid from capitation, although this was not claimed extensively.

Advertisement expenses
Advertisement expenses were paid centrally. The LEA used large block advertisements and discouraged verbosity and repeats unless there were special reasons.

Interview expenses
LEA policy was for a maximum of five candidates for posts below deputy head. The school's policy was normally to call that number, sometimes less.

*Premises and grounds costs*

Premises-related salaries
The school's establishment of cleaners and caretakers was based on a formula negotiated with NUPE by the LEAs of the South West. This had been modified with a work study bonus agreement. The establishment of ground staff, based on a county work study survey, was two full-time groundsmen and one part-time in the summer, with a back-up group team for heavy mowing of fields. A proportion of the bursar's and clerical salaries has been allocated to premises for work generated by maintenance.

Repairs and maintenance to premises
The main buildings were built in 1959 and 1970. Maintenance was carried out by the area building surveyor, using funds of the county's architect's department, which were recharged to education. He determined what work should be done for both minor and major maintenance, and placed tenders. The school only dealt with emergency repairs. In the year in question, funds had been drastically reduced and maintenance was limited to essential items. There was a little latitude for the school to attempt to secure its own priorities, but minor improvements and redecorations were out of the question. The 1970 buildings, constructed within tight cost limits, were already throwing up higher maintenance costs.

Grounds maintenance was largely carried out by the school grounds staff, with materials either bought centrally, or bought locally with central funds.

Heating
As the school grew piecemeal, it has four separate oil-fired burners, as well as two temporary classrooms heated by low grade oil, and three heated by gas. The caretaker was very conversant with boilers, and operated them carefully, the main boiler having an electronic miser device. However, there was room for a number of measures to achieve greater fuel efficiency: many external doors were ill-fitting or slow to close; most roofs were still unlagged; the new buildings in particular had poor insulation qualities; room thermostats in the newer buildings were accessible to children.

Swimming-pool costs
Somerset had off-loaded these. The school had to finance the electricity and water, the chemicals, the maintenance of the filter plant

and of the fabric either from capitation (an element was allowed for chemicals) or from private fund-raising, which included charges for children for use out of school, and letting to 'key holders' during the holidays. Despite this private enterprise, the pool still made a loss, which had to be met from capitation.

Electricity

Electricity was mostly charged on the maximum demand tariff. The meter registered the highest half-hour of demand during each month, rather like a maximum-and-minimum thermometer. Charges in 1979/80 were, for each kw-hour of maximum demand, £4.22 in December, January; £2.24 in November, February and March; 55p in other months. The danger time was lesson one, if heating, lighting and power-tool demands came on fully. In addition, there was a unit charge, for the total units consumed, of approximately half the normal flat-rate tariff. A small number of appliances creating a heavy load, for example domestic science cookers, school kitchen cookers, were on the flat-rate tariff.

The other expensive area of heating and lighting expenditure was community education in the evening. However, there was no easy way of monitoring this, unless meters were read every day. Even that was not possible for the boilers, because they had no accurate fuel guage. In the evening various zones of the school could be isolated, but normally heating one room within any one zone of say half a dozen rooms entailed heating the lot, unless a great deal of trouble and effort were taken.

Water

Water bore a volume related charge, established by a water meter. The tariff was a standing charge based on the size of the supply, and a second charge on the volume consumed multiplied by the charge per unit.

Sewerage

Sewerage charges were calculated as a rate in the £ of rateable value.

*Assistance to pupils*

School uniform grants

Since the school retained school uniform in the lower school, and a semi-uniform in the upper school, county grants of £20 were still payable on entry, with £10 renewal every two years. Only about half of those entitled to free meals claimed uniform grants, possibly because many children became entitled in primary school, and so a separate application had to be made for uniform at 11 + .

Maintenance grants
Maintenance grants for the sixth form enjoyed a better take-up, perhaps because the more middle-class element in the sixth form was better able to cope with the application, and also because the sum at stake was much larger (a sliding scale rising to £400).

Free meals
The largest element of assistance was obviously free meals. This allowance was well known among parents but in the year in question was subjected to quite a severe means test, and there was certainly some disillusionment over the severity of the scale. Undoubtedly some families who were entitled to claim did not do so. In some cases this would be affected by children living near the school and preferring to go home during the lunch hour. A good standard meal was served, but obviously it did not please everybody! A number of children who actually qualified for school meals did not in fact eat them every day (about 10 per cent).

*School meals*
During 1979/80 the LEA was still required to provide 'as a midday dinner a meal, suitable in all respects as the main meal of the day' (Schools Regulations).

The school had its own kitchen. This operated as a separate cost centre with a financial system completely independent from the school's main finances. The cook-supervisor costed her own operations, kept her own accounts, and reported to the area and county catering officers. Staffing was based on a scale relating to meals served (and to a small degree, packed lunches eaten). Food was provided by county contract suppliers. Equipment was replaced centrally.

A daily choice between two traditional school meals was served. Pupils bringing sandwiches were also accommodated within the dining hall. Meal numbers were highest in September, falling off slowly during the year. There was a sharp fall from May onwards, with the absence of examination candidates and the greater appeal of packed lunches in the summer. It proved difficult to adjust staffing fully and promptly for this.

*School transport*
This was administered by the county surveyor's department, with the administrative expenses recharged.

The school's catchment area stretched from three to eight miles. The LEA met its statutory obligations to transport pupils of compulsory school age, (those who lived more than three miles from the school measured by the nearest walking route,) and exceeded its statutory obligation by carrying sixth formers and by stretching the three mile limit for a particular village when there had been vociferous demonstrations centuries before. During 1979 it was stated that this last privilege would be withdrawn – but it was still surviving in the summer of 1981.

A total of 272 children were transported by school buses (four private operators' coaches, two private minibuses, one local authority minibus and one private car paid by a neighbouring authority). In addition, 41 pupils were carried on public service vehicles with season tickets. Some of the vehicles made a double run, and a supervisor had to be paid for later supervision.

*Community education*

For 1979/80, Holyrood had a conventional adult education centre, with evening classes organized by the principal of a nearby adult education college. In addition, the school was also let to organizations and to individuals under county regulations, administration of this being provided by the school office. Both these two elements were prolific loss makers. In the case of adult classes, there were regulations laying down the minimum size of groups and, of course, the fees to be charged. In 1979/80 these were £12 for a twenty-week course (senior citizens £4.80, school students free). In practice, such charges did not quite recoup the salaries payable to the evening class teachers, and certainly did not cover the heating, lighting and maintenance costs, or central establishment costs such as telephone, publicity, clerical costs or the share of the FE principal involved. In the case of lettings, policy was determined by the LEA. They laid down three scales, group 1 for adult classes and for youth groups, group 2 for worthy community groups such as Women's Institutes and group 3 for private commercial or fund-raising ventures. The scales also varied, depending on whether they were weekday lettings, lettings after 10.00 p.m., or lettings on a Sunday. This was obviously a complex system to operate which also allowed a good deal of local discretion. School staff were therefore torn between a desire to increase the use of the school by the local community and a desire to reduce the additional running costs which such lettings caused. County policy on lettings has changed since that time, but the dilemma still remains unresolved, and I suspect still exists in many schools.

*Donations*

The main donation during the year was from the Parents and Friends Association. It held a large 'spectacular' in September, which raised £2,800, which was allocated to various projects nominated by the staff. In addition, it contributed another £140 towards running the school minibus and prizes. Parents also contributed in kind through providing atlases, school textbooks to some minor degree, and files. This is difficult to quantify, but has been set at £1,000. Pupils contributed part-payment to school visits, and also paid 'match fees' for school matches.

## *Unit costs*

From the total costs in Table 2:1 costs per pupil can easily be derived.

**Table 2:2** Unit costs per pupil, Holyrood School, 1979/80

| | |
|---|---|
| *Whole school* | |
| Total cost, one year | £868,860 |
| Total cost, one school week | 22,865 |
| Total cost, one school day | 4,573 |
| *Per pupil (1088 pupils on average on roll)* | |
| Cost of educating one pupil,* per year | £798 |
| Cost of educating one pupil, per school week | 21 |
| Cost of educating one pupil, per school day | 4.20 |
| Cost of educating one pupil, for one 35-minute period | 52p |
| Cost of educating one pupil, for one minute | 1.5p |
| Cost of educating one pupil, for one period per week for a year | 20.00 |
| Cost of educating one pupil, for 4 periods per week for a year (a typical course) | 80.00 |
| Cost of educating one pupil for 4 periods per week for 5 years (example of a 5-year course, e.g., French) | 400.00 |
| *Per class of any size with one teacher*† | |
| Cost of educating one class, for one 35-minute period | £12 |
| Cost of educating one class, for 4 periods (e.g. a week's French) | 48 |
| Cost of educating one class, for one period per week for a year | 450 |
| Cost of educating one class, for 4 periods per week for a year (a typical course) | 1,800 |
| Cost of educating one class, for 4 periods per week for 5 years (an example of a 5-year course – French) | 9,000 |

*Source:* Total costs in Table 2:1. Per pupil costs: total costs divided by 1088 pupils. Per class costs: total costs divided by 73,188 (1926 weekly teacher periods × 38 weeks)

* This is an overall average unit cost, ignoring differences in costs for different age groups. It has been argued that sixth-formers, for example, should be weighted to allow for more favourable staffing and capitation, and that 1.6:1 would be an appropriate ratio (see Appendix B). In this particular instance the effect is relatively marginal – the average cost of an 11 to 16 pupil would be £762. Of course in, say, a 13 to 18 school with a large sixth form it would be much more substantial.

†In fact the average size was 22.88. Classes below the average size involve less charges (less need for capitation, accommodation, back-up services, etc.) although, of course, the actual pupil-cost for these under-sized classes would be greater. Similarly classes of, say, thirty involve more charges although their pupil-cost would be lower.

Unit costs highlight what we already knew – that education is a very expensive pastime. If the school closes with snow for one day, that is over £4,000 of ratepayers' money wasted; if a pupil truants for one day, £4 goes with him; if a teacher is away for a week and his classes learn nothing, his sick-bed costs us £380; if a student takes a course and at the end of the year is measurably no better than when he started, that is £80 ill-spent.

## *Marginal unit costs*

It can be argued that the total unit costs above are interesting, perhaps thought provoking, but not particularly useful. Although they give us a feel for school costs, they do not provide us with a tool that we can easily use. They do not tell us, for example, how much more or less we shall have to spend if there is a pupil more or less in the school. Perhaps marginal unit costs can do that? However, establishing marginal unit costs is not easy in theory, and even less in practice.

A gain or loss of pupils during the school year will normally make very little difference to a school's costs, because the LEA will make no adjustment for them. The only exception would be an avalanche of pupils, when additional resources would be necessary. But if a school's September numbers rise, and the rise was foreseen, teaching costs should immediately respond. (In primary schools it may require a minimum number of new pupils before there is any change.) If there is a 10 per cent increase in numbers, there should be an equivalent increase in teaching establishment – although not a full 10 per cent increase in costs, since the additional teachers will probably be on scale 1, and tend to be on the lower part of the scale. Supply teachers' salaries and travelling expenses should rise roughly in proportion with teacher numbers. Advertisement and interview expenses will rise more than 10 per cent. Per capita allowances should rise by 10 per cent (but almost certainly not the centrally held funds for furniture, equipment, special needs, etc.). Examination fees will rise to match any increase in the year group. Postage and telephone charges will not be strongly affected, but should follow to some degree.

Premises costs are a different story. They will be largely unchanged – until the critical point at which new buildings are necessary. Until then there will be some slight increase in heating, lighting and water costs, but not by any means in proportion to the increase in pupils. At first there often will be temporary classrooms; these are relatively inexpensive, especially if redeployed from elsewhere. But when a new permanent building is necessary, costs soar – salaries, rates, heating and lighting, cleaning – and of course, debt charges (although this will not be apparent for this school's costs under the system of allocation used above). Grounds costs will often be unaffected, however.

Other costs will respond more quickly. Assistance to pupils should increase exactly in proportion to the rise in pupil numbers. School meals net costs and school transport costs will certainly increase, but not in proportion as they offer some economies of scale. Community education will be unaffected. Expenditure from donations should rise in some proportion to the increase in school size. LEA overheads will not increase initially, until there is sufficient increase in pupil numbers across the authority to bring the administration under strain. Any increase will still lag well behind the arrival of the pupils.

If numbers fall the opposite occurs, but with a marked difference. Teaching costs would fall in fair proportion to falling pupil numbers, providing the fall is small and can be absorbed. Even here there will be a lag, with continuing allowances. If the reduction is a considerable one, however, it may not be possible to redeploy staff, and the lag will be much greater. Assistance to pupils will fall proportionately, and school meals and school transport to some degree, but their overheads will remain fixed. Premises costs largely remain unaltered, apart from marginal changes to heating, lighting and water costs until or unless premises are sold or leased, or temporary classrooms are removed. Central LEA overheads will be very slow to respond to falling pupil numbers unless there is a very determined pressure from elected members to push the costs down.

Table 2:3 attempts to set out the marginal costs for Holyrood School 1979/80 in the event of an increase or decrease in pupil numbers of 30 per cent. But many of the figures are speculative. And I have chosen the simple model, where no buildings are added or removed! This table shows that in practice marginal costs are very difficult to predict. They depend upon the individual circumstances of the school, and particularly of its staff; on the degree and rate of change; on the general situation across the LEA; upon LEA policies; upon national policies, including cash limits; upon a hundred-and-one factors. As always, teachers' salaries will be the predominant factor. But at present we do not have in the education service the sound data base or the techniques to use marginal unit costs to predict future expenditure accurately. Significantly when LEAs calculate their 'continuation budget' (the budget to finance the present standard of provision, but adjusted for changes in pupil numbers) they often do not make a sophisticated marginal cost adjustment, but only crudely for the obvious changes – for example, in numbers of teachers, capitation, etc.

**Table 2:3** Marginal costs for Holyrood School, 1979/80 (model of 30 per cent change in numbers)

| | TOTAL COSTS AS IN TABLE 2:1 *(numbers on roll, 1088)* | | ROLL FALLING BY *30% (to 762)* | | ROLL RISING BY *30% (to 1414)* | | |
|---|---|---|---|---|---|---|---|
| | *Total costs (£s)* | *Costs per pupil (£s)* | *Total costs (£s)* | *Costs per pupil (£s)* | *Total costs (£s)* | *Costs per pupil (£s)* | *Likely changes?* |
| LEA OVERHEADS | | | | | | | |
| Central administration (all items in Table 2:1 except debt charges) | 54,400 | 50·0 | 48,960? | 64·3 | 59,840? | 42·3 | +/– 10%? |
| Debt charges | 102,700 | 94·4 | 102,700? | 134·8 | 102,700? | 72·6 | No change unless premises taken out of use, or new buildings provided |
| SCHOOL-BASED COSTS | | | | | | | |
| *Teaching costs* | | | | | | | |
| Salaries, teaching, including supply | 428,520 | 393·8 | 330,000? | 433·1 | 530,000? | 374·8 | +/– 23% |
| Salaries, non-teaching support | 48,120 | 44·2 | 43,300? | 56·8 | 52,930? | 37·4 | +/– 10%? |
| Capitation, net | 34,400 | 31·6 | 24,080 | 31·6 | 44,720 | 31·6 | +/– 30% |
| Examination fees, net | 4,720 | 4·4 | 3,340 | 4·4 | 6,200 | 4·4 | +/– 30% |
| Postage and telephone | 2,690 | 2·5 | 2,560? | 3·4 | 2,820? | 2·0 | +/– 5% |
| Travelling/advertisements/ interview expenses | 1,530 | 1·5 | 200? | 0·3 | 3,000? | 2·1 | ? |
| Total teaching costs | 519,980 | 478·0 | 403,480 | 529·5 | 639,670 | 452·4 | |

| | | | | | | | |
|---|---|---|---|---|---|---|---|
| *Premises costs* | | | | | | | |
| Salaries | 40,940 | 37·6 | 40,940 | 53·7 | 40,940 | 28·9 | No change unless premises increased/ decreased |
| Rates | 28,560 | 26·2 | 25,700? | 33·7 | 28,560? | 20·2 | – 10%? |
| Maintenance, premises and grounds | 26,290 | 24·2 | 26,000? | 34·1 | 26,500? | 18·7 | Slight changes |
| Heating and lighting | 14,390 | 13·2 | 13,670? | 17·9 | 15,110? | 10·7 | + / – 5%? |
| Water | 1,450 | 1·3 | 1,230? | 1·6 | 1,670? | 1·2 | + / – 15%? |
| Cleaning materials and equipment | 2,550 | 2·3 | 2,300? | 3·0 | 2,810? | 2·0 | + / – 10%? |
| Swimming-pool | 1,060 | 1·0 | 1,030? | 1·4 | 1,090? | 0·8 | Slight changes |
| Total premises and grounds costs | 115,240 | 105·9 | 110,870 | 145·5 | 116,680 | 82·5 | |
| *Assistance to pupils* | 7,640 | 7·0 | 5,350 | 7·0 | 9,930 | 7·0 | + / – 30% |
| *School transport* | 35,290 | 32·4 | 30,000? | 39·4 | 40,580? | 28·7 | + / – 15%? |
| *School meals net* | 26,910 | 24·7 | 21,530? | 28·3 | 32,290? | 22·8 | + / – 20%? |
| *Community education net* | 2,500 | 2·3 | 2,500 | 3·3 | 2,500 | 1·8 | |
| *Donations* | 4,200 | 0·2 | 3,360? | 4·4 | 5,040? | 3·6 | + / – 20%? |
| Total school costs | 868,860 | 798·6 | 728,760 | 956·4 | 1,009,230 | 713·7 | |
| Change in total and per pupil costs | | | – 16·1% | + 19·8% | + 16·2% | – 10·6% | |

## *A last word*

Superficially the analysis of the single school discussed in this chapter suggests an almost predetermined cost structure. Given the history and organization of the school, given national and LEA policies, its costs suggest a pattern which rolls on from one year to another. Yet that impression would be quite untrue. The next chapter shows that if one examines other schools, one finds considerable variations in both unit costs and the cost structure. And once one realizes that there are very few of the cost forces or constraints which cannot be altered in some way or other, then . . .

# 3 Comparisons between Secondary Schools

How alike are schools' costs? How typical is Holyrood School, compared with others of the same type and size in its own county, or in other local authorities? Or compared with schools of different types, different sizes, or with different environments? The short answer is that we do not really know. Not even the Secretary of State for Education knows. But we can explore.

## *Comparisons between LEAs*

We need a yardstick for comparisons. The obvious yardstick is average unit costs per pupil. Pupil units are easily established and directly comparable. They are also linked firmly to the chalk-face principle – it is pupils we are concerned about, and right that unit costs should be linked with them. Other units can be used – for example, floor area for premises costs – but they are more troublesome to calculate, more prone to inaccuracy, and in some ways not as relevant.

There are plenty of unit costs available. The best known are those provided by CIPFA. These cover all secondary-school costs, including transport, but excluding school meals, debt charges, fees for pupils in direct grant or independent schools, boarding education, central administration and inspection, psychological and careers services. They therefore omit over 20 per cent of the total costs listed in the previous chapter, but they are still substantial enough. The unit costs below are based upon local authority estimates for 1980/81 (actual expenditures may differ slightly). The CIPFA statistics have frequently been criticized, on the grounds that returns from LEAs are sometimes incomplete, and often classify expenditures differently. However, great efforts have been made to improve them in recent years. They are certainly the best statistics available, produced annually and promptly by an independent professional body.

Figure 3:1 sets out secondary-school unit costs per pupil for all LEAs, 1980/81. The disparity of unit costs between groups of local

**Fig. 3:1** Secondary-school unit costs, net expenditure per pupil, for LEAs in groups, 1980–81 (includes middle schools deemed secondary)

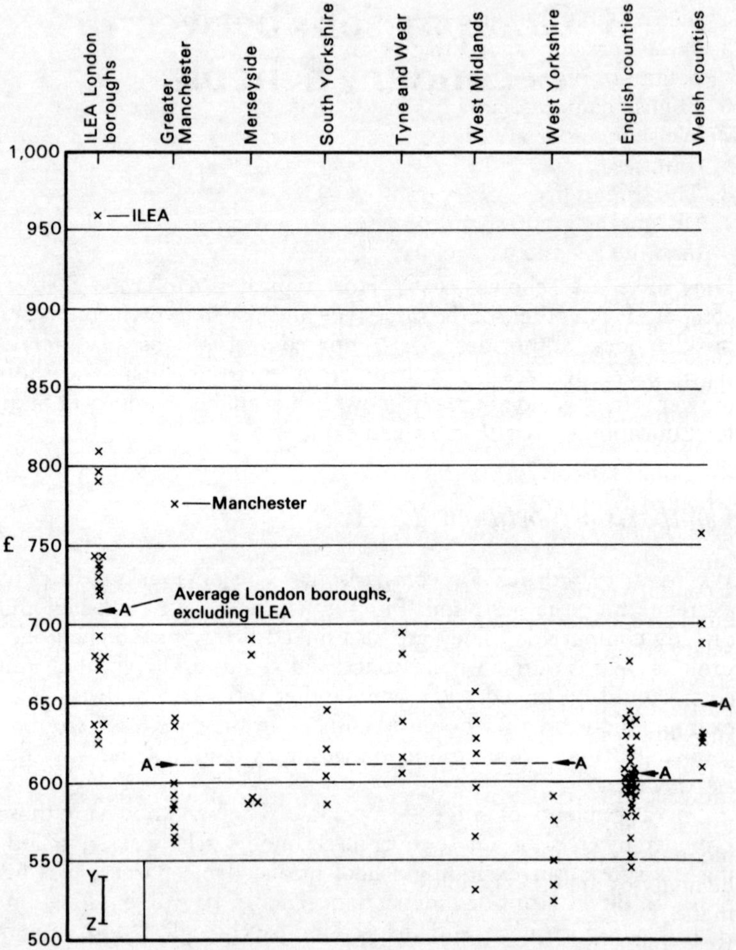


*Source.* CIPFA Education Statistics 1980/81 Estimates.

*Note.* Y/Z Average national expenditure per pupil on books, stationery, equipment and materials

A Average for group(s)

authorities and also between LEAs within the same group is striking. There are a number of obvious features:

1 Unit costs in the Inner London Education Authority are considerably higher than any other authority
2 London Borough unit costs as a group are higher than any other group

3 Manchester is a considerable amount higher than its satellite authorities, and indeed all other metropolitan authorities
4 There is substantial variation between the different groups of metropolitan authorities
5 West Yorkshire shows the lowest unit costs of any group, metropolitan or other
6 English counties show the lowest degree of variation
7 Welsh counties are on average considerably higher than English counties
8 The spread in every group is considerable, with the highest cost LEA in the group spending from 10 to 37 per cent more per pupil than the lowest cost member.

The effect of these differences in real terms is shown by the line *YZ* on the graph. Its length is equivalent to the average expenditure on capitation items for an English secondary-school pupil. So, if one of the 'low' authorities on the graph increased its unit costs by that margin – and many of its sister LEAs in the same group will be at least that amount above it – it could double the capitation expenditure in its schools, or insert extra teachers at the rate of four for each school of a thousand pupils. Education is bound to cost more in some areas than others, given sparsity of population on one hand and inner-city problems on the other. Yet 73 per cent of expenditure on secondary education (CIPFA figures, described above) arises from employee costs, which are almost entirely based on nationwide salary scales, except for the London allowances. This should have a strong levelling effect upon all LEAs outside of London (with the partial exception of LEAs which educate a high proportion of 16 + students in FE colleges). This is certainly not the case: all LEAs are equal, but some are more equal than others. The overriding impression is of historical diversity and arbitrary irregularity – the unacceptable face of local autonomy. Further illustrations of these inequalities can be found in Chapter 5 of James Hough (1981) where he analyses the CIPFA statistics for 1975/76 in considerable detail, in the 'League Tables' produced by the National Union of Teachers' Research Unit, and in Howick and Hassani's paper 'Education spending: secondary' (1980).

A number of studies have suggested reasons for these disparities. Eileen Byrne in *Planning and Educational Inequality* (1974) studied expenditure in three LEAs, and suggested factors such as preferences for certain types of schools; priority for prestige projects or for general improvement; the relative poverty of an LEA, and inequalities of the rating system; and a low starting-base. Her later study with Williamson and Fletcher, *The Poverty of Education* (1975) illustrated the importance of the expectations of an LEA, this reflecting the attitudes of officers, of elected members, and of the community. K. G. Ilett, Assistant Education Officer in Walsall, in an M.Ed. dissertation (1981) examined various aspects of costs in Walsall, comparing them over several years against national and all metropolitan borough figures (Chapter 2). In some cases he was able to suggest an explanation – for example, lower mean cost of teacher salaries because Walsall's larger teacher intakes reduced average teacher 'quality' in terms of age and qualifications (page 25); new emphases after local government reorganization, or a change of political control. In others, there was no apparent reason – for example, unit costs for primary teachers' salaries were well below national and metropolitan borough figures (though secondary teachers' salaries slightly above) – except for the force of 'tradition'.

## *Comparisons within LEAs*

These LEA costs are averages; and averages conceal extremes. They do not show us whether costs are grouped around the average, or whether there is a wide variation within the authority itself. This is the central question to which Hough addressed himself in his important study, the core of which lay in Chapter 6, where he analysed data on the costs of individual secondary schools for four authorities, 1974-77. His cost-base was similar to CIPFA's, but a little narrower as he excluded transport.

Hough found there were marked variations within each authority. In effect, he made nine separate studies (three LEAs analysed in depth for three separate years). The variations are shown in Table 3:1.

**Table 3:1** Variation in school unit costs within three LEAs

| | YEAR | UNIT COSTS OF INDIVIDUAL SECONDARY SCHOOLS, £ PER PUPIL | | | RATIO, HIGHEST TO LOWEST UNIT COSTS |
|---|---|---|---|---|---|
| | | *Lowest* | *Mean* | *Highest* | |
| LEA A | 1974/75 | 140 | 299 | 484 | 3·5:1 |
| | 1975/76 | 260 | 380 | 519 | 2·0:1 |
| | 1976/77 | 325 | 442 | 1372 | 4·2:1 |
| LEA C | 1974/75 | 216 | 286 | 472 | 2·2:1 |
| | 1975/76 | 281 | 354 | 595 | 2·1:1 |
| | 1976/77 | 307 | 404 | 731 | 2·4:1 |
| LEA D | 1974/75 | 111 | 276 | 419 | 3·7:1 |
| | 1975/76 | 164 | 343 | 576 | 3·5:1 |
| | 1976/77 | 221 | 379 | 561 | 2·5:1 |

*Source:* J. R. Hough *A Study of School Costs* (NFER-Nelson, 1981), Table 6.1.
*Note:* Sixth-formers weighted at 1·6:1 for 11 to 16 pupils.

**Table 3:2** Variation in unit costs for homogeneous groups of schools within one LEA

| | | *Mean units costs (£s)* | | | *% higher than lowest groups in the LEA* | | |
|---|---|---|---|---|---|---|---|
| | | *1974/75* | *1975/76* | *1976/77* | *1974/75* | *1975/76* | *1976/77* |
| LEA A | Secondary modern | 285 | 362 | 410 | – | – | – |
| | Grammar | 304 | 378 | 408 | 7 | 4 | – |
| | Comprehensive | 321 | 406 | 489 | 13 | 12 | 19 |
| LEA C | High schools | 266 | 320 | 368 | – | – | – |
| | Upper schools | 344 | 409 | 466 | 29 | 28 | 27 |
| | Secondary modern | 262 | 333 | 384 | ( – 2) | 4 | 4 |
| | Grammar | 319 | 401 | 435 | 20 | 25 | 18 |
| LEA D | Middle | 237 | 293 | 309 | – | – | – |
| | Comprehensive, 11 to 16 | 272 | 341 | 378 | 15 | 16 | 22 |
| | Comprehensive, 11 to 18 | 311 | 391 | 437 | 31 | 33 | 41 |

*Source:* J. R. Hough, *A Study of School Costs*, Table 6.2
*Note:* Sixth-formers weighted at 1·6:1 for 11 to 16 pupils.

For five of the studies, the unit costs of the highest cost schools were double that of the lowest; for three of them, they were over three times as great; and one, four times. The findings need treating cautiously. Although sixth-form pupils were weighted at 1·6:1 against main school pupils, there may still have been some distortion caused by the older pupils. Looking just at extremes, it was possible for a rogue school to exaggerate the range, perhaps a small middle school at one end, and a grammar school at the other. There was always the risk of error. However, having made all the allowances, the range of variation is still surprising.

Hough then divided the schools in each LEA into homogeneous groups, such as secondary modern, grammar/technical, comprehensive 11 to 16, comprehensive 11 to 18, etc. There were appreciable differences between the means of such groups within each local authority. Table 3:2 shows that in authority C, upper schools and grammar schools were 20 per cent or more above high schools or secondary moderns in unit costs per pupil, even allowing for the weighting of sixth-formers. Similarly in authority D, 11 to 18 comprehensives were about 15 per cent more expensive per pupil than the 11 to 16s.

Even within each group the variation was still considerable. In most of the groups, the highest unit costs were 50 per cent or more greater than the lowest. Caution is still necessary. It is possible for a school which is wrongly classified or which has recently changed from one type to another to exaggerate the range of the group. But the detailed statistics do suggest that there is a good deal of variation right across most of the groups.

Similar variations in unit costs within an LEA were exposed by the Kent County Council's feasibility study on the voucher system (1978). The study attempted to establish the equitable value of a voucher to cover the bulk of a school's teaching costs and premises costs, but excluding LEA overheads, transport and meals. There was such sharp variation in schools' per capita salary and loan commitments that the amount of the voucher remaining for other purposes varied from £63.80 to £128.54 per pupil net among the sample secondary schools. Similarly B. Atkinson and J. H Butel found costs per pupil varying from £664 to £442 in 1978/79 in forty-nine 11 to 16 schools within one LEA which had all been comprehensive for at least five years (*Education*, 6 November 1981). Although variations in teachers' salary costs were the most powerful factor, variations in premises costs were actually wider.

Another inter-school comparison was made by J. K. Roberts in a dissertation, 'Secondary School Costs', in 1980. He took a restricted view of school costs, only including those 'over which those concerned in running the school can be expected to exercise some degree of control . . . and therefore which ought to be broadly comparable between schools'. He therefore excluded loan charges, rates and rents, central administration and inspection, training of teachers, grants to pupils, school meals, transport, the careers and psychological service and maintenance of grounds. This emphasized teaching costs which made up 85 per cent of the costs he selected. Roberts' study of four matched pairs of Northamptonshire schools did not unfold the range of variation that Hough found. 'Even using unweighted figures, the most expensive school in the group cost only about 30 per cent more than the least expensive.' Probably this was because the group was relatively small and also because the costs surveyed were limited in their range. Perhaps a more important

**Fig. 3:2** Unit costs per pupil, Somerset secondary schools 1977/78

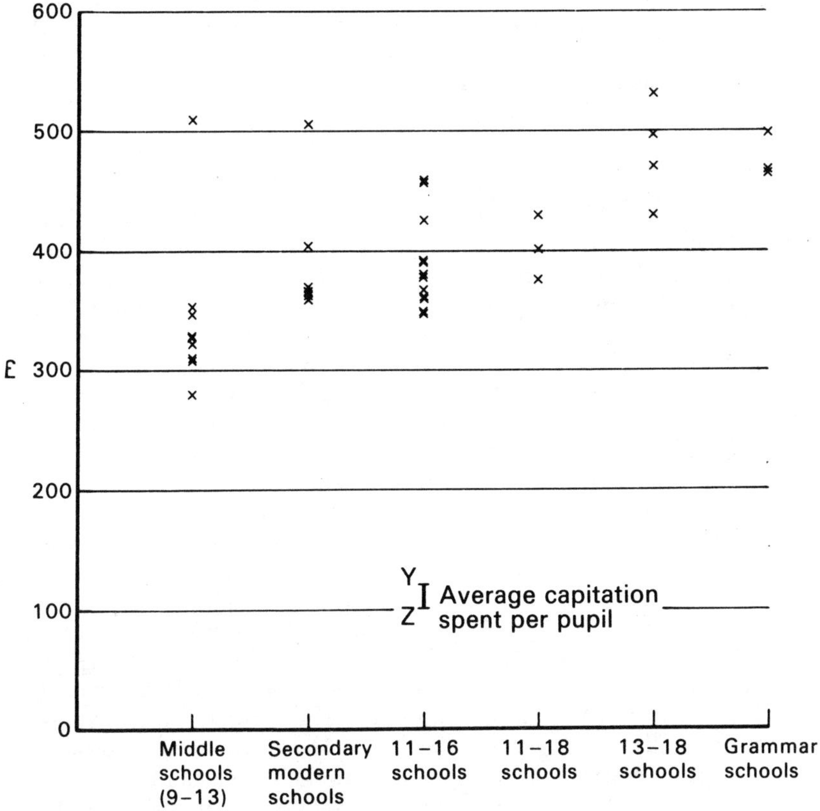


*Source:* Somerset Treasurer's Department (unpublished).
Included: Teacher's and non-teaching salaries, premises and grounds maintenance, heat and light, rates, capitation, examination and some minor expenses.

finding was that 'variations between schools paired together as being of similar size and stage of development were less than 7 per cent.'

Mike Pollard of the Somerset County Council Treasurer's Department made a comparative analysis of pupil costs in Somerset secondary schools for 1977/78. He grouped the schools by types. The results are summarized in Figure 3:2. These support the main findings of Hough, namely:

1 There is very considerable variation between the most and the least expensive school within an authority
2 Different types of schools tend to have different cost patterns
3 Within each type, there are still considerable variations.

However, given a reasonable knowledge of the schools in one's own education authority, many of the discrepant results are easily explicable. If these are excluded, one sees the bunching of unit costs which Roberts found in similar schools.

## *Comparisons by size*

A general belief in economies of scale in schools seems quite widespread. It is probably based upon the simple observation that in most other industries there are trends towards larger units on grounds of financial efficiency. The move to close small primary schools has been largely driven by the desire to provide primary education more economically – although justified by the twin argument that small schools are limited educationally. At secondary level, at the height of the comprehensive debate, one of the arguments, usually in very general terms and unsupported by hard evidence, was that the larger schools were more efficient financially, and that this would make for a better quality of provision for the same expenditure.

Hough in his *A Study of School Costs* devoted the whole of Chapter 7 to what he calls economies of size. He produces good evidence that economies of scale operate in capital provision. 'The Department of Education and Science still expect pupil construction costs typically to be smaller the larger the school size.' However, when he turned to current operating costs, despite a thorough review of the American literature, and despite an exhaustive statistical examination of data for his four LEAs, he was unable to draw very firm conclusions in relation to secondary schools. Some of his relatively homogeneous school groups provided clear evidence of economies of size, but some did not. The statistical difficulties proved quite considerable. His failure to produce strong and extensive evidence of economies of scale in relation to secondary-school size is the last in a long line of previous attempts.

Yet on the face of it, it is rather surprising. Common sense will tell anyone with experience of schools that there ought to be economies of size. We would expect to see the following:

1 Some reduction in LEA overheads from administration of a smaller number of units.
2 Slimming of schools' staffing costs. Salaries of heads and deputies rise with increased numbers, but not in direct proportion. Larger schools tend to have fewer points for special responsibility allowances per hundred pupils than smaller schools. The booklet produced by the Secondary Heads' Association, *Big and Beautiful* (1979) made this point strongly:

   > A general count was done of points in all secondary schools in the authority. The points available for promotion vary from 1·7 per member of staff in the smaller schools to 0·9 in one of the very largest, and the group 12s and above have an average 1·2 to 1·3. (page 24)

3 One would expect that many functional costs of a school would not rise in proportion to numbers. Water, postage and telephones, maintenance of grounds, swimming pool and meals costs would be good examples. The only way in which one can envisage a larger school creating higher per pupil costs is (*a*) through increased internal communication costs, (*b*) by a duplication of facilities, and (*c*) Parkinson's Law.

My impression is that large schools do provide economies, but that these are often overlaid and outweighed by other factors connected with the growth of the school. Many large schools have grown as a result of comprehensive reorganization, and at the point of reorganization, heavy costs were often grafted on:

1 Because of projection of group size and points range.
2 From lavish initial kitting out. Some comprehensives were controversial, and the authority made sure that the new school could not be criticized for lack of provision. It had to satisfy parents that its laboratories would be as good as the grammar school and its workshops and art rooms as good as the secondary modern it replaced. If you like, C $\rangle$ G + M.

   Some of the early comprehensives were fitted out as show schools. There were also anxieties within the authority, for example, over size, and this explains some of the sometimes expensive provision for internal telephone systems and social accommodation. Also, any new school will tend to be built at the standard of the best current practice within the cost limits available. Therefore it is always likely to be more expensive to run than its more elderly sisters.

3 Because large schools have more leverage. Heads and senior staff are better paid; some large schools acquire county or national fame; the governing bodies tend to be more prestigious and therefore attract higher calibre governors (some LEAs only!). In many cases this has given larger schools stronger leverage for securing an increase in points, equipment or funds, etc.

4 Because quite a number of large schools are on split sites.

## *Comparisons by average unit costs per pupil*

The previous sections make clear that average unit costs will not be a very useful management tool until they can be used in a much more sophisticated way. A lot more research needs to be done, and agreement reached on which costs should be included and excluded. Local knowledge will always be essential for their interpretation. And caution will be necessary! Two schools with identical unit costs may start from different bases, and so make quite different provision. In particular, the heavy preponderance of teachers' salaries may mask other differences.

*Example*. Juventus High School has a young staff, and so lower salary costs, offset by generous capitation provision, good ancillary help and excellent buildings. Senescence Comprehensive has an elderly staff, all on the maximum of their scales, but miserable capitation, scanty ancillary help, and decrepit buildings. Yet both may have the same average unit costs.

However, average unit costs may come into use more rapidly than we think. For LEAs are saddled with the new Block Grant System introduced for 1981/82, whether they like it or not. In effect this establishes financial spending norms (Grant Related Expenditure) for each LEA – they do, of course, vary between LEAs because of special factors – and penalizes LEAs which exceed them by reducing the grant payable for above-norm spending. This tends to penalize LEAs with high unit costs. Indeed, it is possible for LEAs to calculate the average unit costs represented by the norm. This will in effect establish a 'standard cost' – a concept much used in industry to establish target costs and to measure variances from them. As the new GRE system becomes established one can foresee LEAs looking sharply at variances from school standard unit costs. However, such average costs will still suffer from the defects mentioned above. Comparisons between schools will be more useful if they are broken down under functional headings.

## *Comparisons by function*

*LEA overheads*

Within an LEA overheads fall evenly on all pupils. It could be argued that some schools incur greater administrative costs but it would be difficult and probably profitless to assess this. However, across LEA boundaries the per pupil costs of LEA administration vary considerably. Tom Hinds, Second Deputy Chief Education Officer in Cambridgeshire, analysed the CIPFA educational estimates for 1980/81. Total administrative costs as a percentage of net educational expenditure were as follows:

| | |
|---|---|
| London boroughs | 4·6% |
| ILEA | 6·5% |
| Metropolitan districts | 3·9% |
| English counties | 3·6% |
| Welsh counties | 4·2% |
| Average, all authorities | 4·0% |

Within these averages there is much sharper variation, for example:

| | | | | |
|---|---|---|---|---|
| Derbyshire | 2·6% | Gloucestershire | 4·9% | (almost double) |
| Dudley | 2·6% | Coventry | 5·3% | (more than double) |

Of these central expenses, 45 per cent was taken up in re-charges – charges made upon education departments by other departments for services rendered.

These statistics need interpreting with caution. However, if an LEAs central administrative costs could be brought down from, say, 5 to 4 per cent of its total expenditure, and the finance recycled, the impact on individual schools could be substantial. There appears to have been surprisingly little research into comparative administrative costs (best compared 'per pupil'). My impression is that where there is heavy reliance upon district education offices, administrative costs tend to be high. There are undoubtedly considerable variations between authorities' per pupil costs for library and museum services, educational and psychological services, in-service training for teachers, teacher centres, residential centres, etc. Hinds has pointed out that there are wide discrepancies in the proportion of administrative costs devoted to inspectors and advisers. English counties average one inspector/adviser to 3,555 pupils; metropolitan districts one to 2,820 pupils (a quarter as much again). Differences between individual authorities are even more marked:

| | | | |
|---|---|---|---|
| Warwickshire | 1:4,585 | Gloucestershire (80 per cent more) | 1:3,024 |
| Birmingham | 1:4,440 | Wolverhampton (nearly three times greater) | 1:1,596 |

However, as he points out, lower expenditure on this item may mean poorer quality control.

*Teaching costs*

Teachers' salaries

Since these are by far the largest element in a school's costs, and since they are often the main cause for the discrepancies and variations between schools and between local authorities described earlier, they deserve attention. Oddly, although a lot of detailed information is marshalled within the DES for expenditure projections, and within the local authorities and teachers' unions for salary negotiations, there is seldom detailed consideration of the effect of the teachers' salary system upon the costs of individual schools. Teachers often underestimate the effect of 'employers' contributions' on the teacher's salary bill.

Differences in teachers' salaries costs for schools of comparable size arise from a range of factors:

1 London allowances, paid on three scales for London and its fringe.
2 Group of school, affecting salaries of head and deputy heads, based on a weighted 'unit total' for numbers in different age-groups, averaged over a three-year period. This could add nearly £3,000 to the salary bill of a school just scraping into a group compared with one of comparable size just falling short (April 1981 salary scales).
3 LEA option to appoint senior teachers, group 10 and above, and third deputy, group 9 and above. In practice, policy varies from the generous to the niggardly, and there is sometimes variation within an LEA itself. Generous LEAs would be adding another £1,700 or so to the school's costs. On average, LEAs appoint about a quarter of the possible third deputies, and a half of the senior teachers.
4 LEA option to increase a school's total responsibility allowances. Most secondary schools are in a range (determined by the unit total) with fifteen points difference between the maximum and minimum points which can be provided. As each point is equivalent to approximately two increments with on-costs, an authority adopting the most generous policy would be paying about £10,000 more per school.
5 LEA policies on pupil/teacher ratio. The basic scales on which LEAs staff their secondary schools vary considerably. This variation is then compounded by their policies and attitudes towards special needs of particular schools, pressures from individual schools or influential councillors, difficulties of schools with falling rolls, the need to carry redeployed staff when schools are reorganized, etc. As a result, there are marked var-

iations in secondary pupil – teacher ratios between authorities. These statistics are usually published in the form of league tables. It is more realistic, however, if one adapts them to show the effect they produce upon a school, say, of 1,000 pupils (see Table 3:3)

**Table 3:3** Variation between LEAs in pupil–teacher ratios for secondary schools

| If an 11 to 16 school of 1,000, is transplanted from: | | |
|---|---|---|
| Leeds to Birmingham, | it gains 4·9 teachers, costs another | £34,000 p.a. |
| Leeds to Manchester, | it gains 11·7 teachers, costs another | £81,000 p.a. |
| Bradford to Sunderland, | it gains 5·8 teachers, costs another | £41,000 p.a. |
| Bradford to Newcastle, | it gains 12·1 teachers, costs another | £85,000 p.a. |
| Wakefield to Stockport, | it gains 5·0 teachers, costs another | £35,000 p.a. |
| Wakefield to Salford, | it gains 11·1 teachers, costs another | £78,000 p.a. |
| Suffolk to Bedfordshire, | it gains 3·2 teachers, costs another | £22,000 p.a. |
| Suffolk to Hertfordshire, | it gains 6·9 teachers, costs another | £48,000 p.a. |

*Source:* DES pupil–teacher ratios from form 7, based on actual teachers employed in schools, January 1980, quoted by NUT Research Unit.
It has been assumed that the additional staff are on scale I, at approximately £7,000 each per annum, including on-costs.

6 LEA administrative procedures. Its efficiency in making staff allocations; clawing back over-scale staffing; interpreting schools' projected numbers realistically; curbing special pleading; handling redeployments – all can affect the size of a school's salary bill.

7 LEA policy on comprehensive reorganization. Under reorganization a school's numbers are projected, so that its group and points scores can be brought forward. The net effect is to make the school more expensive for its present size, though not for its future size.

8 Age composition of staff. This is an historical accident, but it plays quite a significant part in cost differences between schools. For example, the HMI secondary education survey (1979) reported 'teachers in grammar schools, and to a lesser extent in modern schools, tended to be older and to have had longer experience than teachers in comprehensive schools'. Currently, with many fewer new entrant teachers joining schools, this composition becomes more important and the salary drift more significant. DES calculations in 1977 estimated salary drift at 0·7 per cent and 0·8 per cent in 1980/81 and 1981/82.

9 Promotions and retirements. These reduce total salary costs in a school, because replacements tend to come in at a lower incremental point. Difficult to calculate.

10 Early retirement. Operated extensively by some authorities. It obviously reduces salary costs. The bulk of an early retirement pension is paid from national superannuation funds, but the 'added years' are paid by the LEA.
11 LEA policies creating 'protected' salaries – teachers above scale 1 whose responsibility post is removed but whose original salary continues. Usually protected salaries are caused by reorganization, amalgamation or closure.
12 Variations in qualifications. The HMI secondary survey pointed out that in modern schools, 30 per cent of teachers were graduates or B.Ed.; in full range comprehensives, 50 per cent; in grammar schools, 79 per cent. Between individual schools variations would be wider, caused by different recruitment policies and ability to attract applicants.

In Chapter 3 of his dissertation Ilett examined some of these variables in staffing costs. For example, he noted that the scale 1 equivalent salaries (shorn of allowances) for one of his three schools were lower than in the others, even though they included social priority allowance, because the teachers in this school were less well qualified and less experienced (page 52). Such a school also developed a smaller sixth form and so obtained fewer points and a smaller staff, so once again its teachers' salary unit costs were lower.

Without question there are very considerable variations in the salary costs of apparently comparable schools within any one LEA. Hough discovered considerable variations in the four LEAs he studied. He found that teachers' salaries as a percentage of total costs (as he defined them) varied from 48 to 66 per cent. He also found 'that to some extent although not uniformly so, the percentage is higher in grammar schools or upper schools'. Pollard's figures for Somerset for 1977/78 showed this variation in detail. Teachers' salary costs per pupil, for example, were fairly uniform for the middle schools, with a low of £225 and a high of £249. There was more variation in the other groups, particularly in the 11 to 16 comprehensives: a low of £255, and a high of £346 (ex grammar school), or perhaps more realistic £298 (ex secondary modern).

Teachers' salaries: employers' contributions to superannuation and national insurance

Nationally determined. Variations between LEAs and individual schools will be minimal. Currently estimated at 21 per cent of salaries.

Supply teachers' salaries

Costs vary according to:

1 The supply policy of the LEA. Some LEAs cover all or most

absence for illness; others cover absence for courses. Few cover both, some cover little.
2 Health and morale, and attitudes to absence within each school. Some schools are more tolerant about covering their own absent staff. Others may even stretch the regulations.
3 Availability of supply teachers (better in urban areas).

Salaries: non-teaching support

Although salary scales are laid down nationally, once again there is considerable variation between LEAs, and perhaps even more within them. Some authorities have a standard scale for provision. Others have largely ad hoc allocations, which they are now gradually rationalizing. Hough found that teachers' salaries and non-teaching salaries were positively correlated for nearly all groups and sub-groups of schools. 'The implication is clearly that where a school has a highly qualified and highly paid teaching staff and/or favourable pupil/teacher ratio, it also has a high level of support staff, and vice versa'. Interesting!

Capitation and central allowances

Capitation is the life-blood of a school. The total costs of a school can in the main only be translated into learning experience through the medium of capitation. Apart from PE classes and any lessons which rely solely on the teacher's voice, learning activities can only take place with the aid of the books, equipment and materials which capitation buys.

Each authority decides annually its own capitation allowance per pupil, normally different for pupils 11 to 16 and for sixth-form students, although some authorities give an improved rate for 14- and 15-year-olds. The number of pupils is usually those on roll in September of the financial year. This means that at a time of falling rolls, the allowances fall five months early. With rising rolls, the school gains. The LEA normally builds into the per pupil allowance an increment for inflation. It is usually based on inflation for twelve months ending November preceding the beginning of the year. The inflation increment therefore acts in a similar way – schools suffer when the rate of inflation is rising and catch up when it is falling.

Inequalities between individual LEAs are notorious. Among the London boroughs in 1980/81, for example, Brent planned to spend almost twice as much on books and equipment per pupil as Hillingdon; and outside London, Buckinghamshire planned to spend almost twice as much as Suffolk or Cumbria; Bury twice as much as Trafford; South Tyneside twice as much as Bradford. In theory, the per capita allowances should at least create equality within LEA boundaries. In practice this is offset by extensive central funds allocated in a much more irregular manner. There may be allocations, for example, for reorganized schools or schools in deprived areas; or for a particular feature such as libraries or computers; or by advisers giving out where they see particular needs; or in response to pressures from schools. In theory such discriminatory provision has much to commend it. In practice often one adviser or department does not know what others have given. Some schools are adept at scooping the pool. Some indeed even acquire the reputation of being 'demanding' schools. Pollard's figures for Somerset, 1977/78, again illustrate this diversity. Middle school per pupil spending varied from £10 to £23, comprehensives from £17 to £28.

The items which capitation is meant to provide vary somewhat from LEA to LEA. All include provision for books, stationery, equipment and materials; most include some furniture, some include educational visits, cleaning materials and equipment, and, more recently, postage and telephone charges. Some of these latter items are often allocated on a different formula. Procedures vary, too, over aspects such as carrying forward of surpluses; crediting of income; and allowing spending across a whole range of items. Most authorities have some sort of 'good value' buying arrangements, either by direct contracts or by membership of consortia. Some of the larger authorities have excellent buying departments. In many cases schools have to place their orders for certain items with designated suppliers.

Examination fees

These are an expensive item. For example, in Holyrood's case they were equivalent in 1979/80 to 14 per cent of the school's capitation and allowances.

Examination costs are affected by a number of variables:

1 LEA policies to damp down the total number of entries, discourage 'fails' or absenteeism, restrict choice of examination boards; also partially to recoup fees by charging for retakes or for entries above a certain number.
2 School policies, for example, the number of subjects taken (this will depend partly on the school's curriculum), the choice of GCE board(s); the toleration of weak or 'no hope' entries (often used as a social control device); and observance of LEA regulations!
3 Socio-economic catchment area, which obviously affects the demand from children and parents to take examinations. It is slightly odd that the areas where parents are best able to pay for examination fees will be those where the examination costs are the highest.

Postage and telephones

Postage costs should have a general correlation with the size of the school. There are probably considerable variations in practice.

Many LEAs have a centralized distribution system for mail to and from offices.

Many comprehensives are equipped with extensive telephone systems which involve substantial annual hire charges. Call charges relate to the number of dialling out points, and to general control within a school. Abuse can be expensive! There is a strong trend for LEAs to devolve postage and telephone costs to schools, with an allowance.

Travelling allowances

There is considerable variation between LEAs and between schools. LEAs determine their own policy on travelling allowances, although recently a Council of Local Education Authorities code of practice has been drawn up. Different rates are paid for different purposes. Some authorities, particularly metropolitan, pay quite generous subsistence allowances for teachers. However, costs will also depend upon school practices. In most authorities, allowances are paid centrally, and often not logged against individual schools.

Advertisement expenses

Advertisement expenses are affected by LEA policy on the form and length of advertisements, and also by turnover in a particular school. Interview expenses are affected by LEA and school policies on the maximum number to be interviewed. One interview will commonly cost £200 to £300 (although it often decides an investment of many thousands of pounds). Far-flung outposts cost more, presumably.

*Premises and grounds costs*

The total impact of these is usually underestimated, because they are split up under a number of headings. In particular over a third of premises-related costs are debt charges, often excluded for the reasons mentioned earlier. The full breakdown is shown in Table 10:2.

Salaries

Salary scales are determined nationally. A school's establishment of caretaking and cleaning staff, however, depends on regional agreements relating it to area, but with some LEA variations.

> *Example.* Under the South Western Provincial Council Manual Workers Agreement, the first 8,100 square feet of a school's area provides a caretaker, and each 200 thereafter one weekly cleaning hour. There are some LEA variations, for example, Cornwall only allows 300 square feet per additional hour – and some LEAs reallocate the finance through work study schemes.

These square footage formulas are about to be superseded by more local agreements.

Grounds establishments are based on a formula individual to each LEA. Many LEAs arrange for grounds work to be done in part or whole by teams. In some cases it is undertaken by an estates or maintenance department. N. Bartman and T. Carden (*Education*, 16 October 1981) estimated labour costs of grounds maintenance at about £750 per hectare (£300 per acre) at 1980 prices, plus another £250 per hectare for non-labour costs. Further details will be provided in the forthcoming revised DES Building Bulletin 28.

Rates

The gross rateable value of a school is based upon its permanent 'internal class space area', adjusted for high or low site value; reduced if services are lacking, or if 'aged and obsolescent'; supplemented for kitchen, sports hall, swimming pool, rifle range/armoury [sic!], playing fields, community and temporary classrooms. This gross value is then abated by a 'superfluity allowance' which broadly reduces it in proportion to the extent that numbers of pupils are below recognized capacity, and a 'statutory deduction' which reduces it by a sliding amount (about 40 per cent for a small school to 17 per cent for a large one), to produce the rateable value. Of course the major part of the rates paid by an LEA for its schools returns to the authority, although not directly to the education budget.

Maintenance of premises

Costs will vary considerably from school to school, and not just in relation to the age of the building. Indeed, old buildings can often have low maintenance costs. Other factors will be the funds available from the county architect's, maintenance or estates department; the policy on the frequency of redecoration (for example, Army redecoration works on a seven year cycle); historical factors such as the construction of the buildings, reliability and quality of equipment and fittings; maintenance problems; the energy of the local man in dealing with maintenance questions; vandalism and misuse; the pressure from the school head and governors. Bartman and Carden suggested that some authorities may spend four times as much as others to maintain the same area, although for most shire counties costs appear to range from £1·8 to £4 per square metre at 1979/80 prices.

Heating

Costs depend upon:

1 DES cost limits for buildings, which affect insulation and energy saving.
2 Local authority architects' policies on ideal heating systems, sub-

sequent conversions to alternative energy sources, and on insulation in buildings.
3 Local authority policies on energy conservation, for example, prominence of fuel efficiency officers, monitoring of energy consumption, advice to head teachers, training for caretakers, investment in control devices, improved insulation, etc.
4 School practices, for example, information and training for staff, teachers' and pupils' attitudes and actions, caretakers' practices, pattern and times of school day, use of buildings outside school hours, etc.
5 Regional cost variations for various fuels.

And no doubt many other factors.

Many LEAs have introduced effective energy-saving policies. Some have introduced incentive schemes. Berkshire has given secondary schools targets, in volume units, and allowed schools to keep half the cash value of any savings.

Electricity

This will be affected by a similar range of factors. Within most schools the crucial factor is the correct choice of tariff and policies designed to minimize the charges of the maximum demand tariff.

Water

Being a volume-related charge, this is mainly affected by use of lavatories and school kitchens.

Swimming pools

These are an expensive hobby, creating costs for water, electricity, chemicals, fabric maintenance and possibly heating and lighting, and tuition. Normally most of these expenses are borne by the LEAs' central funds, but in some LEAs some or all are borne by the schools' theoretically adjusted capitation.

*Assistance to pupils*

The grants listed below are not normally coded against a school's costs.

Free meals

A national minimum scale for a family's net income establishes entitlement to free meals, broadly equivalent to that for Family Income Supplement and Supplementary Benefit. Some local authorities, however, go beyond this. LEAs are obliged to provide free meals 'so as to ensure that such provision is made for him [pupil] in the middle of the day as appears to the authority to be requisite'. Free meals costs in a particular school are obviously affected by other factors:

1 The socio-economic catchment area

2 Policies of the LEA and school in publicizing free meals, and encouraging take-up
3 Attractiveness of the meals
4 Ability of pupils to take other alternatives, for example, going home or eating outside of school.

Maintenance allowances

Payment is not mandatory. Maintenance allowances are, however, normally available for pupils over school-leaving age. The usual practice is a sliding scale, rather like students' grants, based on net family income.

The actual scale used by local authorities varies considerably. Variables as for school meals are the social catchment of the sixth form and the policy of the school in advertising and encouraging take-up. It is my impression that practice varies considerably from school to school. In some cases parents are almost unaware of their rights.

Miscellaneous additional grants

Some authorities pay grants for travel abroad, for attendance at courses or residential centres, for camps and visits, for sixth-formers' interviews. These bursaries, normally means-tested, vary in scope from authority to authority. In some they have now virtually disappeared.

Uniform grants

Again these are not mandatory. However, it is the normal practice among LEAs to provide a uniform grant for schools where there is compulsory school uniform. The grant is payable on entry to the school and at intervals thereafter. It is usually not particularly substantial, and certainly not enough to provide a full school uniform. Practice varies from LEA to LEA and actual costs depend upon the size and frequency of the grant, the income scale on which it is based, whether school uniform exists in a particular school or not, the catchment area, and advertisement of the grant.

Take-up of uniform grants is less than for free school meals, probably because the grant itself is worth much less annually, and also because it is sometimes more trouble for the claimant to collect. In extreme cases a grant for necessary clothing may be paid.

*School meals*

This is the one area of school costs which is changing rapidly at the present time and which shows itself capable of radical change. One does not get that helpless feeling that there is very little that can be done. The Education Act 1980 has altered the legal requirement. An LEA is no longer required to provide a school meal (other than free meals, above). 'It may provide . . . pupils . . . with milk, meals and other refreshment'. It is, however, required to provide appropriate facilities for the consumption of packed lunches, etc. As a result, authorities currently vary considerably in their approach, ranging from the radically abolitionist at one end to the conservationist at the other. Even within local authorities there is not always the same policy. In the same county there may be some schools where the meal has been abolished, apart from free meals which are brought in as a packed lunch; others where the cafeteria system operates; others where there is the traditional school meal. The main cost factors in school meals are:

1 Central administrative costs
2 Kitchen staff salaries
3 Salaries of supervisors, although these are often employed away from the dining hall
4 Clerical assistance – operating tills, keeping accounts, banking money
5 Premises – repair and maintenance, heating and lighting, water, rates, labour charges
6 Replacement of equipment and vehicles, commonly financed as a revenue contribution to capital outlay for major items, though not of course for small kitchen equipment
7 Clothing and laundry
8 Food.

Offsetting this is, of course, sales of meals to pupils and staff. Teachers are entitled to a free meal under certain circumstances. The actual agreement between unions and the DES (1968) states 'teachers who undertake the oversight of pupils during the mid-day break should be entitled to have a free school dinner'. Some LEAs also allow visiting officers (for example, advisers, careers officers) to dine free, in lieu of a lodging allowance. In practice the interpretation varies considerably from LEA to LEA and from school to school. Some LEAs allow a limited proportion of staff lunches to be free; others interpret the agreement more liberally. There will also be local factors, such as the attractiveness of the meal, dining conditions, distance of school from home, encouragement or discouragement of the free meal take-up by head, unions, etc. As a result this not inconsiderable cost factor does vary quite an amount from one school to another.

At the present time, the abolitionist approach to school meals has certainly produced savings, but offset by considerable residual costs, such as free meals, playground supervision, and fixed overheads. It seems quite likely that the more moderate approach is realizing greater savings by reducing the cost of the service and maximizing income.

*School transport*

The 1944 Education Act requires that LEAs 'shall make such arrangements for the provision of transport . . . as they consider necessary'. The sting lies in the school attendance clauses. These allow that parents cannot be prosecuted if their child's school is not within walking distance and no suitable transport arrangements have been made. Walking distance is three miles (two miles under 8 years), measured by the nearest available walking route, regardless of safety or class of road.

LEAs have discretion to carry other pupils, for example, those who come just under the statutory limits on routes where buses have capacity, or where roads are deemed to be dangerous, or who are over compulsory school age. In practice, LEA policy on discretionary transport varies, although it is wilting under central government financial pressure. Authorities also have the right to charge for discretionary transport and there is a growing tendency for these charges to be made, although offset with some administrative costs.

The transport itself is mainly provided by buses contracted by local operators. In many rural areas there is not a wide choice of operators, and a semi-monopoly situation often exists. Other children are carried by the LEA's own coaches, minibuses, or school meals' vans, and by season tickets on public transport. In more rural counties, there is also a network of private cars, taxis and bicycle allowances. It is a very expensive and complicated operation and some LEAs have computerized the system to make the best possible use of their bus runs, claiming savings in the process.

*Community education*

If school costs are a forest, then community education is a jungle. Where can you find such varieties of form, ranging from lush and extravagant to the stunted and bizarre?

Community education can comprise adult education centres, classes and similar activities; youth wings, youth activities; dual-use combined local authority and local council sports centres; dual-use community centres, libraries, etc.; lettings of premises to organizations or individuals.

In dual-use schemes, defined as those where an authority other than the LEA has made a substantial capital or revenue input, the financial arrangements are often tidy. Commonly a centre has its own budget, fed partly from the LEA, partly from the other council, together with its income, with its own employees and with its own metering of heat and light, etc. The cost of shared premises can often be apportioned between the LEA and the centre. The school will have free use of the facilities at set times. In other examples, the LEA actually pays for its school's use of the centre. Although these dual-use arrangements vary, they tend to create a reasonably neat separation of community costs.

In many schools, however, this is not the case. It may be possible to have salaries which are clearly identifiable as community education, for example, heads of adult community education, youth tutors, frequently some clerical, caretaking or supervisory salaries. Similarly, with postage, stationery, printing, furniture and equipment and materials costs. However, there is often no attempt to apportion premises costs for community education. Some LEAs have attempted this. Leicestershire, for example, recharged 10 per cent of rates, repairs and maintenance, together with a fixed amount for rent from the schools to the community education and youth service sections of the further education budget. It also recharged 10 per cent of fuel, water, cleaning materials costs, and 25 per cent electricity costs. This recharging, which in 1979/80 was in the order of £10,000 on average for each community college, was a book-keeping transfer. It was not generally notified to the colleges themselves. Its basis can be questioned. Rates and notional rent can be considered a 'sunk' cost, which would still be committed even if community education was withdrawn. Other items are clearly increased because of community usage, but the basis for recharging is subjective. The introduction of separate metering is really necessary to provide realistic costs for heating and lighting. This failure nationally to produce detailed and realistic cost information has prevented the production of good community education unit costs on a student hour and class/activity hour basis. Such figures as are quoted are seldom derived from full costs, and usually omit or estimate premises costs, central and even local administration. When community education salaries and allowances were included, together with caretaking and clerical cost, the average community costs of the Leicestershire colleges recharged for 1979/80 ranged between £23,000 and £49,000, with an average of £34,000.

The tendency is for greater local control of community education finance. It is not uncommon for community education colleges or adult education centres to be given a block budget comprising an allocation of teaching and non-teaching salaries, materials, equipment, printing, office expenses etc. with facility for virement between one item and another. It is also common for a 'net budgeting' system to operate, whereby centres may retain and re-spend any surplus income beyond budgeted income/expenditure. It was formerly common for LEAs only to expect class fees to cover a portion of the teacher's salary, but because of financial pressures this proportion has increased, and in many cases it now has to be met fully. In one sense this is a retrograde step, because it has increased fees and often restricted programmes or discouraged enrolment, as well as increasing the proportion of overheads in class costs. On the other, it can facilitate growth, because there is no longer any budgetary limit upon local decision to increase the number of classes offered.

With its three latest colleges Leicestershire has introduced a system by which each college is given its own budget, very much on the further education model. Here the budget is prepared and discussed between the college and the LEA, based on projected demand for the following year. Estimates have to be approved by the governing body and by the county council. This procedure offers some room for negotiation, and encourages forward planning. In the short term it assists the local authority in controlling expenditure, and allows scope for virement within revenue categories though not currently between them.

*Donations*

These are legion, and underestimated. Some schools are linked with charitable trusts which provide considerable supplements to income. Others have occasionally tapped specific trusts or charitable bodies. Almost all benefit from parents' associations or activities. Contributions can amount to several thousand pounds per year. In addition, teaching staff may generate their own activities for specific events, such as a fair or a concert, or minor events, where pupils contribute to swimming sessions or to the use of facilities or fees for matches. There are also commercially promoted schemes to raise funds by collecting labels, coupons, etc. An important source of funds is the appeal launched to the parent body or the community at large, usually for capital projects. Another source of funds is industry. This can take the form of direct sponsorship or of contributions for a specific project. A few schools have experimented with large lotteries, and most schools have a draw from time to time. There are individual donations, either large donations from a wealthy benefactor or the many small donations of parents, sometimes linked with a covenant scheme. The best known examples in the State system are perhaps the 'enrichment' schemes operated by a number of schools in Avon, advised by professional fund raisers and matched by a generous local benefactor. One of these has already raised £50,000 capital. Finally, and certainly not the least, we have contributions of individual parents for specific items which their children need, for example, stationery, atlases or textbooks, games equipment, all items which other schools would provide out of capitation. These last are probably illegal. The Education Act of 1944 states, 'No fees shall be charged in respect of admission to any school maintained by an LEA or any County College or in respect of the education provided in any such school or college.'

Most schools underestimate the aggregate importance of donations. I would estimate that many schools manage to supplement their capitation by 10 to 20 per cent.

## *The cost structure of independent schools*

Information on the costs of independent schools is not readily available. Some information has been published on the finances of public schools (Graham Kalton (1966) and Glennerster and Wilson (1970)), but it was not very detailed and is now somewhat out of date. ISIS (Independent Schools' Information Service) publishes some information about fees. In January 1980, for example, fees for day boys at public schools averaged £1,200. However, information on comparative costs of individual schools is not available, partly because it is not published and no doubt also because of competition between schools. Also public schools vary enormously between themselves in size, type, balance of day boys and boarders, age of buildings, endowments, etc. There is probably even more variation between costs of independent schools than within the ranks of maintained schools. The Public Schools Bursars' Association does exchange some information, but not cost comparisons. Schools of the Woodard Foundation apparently make some comparison of unit costs within some of their divisions, although such information is not readily available.

The headmaster of one independent school very kindly made his school's accounts available to me. These are presented in Table 3:4, using broadly the same headings as for the maintained school in Table 2:1. The costs of the two schools have been set out side by side, with slight adjustments. The public school in question contained 661 pupils in the school year 1979/80, of whom 210 were in the sixth form. Approximately 113 boys were boarders. It occupied substantial buildings, most of them dating from the last century and therefore not incurring loan charges.

It needs to be emphasized very strongly that any comparisons should be made with great caution. First, there is no indication that either the independent or maintained school is typical. Secondly, we are not comparing like with like. The independent school is rather like a grammar school in its general organization and the proportion of its sixth form. A comparison of a grammar school and a 11 to 18 comprehensive would show some similar differences. Thirdly, the independent school has a boarding establishment and some costs had to be allocated between the day school and the boarding houses. The accuracy of the allocation affects such figures. Finally, it is obvious that certain expenses in the maintained school are not necessary in the independent school. Examples are: LEA administrative overheads (although it can be argued that as these have been allocated on the 'full cost' principle to the maintained school they are an integral part of its costs); assistance to pupils; transport costs; subsidized meal costs; community education costs. So the two sets of costs are not really for close comparison. However, some differences are worthy of comment.

**Table 3:4** The costs of one independent and one maintained secondary school, 1979/80

| | *Net costs (£s)* | | *% of total net costs* | | *Costs per pupil (£s)* | | *Costs per weighted pupil (£s) (d)* | |
|---|---|---|---|---|---|---|---|---|
| TEACHING AND ADMINISTRATIVE COSTS | I | M | I | M | I | M | I | M |
| LEA administration and inspection | N/A | 25,000 | N/A | 2·9 | N/A | 23·0 | N/A | 21·9 |
| LEA library, museum, residential, psychological and careers services, INSET and education/resource centres | N/A | 17,500 | N/A | 2·0 | N/A | 16·1 | N/A | 15·3 |
| Salaries, teaching | 341,660 | 428,520 | 59·8 | 49·2 | 516·9 | 393·9 | 434·1 | 375·9 |
| ditto, bursar and clerical support | 16,620 | | 2·9 | | 25·1 | | 21·1 | |
| ditto, laboratory assistance | 7,680 | | 1·3 | | 11·6 | | 9·8 | |
| Total salaries, non-teaching support | 24,300 | 48,120 | 4·3 | 5·5 | 36·8 | 44·2 | 30·9 | 42·2 |
| Books | 7,460 | | 1·3 | | 11·3 | | 9·5 | |
| Stationery, materials and equipment | 24,510 | | 4·3 | | 37·1 | | 31·1 | |
| Repairs and replacement of furniture | 3,430 | | 0·6 | | 5·2 | | 4·3 | |
| Revenue contribution to capital outlay on furniture and equipment | 3,180 | N/S (a) | 0·6 | (a) | 4·8 | (a) | 4·0 | (a) |
| Games and sport expenses | 13,010 | | 2·3 | | 19·7 | | 16·5 | |
| Duke of Edinburgh Award (expedition) | 300 | | 0·1 | | 0·4 | | 0·4 | |
| Combined Cadet Force | 2,130 | | 0·4 | | 3·2 | | 2·7 | |
| Outward Bound | 1,240 | | 0·2 | | 1·9 | | 1·6 | |
| Other expenses | 3,160 | | 0·6 | | 4·8 | | 4·0 | |
| Medical | 240 | | – | | 0·4 | | 0·3 | |
| Gross (b) total, books, stationery, materials, equipment, sports, expeditions, etc., costs | 58,660 | 39,850 | 10·3 | 4·6 | 88·7 | 36·6 | 74·5 | 35·0 |

| | *Net costs (£s)* | | *% of total net costs* | | *Costs per pupil (£s)* | | *Costs per weighted pupil (£s) (d)* | |
|---|---|---|---|---|---|---|---|---|
| | I | M | I | M | I | M | I | M |
| Gross (b) total, examination fees | 4,580 | 5,550 | 0·8 | 0·6 | 6·9 | 5·1 | 5·8 | 4·8 |
| Postage and telephones, printing, office stationery | 13,270 | 2,690 (c) | 2·3 | 0·3 | 20·1 | 2·5 | 16·9 | 2·4 |
| Advertisements, interview expenses and entertainment allowances | 1,970 | 1,530 (d) | 0·3 | 0·2 | 3·0 | 1·4 | 2·5 | 1·3 |
| Audit expenses | 850 | N/A | 0·1 | N/A | 1·3 | N/A | 1·1 | N/A |
| Total, teaching and administrative costs | 445,290 | 568,760 | 77·9 | 65·3 | 673·7 | 522·8 | 565·8 | 498·9 |
| PREMISES AND GROUNDS COSTS | | | | | | | | |
| Salaries, caretaking and cleaning | 19,410 | 30,820 | 3·4 | 3·5 | 29·3 | 28·3 | 24·7 | 27·0 |
| ditto, grounds | 9,420 | 9,620 | 1·6 | 1·1 | 14·2 | 8·8 | 12·0 | 8·4 |
| ditto, maintenance | 4,730 | N/A | 0·8 | N/A | 7·2 | N/A | 6·0 | N/A |
| ditto, bursar and clerical support | 3,170 | 500 | 0·6 | 0·1 | 4·8 | 0·5 | 4·0 | 0·4 |
| Total salaries, premises and grounds | 36,730 | 40,940 | 6·4 | 4·7 | 55·5 | 37·6 | 46·7 | 35·9 |
| Rates | 8,010 | 28,560 | 1·4 | 3·3 | 12·1 | 26·2 | 10·2 | 25·1 |
| Maintenance, premises | 23,610 | 24,700 | 4·1 | 2·8 | 35·7 | 22·7 | 30·0 | 21·7 |
| ditto, grounds | 7,260 | 1,590 | 1·3 | 0·2 | 11·0 | 1·5 | 9·2 | 1·4 |
| LEA services to grounds | N/A | 2,700 | N/A | 0·3 | N/A | 2·5 | N/A | 2·4 |
| Heating, lighting, water and cleaning | 16,680 | 18,390 | 2·9 | 2·2 | 25·2 | 16·9 | 21·2 | 16·1 |
| Swimming-pool expenses | N/S | 1,060 | N/S | 0·1 | N/S | 1·0 | N/S | 0·9 |
| Insurance | 2,380 | N/S | 0·4 | N/S | 3·6 | N/S | 3·0 | N/S |
| Debt charges and revenue contributions to capital outlay on buildings and grounds | 21,090 | 102,700 | 3·7 | 11·8 | 31·9 | 94·4 | 26·8 | 90·1 |
| Laundry | 850 | N/S | 0·1 | N/S | 1·3 | N/S | 1·1 | N/S |
| Total, premises and grounds costs | 116,610 | 220,640 | 20·4 | 25·3 | 176·3 | 202·8 | 148·2 | 193·6 |

| | Net costs (£s) | | % of total net costs | | Costs per pupil (£s) | | Costs per weighted pupil (£s) (d) | |
|---|---|---|---|---|---|---|---|---|
| | I | M | I | M | I | M | I | M |
| ASSISTANCE TO PUPILS (including LEA overheads) | N/A | 10,640 | N/A | 1·2 | N/A | 9·8 | N/A | 9·3 |
| SCHOOL TRANSPORT (including LEA overheads) | N/A | 37,690 | N/A | 4·3 | N/A | 34·6 | N/A | 33·1 |
| SCHOOL MEALS | | | | | | | | |
| LEA overheads | N/A | 1,800 | N/A | 0·2 | N/A | 1·7 | N/A | 1·6 |
| Food | 16,640 | 12,080 | 2·9 | 1·4 | 25·2 | 11·1 | 21·1 | 10·6 |
| Salaries, supervisors | N/A | 2,260 | N/A | 0·3 | N/A | 2·1 | N/A | 2·0 |
| ditto, kitchen staff | 16,190 | 16,010 | 2·8 | 1·8 | 24·5 | 14·7 | 20·6 | 14·0 |
| Premises, equipment, cleaning, office overheads | 2,280 | 4,540 | 0·4 | 0·5 | 3·5 | 4·2 | 2·9 | 4·0 |
| Total expenditure | 35,110 | 36,690 | 6·1 | 4·2 | 53·2 | 33·8 | 44·6 | 32·2 |
| Less income received | 25,320 | 7,980 | 4·4 | 0·9 | 38·3 | 7·3 | 32·2 | 7·0 |
| Net total, school meals costs | 9,790 | 28,710 | 1·7 | 3·3 | 14·8 | 26·4 | 12·4 | 25·2 |
| COMMUNITY EDUCATION, NET | N/A | 4,500 | N/A | 0·5 | N/A | 4·1 | N/A | 3·9 |
| Full cost totals | 571,690 | 870,890 | 100·0 | 100·0 | 864·5 | 800·5 | 726·4 | 763·9 |

*Notes:*

1 I = Independent schools, as described above
M = Maintainted school, as per Table 2:1
N/S = Not separated. N/A = Not applicable

2 Costs per weighted pupil. Sixth-form pupils have been weighted at 1·6:1. This gives the independent school a weighted total of 787, and the maintained school a weighted total of 1,140 (see Appendix B).

3 Letters in table represent the following:
(a) Some of the LEA loan charges would be for equipment and furniture, but proportion cannot be separated.
(b) Gross totals – before income deducted.
(c) Postage and telephone only. Printing and office stationery, perhaps £700, included in books and stationery.
(d) No entertainment allowance!

*Teacher salaries*

As expected, teacher salaries were considerably higher per pupil for the independent school - 30 per cent more - but if they are compared on a weighted pupil basis, the figure shrinks to only 15 per cent. Although the maintained school had its expensive staffing areas - for example, remedial teaching and a higher proportion of time spent on practical subjects - the difference is less than expected. The independent school in question did not seem to put heavy emphasis on small class size. Non-teaching costs, in contrast, were appreciably higher in the maintained school.

*Books, stationery, materials, equipment, sports and expedition expenses*

This is perhaps the most striking feature of the two sets of cost information. The total expended in the public school was nearly two and a half times as much per pupil as that spent in the maintained school, and still twice as much on the weighted pupil figures. In this expenditure a particularly striking feature was the large amount spent on games, sport (including transport) and outdoor activities. If one links this with costs later in the table, such as groundsmen's salaries, grounds' maintenance and debt charges, and revenue contributions to grounds, the total amount spent in this area in the public school was very much greater.

*Postage, telephone, printing and office stationery costs*

These costs seemed much higher in the independent school. This may be partly explained by the fact that it needed to put on a much better public face, and also because it had to deal frequently with its parents over fees and other matters by post.

*Rates*

Rates in the independent school were very much less. This no doubt reflects rate relief, and also in part the age of the buildings.

*Maintenance of premises*

Figures are not really comparable because obviously these can fluctuate from one year to another. It is interesting to note, however, that the public school expended nearly £5,000 a year on its own direct labour salaries, so that a much higher proportion of the maintenance costs would be for materials used by its own staff rather than work by outside contractors.

*Debt charges*

Debt charges are nearly five times greater for the maintained school, reflecting the relative youth of Somerset's secondary buildings. About half of the figure shown for the public school was in fact contributions from revenue to capital outlay, rather than debt charges.

*School meals*
School meals figures are difficult to compare without using the number of meals served.

We should be extremely cautious about drawing any conclusions from such sets of figures. I have only included them because I am not aware that any such comparison has been attempted before and in the hope that this may spur other researchers to carry out a thorough survey. The first need is to produce some comparative costs from independent schools. Indeed, it is surprising that they have not already produced these themselves. Since they are in the business of securing good value for money, one would have expected them to have compared costs for heating and lighting, for example, to get some idea of their own efficiency. However, the differences between independent schools mentioned earlier will make such cost comparisons difficult.

## *Conclusions*

Faced with this range and variety of schools' cost structures, what conclusions should we make? First . . .

*Grounds for despair*

1 Over 50 per cent of a school's costs normally comes from teachers' salaries.

2 Irregularity of LEA policies
These obviously create differences in comparable schools *across* authority boundaries. But they also create considerable differences within LEAs themselves. LEAs are still digesting the reorganization of 1974, and differences between schools in different areas reflect the different provision which existed previously. Sometimes new policies are introduced piecemeal, creating differences between one school and another – extension of community education would be a good example. Also LEAs allow considerable variation from their avowed policies, sometimes for positive discrimination, sometimes reacting to pressure from politicians or schools, sometimes by accident or default.

3 Diversity of schools
Obviously types of school are important. A grammar school with a large sixth form will normally be considerably more expensive than a secondary modern. A comprehensive growing from the bottom may take seven years to become fully comprehensive, and even then some of the cost features of its previous existence will show. Middle schools or 13 to 18 schools will be very different from 11 to 16 schools.

Size is also a factor, although research has not thrown up any clear evidence of economies of scale. There are suspicions that schools with around a thousand pupils are cheaper to run per pupil than smaller schools, but that larger schools become slightly more expensive again. However, this is certainly open to debate.

Buildings are important because of the 30 per cent or so of total costs related to them. The main factors here are size; utilization (square footage relating to the number of pupils); whether they are expensive to maintain, exposed or sheltered (both against the elements and human intrusion); single or split site.

Another important feature is the school's social/economic catchment area. It may increase its costs for aids to pupils, a lower pupil – teacher ratio or additional pastoral allowances; it may, however, reduce costs for examination expenses and sixth-form allowances.

Finally, an underrated differential between schools is donations. Some schools have substantial sources of additional funds available, through trusts or very active PTAs or commercial type fund-raising. Although such differentials appear to be small in percentage terms, they can make a very noticeable difference to a school's stock of equipment, textbooks, etc.

4 History and inertia

There is plenty of evidence to suggest that these are two of the most powerful forces affecting the structure of a school's costs. What was, will be.

5 Supply, demand and need

Costs are an expression of supply. They reflect the supply of finance from the central government – of increasing importance – and the local authority, through decisions on rates, priorities and allocations.

Costs are also an expression of demand. Demand varies with pupil numbers. It is also affected by political factors – less with the debate at elections, and more with local pressures between elections. A strong councillor can affect cost-structures considerably. So can trade unions in relation to wage settlements, manning levels, and other cost items. There are other less obvious demand forces – the influential officer or department, influential governors or heads, PTA and former pupil lobbies.

Finally there is the more elusive pull of need. We all need a good education. But what do we need? For how long? At what quality? At what expense? And who decides? By what criteria? And if students do not want what they need . . . ?

*Grounds for hope*

1 Uneven data

Undoubtedly some of the differences are apparent rather than real, arising either from inaccuracies in collection or allocation of data, or idiosyncracies in its presentation.

2 Many costs are manageable
While teachers' salaries may seem monolithic, the remaining central overheads and school-incurred costs are made up of a mass of tiny components, each of which can be influenced.

3 One per cent is a lot of money
One per cent at Holyrood School, for example, is £8,700. One only needs a tiny shift in the balance of expenditure to create substantial gains elsewhere.

4 Scope for change
School costs seem to be immovably caught in a web of national, LEA and school policies, decisions, attitudes. Yet none of these constraints at any of the three levels is immutable. With imagination and determination, all can be altered.

## *What does it all mean?*

We all know what school meals figures mean. If a school meal costs more in one authority than others, then this is a 'bad thing'. What about teaching costs? Premises costs? Even LEA overheads? If one authority spends more on these items, is it reprehensible or commendable? Ian Coutts, Norfolk county councillor, (*County Councils' Gazette*, September 1979), put it nicely: 'Has Bedfordshire something to learn from Lancashire where they educate primary school children at a cost per pupil 30 per cent lower than Bedfordshire? Is Suffolk super efficient in that it educates secondary school pupils at a cost per head 20 per cent less than Surrey?' We do not know what to think. More must be better . . . but cheaper must be better too.

The Americans have been through this long before. In the 1970s there was an outburst of litigation over inequalities in the financing of schools. Litigants brought powerful evidence to show that the financial system of a particular state operated unequally and to the detriment of their children. In California the State Court ruled that 'the State may not . . . permit . . . significant disparities in expenditures between school districts . . . disparities must be reduced to amounts considerably less than $100 per pupil' (Serrano versus Priest, Los Angeles County Court 1974, quoted by Hough). The argument raged, school boards versus States and parents versus school boards. The Washington D.C. State Court gave the important ruling that 'dollars count unless proven otherwise'.

Yet, do they prove otherwise? Is quantity of expenditure any indication of quality of provision? Can we just measure inputs and ignore outcomes? And so our pilgrim journeys into the Quicksand of Efficiency, Effectiveness and Productivity. But first, two short diversions . . .

# 4 The Costs of Primary Schools

Primary school costs are the 'Dark Continent' of school finance. Although it ought to be easier to study them, even less work has been done in this field than in the secondary.

## *Costs of individual primary schools*

Table 4:1 sets out the running costs for three Somerset primary schools for the financial year 1980/81. All are 5 to 11 schools. School A serves a country town, the others villages. LEA overhead costs have been reapportioned in a similar way to the secondary school in Chapter 2, as described in Appendix A.

These figures cannot be claimed to be representative or typical. But they do give some idea of how primary-school costs are made up, and how per pupil unit costs can be affected by school size. Close comparative study of them raises as many questions as it answers.

**Table 4:1** The costs of three primary schools, 1980/81

| | SCHOOL A (516 children; staff: head +17) | | SCHOOL B (194 children; staff: head +6) | | SCHOOL C (59 children; staff: head +2.3) | |
|---|---|---|---|---|---|---|
| | *Total cost* | *Cost per pupil* | *Total cost* | *Cost per pupil* | *Total cost* | *Cost per pupil* |
| LEA OVERHEADS | | | | | | |
| Central administration and inspection | 10,400 | | 3,900 | | 1,200 | |
| Central administration recharged to school meals | 400 | | 150 | | 50 | |
| Central grounds maintenance | 900 | | 300 | | 100 | |
| Library and museum service | 2,250 | | 850 | | 250 | |
| Residential centres | 110 | | 40 | | 10 | |
| Educational psychological service | 670 | | 250 | | 80 | |
| In-service training for teachers | 130 | | 50 | | 10 | |
| Education and resource centres | 350 | | 130 | | 40 | |
| Debt charges and revenue contributions to capital outlay | 14,280 | | 3,030 | | 1,720 | |
| Total LEA Overheads | 29,490 | 57·2 | 8,700 | 44·8 | 3,460 | 58·6 |
| SCHOOL-BASED COSTS | | | | | | |
| *Teaching costs* | | | | | | |
| Salaries, teaching (establishment) | 141,010 | 273·3 | 73,360 | 378·1 | 24,800 | 420·0 |
| ditto (supply) | FNA* | | FNA | | FNA | |
| Teaching support salaries | 2,260 | 4·4 | 970 | 5·0 | - | - |
| Clerical salaries (other than on school meals) | 3,150 | 6·1 | 720 | 3·7 | 470 | 8·0 |
| Capitation and other allowances expenditure (books, stationery, materials, equipment, furniture) less income credited | 5,290 | 10·3 | 2,510 | 12·9 | 980 | 16·6 |
| Postage and telephone | 430 | 0·8 | 210 | 1·1 | 230 | 3·9 |
| Travelling expenses, advertisements, interview expenses | | | | | - | - |
| Total teaching costs | 152,140 | 294·8 | 77,770 | 400·9 | 26,480 | 448·8 |

**Table 4:1** The costs of three primary schools, 1980/81

| | SCHOOL A *(516 children; staff: head +17)* | | SCHOOL B *(194 children; staff: head +6)* | | SCHOOL C *(59 children; staff: head +2.3)* | |
|---|---|---|---|---|---|---|
| | *Total cost* | *Cost per pupil* | *Total cost* | *Cost per pupil* | *Total cost* | *Cost per pupil* |
| *Premises and grounds costs* | | | | | | |
| Salaries (caretaking and cleaning) | 10,680 | 20·7 | 3,320 | 17·1 | 1,970 | 33·4 |
| Rates | 4,330 | 8·4 | 920 | 4·7 | 520 | 8·8 |
| Maintenance premises | 2,730 | 5·3 | 1,390 | 7·2 | 550 | 9·3 |
| Maintenance grounds | 60 | 0·1 | 4,650 | 24·0 | 1,950 | 33·1 |
| Heating and lighting: | | | | | | |
| electricity | 1,770 | 3·4 | 970 | 5·0 | 570 | 9·7 |
| oil | 2,670 | 5·2 | 430 | 2·2 | 460 | 7·8 |
| gas | – | | 280 | 1·4 | 150 | 2·6 |
| Total heating and lighting costs | 4,440 | 8·6 | 1,680 | 8·7 | 1,180 | 20.0 |
| Water | 440 | 0·9 | 380 | 2·0 | 90 | 1·5 |
| Cleaning materials and equipment | 1,250 | 2·4 | 410 | 2·1 | 190 | 3·2 |
| Swimming-pool | 70 | 0·1 | 10 | | – | – |
| Total premises and grounds costs | 24,000 | 46·5 | 12,760 | 65·7 | 6,450 | 109·4 |
| Total *assistance to pupils* (free meals at paying rates) | 4,180 | 8·1 | 650 | 3·3 | 190 | 3·2 |
| Total *school transport* | FNA | | – | | – | |

| | | | | | | |
|---|---|---|---|---|---|---|
| *School meals* | | | | | | |
| Food | 5,920 | 11·5 | FNA | FNA | 1,660 | 28·1 |
| Salaries, supervisors | 4,650 | 9·0 | FNA | FNA | 520 | 8·8 |
| ditto, kitchen staff | 15,650 | 30·3 | FNA | FNA | 4,460 | 75·6 |
| ditto, clerical support (establishment) | 800 | 1·6 | 430 | 2·2 | 50 | 0·8 |
| premises | 10 | – | FNA | FNA | 160 | 2·7 |
| Total expenditure | 27,030 | 52·4 | FNA | FNA | 6,850 | 116·0 |
| Less income received | 11,510 | 22·3 | FNA | FNA | 3,980 | 67·4 |
| Net total school meals costs | 15,520 | 30·1 | Estimate 6,000 | Estimate 30·9 | 2,870 | 48·6 |
| DONATIONS EXPENDITURE | | | | | | |
| Radio | | | 900 | | | |
| Capitation items | 470 | | | | 80 | |
| Swimming items | 380 | | | | | |
| Other items | 1,200 | | | | | |
| Total donations expenditure | 2,050 | 4·0 | 900 | 4·4 | 80 | 1·4 |
| Full cost totals | 227,380 | 440·7 | 106,780 | 550·4 | 40,710 | 670·0 |

*Note:* All salaries include employers' contributions.
*FNA = figures not available.

## *Comparisons between LEAs*

We can again use the CIPFA unit costs, based upon local authority estimates for 1980/81 for the same cost categories as the secondary costs in the previous chapter.

**Fig. 4:1** Primary school unit costs, net expenditure per pupil, for LEAs in groups, 1980–81 (includes middle schools deemed primary)

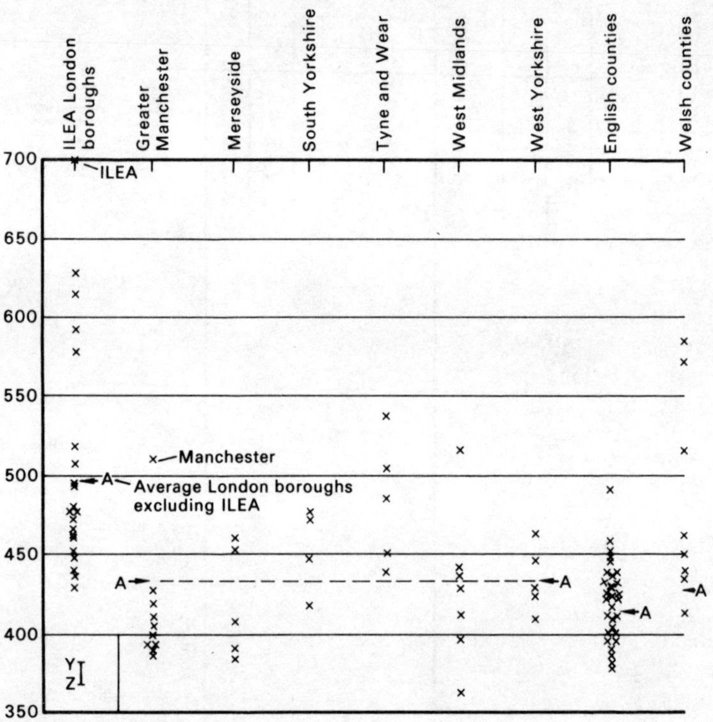


*Source.* CIPFA Education Statistics 1980/81 Estimates.

*Note.* $^{Y}_{Z}$I Average national expenditure per pupil on books, stationery, equipment and materials

A Average for group(s)

Figure 4:1 sets out primary-school unit costs per pupil for all LEAs 1980/81. The disparity between groups of authorities and between LEAs within the same group is again most striking. Many of the features apparent in secondary schools are still present:

1 Unit costs in the ILEA are considerably higher than any other authority
2 London borough unit costs as a group are higher than any other group – although the margin for primary schools is not so pronounced as for secondaries
3 Manchester is a considerable amount higher than its satellite authorities (but no longer has the highest unit costs of all metropolitan authorities outside London)
4 There is substantial variation between the different groups of metropolitan authorities
5 English counties showed the lowest degree of variation of any group
6 Welsh counties' costs are on average considerably higher than English counties
7 The spread in every group is considerable, with the highest cost LEA in the group spending from 13 to 46 per cent more per pupil than the lowest cost member. This spread within groups is proportionately considerably more for primary schools – something like half as great again.

However, although at first sight the pattern of unit costs in Figure 4:1 looks very similar to its secondary counterpart in Figure 3:1, on close examination there are differences.

West Midlands and the West Yorkshire authorities reverse their relationship for primary education compared with secondary. In other words, unit costs of the West Midlands are appreciably higher on average in secondary schools than West Yorkshire, but lower for primary schools.

The anonymous crosses on the graph conceal considerable oscillation for individual authorities. It is best shown by examining a set of league tables such as those produced by the NUT's research unit. Obviously these need treating with care, because where authorities are closely bunched, a relatively minor percentage may cause a substantial position shift. However, some of the results for 1980/81 are still surprising. For example, Harrow was in the middle of the London boroughs (twelfth) for secondary unit costs, but among the highest unit costs (fourth) for primaries. The most striking variations occur in the English counties. Cumbria, for example, was second in the league table for primaries, and thirty-third (out of thirty-nine) for secondary schools; the Isle of Wight, fourth for primaries and thirty-fourth for secondary schools. Conversely, Lincolnshire with lowest unit costs of all for primaries, was eighth highest for secondary schools. Middle schools may be one factor in causing such variations. However, this cannot be uniformly true. Of counties which have no middle schools, Durham was third highest for primary unit-costs, twenty-fourth for secondary; Buckinghamshire twenty-first for primary and third for secondary; Cornwall thirty-fifth and second; Lancashire thirty-seventh and eighteenth.

Because so little research has been done upon the distribution of primary-school costs, it would be dangerous to speculate on what these variations mean. However, it is difficult to believe that such wide variations are explicable solely in terms of a particular LEAs environment, problems and needs. Take the considerable spread in primary-school costs in the Tyne and Wear authorities, for example, or in the West Midlands. Can conditions be so very different? A useful examination of such variations is Howick and Hassani's paper 'Education Spending: Primary' (1976). This stressed the importance of historical factors. It showed for example that over a third of the variation in per pupil primary spending among LEAs in 1976/77 could be explained by the previous pattern in 1968/69. (This was very similar to evidence produced in an appendix to the Plowden Report in 1967.) At the greatest extreme were the Welsh counties with over four fifths of the 1976/77 variation accounted for by that in 1968/69. The outer London boroughs, in contrast, were volatile across the period, and showed no such continuity. There was a general tendency however for the spending of urban areas to increase compared with rural areas over this eight year period. Howick and Hassani also assessed the relationship between LEAs spending per pupil and socio-economic factors. There was positive correlation, particularly with overcrowding and one parent families. Such a relationship was much more positive for outer London than for the shire counties. They also explored correlation of per pupil expenditure with political control of the council, and found that this was strong for Labour controlled outer London boroughs, but again not in the shire counties. Although it is not always easy to see what such variations in expenditure between LEAs mean, it's clear what they mean in another sense. The YZ line in Figure 4:1 again brings home to us that even a slight shift in the unit costs of an authority could lead to the doubling of its expenditure on books, stationery, equipment and materials. It is difficult, too, to believe that if Trust House Forte (Primary Schools) Ltd bought out our LEAs, it would accept or tolerate such a wide variation in production costs.

It is obvious, and clearly established, that primary-school costs are strongly influenced by size. The effect of types is less obvious. Yet the classification of primary schools is almost as complicated as secondary: 19 per cent infant schools 5 to 7; 11 per cent first schools 5 to 8 or 5 to 9; 19 per cent junior schools 7 to 11; 49 per cent primary schools 5 to 11; 2 per cent combined first and middle schools 5 to 11 (figures from HM Inspectorate survey *Primary Education in England* 1978). There are also middle schools 'deemed primary' 8 to 12, excluded from the survey. The HM Inspectorate survey does not comment on costs but it provides some useful information. In rural areas, 77 per cent of primary schools had a one-form entry or less (87 per cent of these were 5 to 11 schools) that is 210 pupils or less. In urban areas only 17 to 20 per cent of primary schools were that small. Fifty-six per cent of schools in inner city areas were located in districts of 'marked social difficulty', compared with 18 per cent for other urban areas and 7 per cent for rural areas.

## *Comparisons within LEAs*

The evidence is depressingly thin, but it supports views in the previous chapter that costs of schools vary very considerably within a particular LEA.

Hough (1981) included some data on primary schools as a by-product of his work on the secondary sector. He considered the cost data for all the primary schools of one authority in 1974/75 and 1975/76, and of a second authority in 1975/76 (380 and 285 schools respectively). In the former, unit costs ranged in one year from a mean of £207 per pupil (with a minimum of £127 and a maximum of £811) and the second year from £259, with minimum of £110 and a maximum of £788. In the second authority, the range was not so wide, with a mean of £197, a minimum of £122 and a maximum of £508.

It is immediately obvious that the range of variation was very considerable, and in fact the coefficients of variation for primary schools were substantially larger than for secondary schools. Hough noted the mean unit costs per pupil were considerably lower for primary schools than secondary; these means would have been even lower but for the fact that they were boosted by the very small primary schools which existed in both authorities and which were very expensive to run in per pupil terms.

T. M. Hinds (1980) gave details of thirteen primary schools from within one authority. If set on a graph with axes of pupil numbers and cost per pupil, these show a broad curve reflecting the increasing pupil cost of small schools. However, within this generalization, considerable variations are apparent. For example, there are pairs of schools of almost exactly the same size with appreciably different unit costs (246 and 250 pupils, costing £225 and £319 per pupil; 204 and 205, £272 and £311). Hinds gave subsidiary unit costs for teaching staff, premises and fixed plant, supplies and services. The variation was again considerable. For example, teaching staff unit costs between schools of 246/250/252 pupils ranged from £186 to £201 to £221. The same group had non-teaching staff costs varying from £23 to £32 to £49. Schools of 190/204/205 pupils had premises and fixed plant costs varying from £27 to £69 to £71. There was less variation for costs of supplies and services, which were fairly uniform apart from two very small schools. Without further information it is impossible to speculate on the reasons for these differences. They may relate to differences in school type, for example, differences in

**Fig. 4:2** Cambridgeshire primary school unit costs per pupil 1979/80 in cost bands (presented to the Finance and Buildings sub-committee, 11 September 1980)[1]

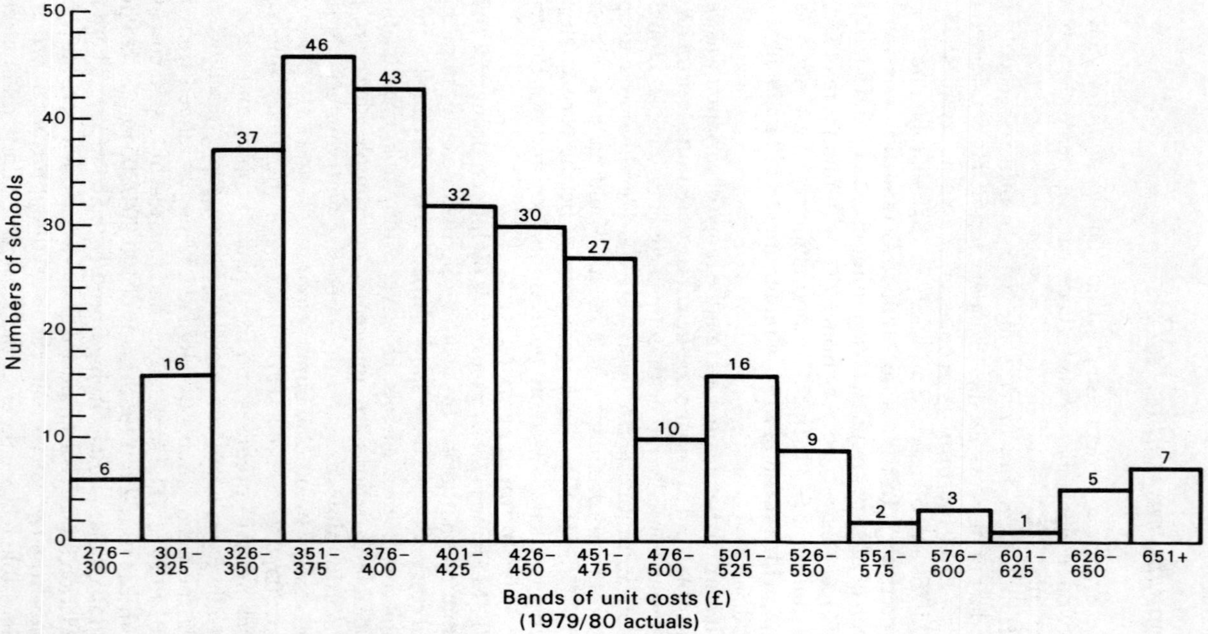


[1] Reprinted by permission of Cambridgeshire County Council

premises or in age structure of staffs. Nevertheless, it is worth pointing out that the differences between schools in each of the pairs quoted above was rather more than the amount that each school spent on capitation.

Cambridgeshire has recently (1980) used its computer to examine the unit costs of its primary schools. A report presented to the Finance and Buildings sub-committee 11 September 1980:

1 Compared the LEA's primary-school unit costs with the national average (using CIPFA statistics)
2 Compared unit costs for teachers' and other salaries, premises, supplies and services, for a selected high, medium and low cost school compared with the average for all primary schools in the LEA
3 Presented a diagram showing the number of primary schools in different cost bands (reproduced in Figure 4:2).

At first sight the information is a little unexciting. There is the customary warning:

> It is clear that the figures have to be interpreted very carefully. No two schools are exactly the same – they may differ in such matters as age and design, method of heating, repair costs, age of staff (e.g. long serving staff are likely to have reached the top of scales). This information is helpful to management for various purposes e.g. dealing with specific enquiries, investigating variations from average, looking at school closures.

The average Cambridgeshire primary school was very close to the national average, in both its financial and non-financial statistics. Yet this is a start – rather more than most LEAs have achieved. Almost certainly if the inquiry is pursued in greater detail, with finer sub-divisions of expenditure and grouping of schools in 'peer-groups', some really useful information could be produced.

## *Comparisons by size*

C. E. Cumming in *Studies in Educational Costs* (1971) established clear evidence for economies of scale in detailed studies of primary schools in two Scottish LEAs. Hough developed this with his work on the primary schools of two English LEAs, and found that 'there is very clear evidence for economies of size in primary schools with the largest schools having the lowest per pupil average costs; no minimum point emerges'. Hough had considerable confidence in his results because of the high significance levels of the data, and also the number of schools included. He also felt confident because primary schools 'tend to form a more homogeneous group, free of, for instance, academic streaming, variations in staying on rates or curricular patterns, or upheavals due to reorganization plans'.

While his finding about economies of scale is not challenged, data supplied by the Norfolk LEA for 1973 and 1975/76 for the research of the Rural Transport and Accessibility Project, University of East Anglia, gave different emphasis. Oliver B. Coles of the project reported that the data indicated 'that costs per pupil dropped very sharply from the bottom of the range to a "floor" at around 100-150 pupils, and then began to rise again'.

## *Comparisons by function*

Many of the secondary-school functional costs described in the previous chapter apply equally in primary schools. Therefore only those which apply particularly to primary schools will be mentioned.

*LEA overheads*
It is not known whether primary pupils take up a greater or a smaller share of LEA overheads than secondary pupils. Nor is the effect of school size upon LEA overheads known.

*Teaching costs*

Teachers' salaries
The Burnham salary scales operate more evenly for primary schools because all pupils aged 5 to 11 count as two units towards a unit total. However, there is a marked stepped effect caused by the transition from group to group and also by pupil - teacher ratio arrangements for smaller schools.

Average teacher salaries tend to be lower. The HM Inspectorate primary survey showed that only 10 per cent of the teachers in the

**Table 4:2** Percentage of teachers on each salary scale in England, 1978/80

| | *Primary* | *Secondary* |
|---|---|---|
| Scale 1 | 40 | 36 |
| Scale 2 | 35 | 27 |
| Scale 3 | 5 | 20 |
| Scale 4 | – | 11 |
| Senior teacher | – | 2 |
| (Scale 3/4/senior teacher) | ( 5) | (33) |
| Deputy | 9 | 4 |
| Head | 11 | 2 |
| (Heads and deputies) | (20) | ( 6) |

*Source:* Department of Education and Science, *Primary Education in England*, A Survey by HM Inspectors of Schools (HMSO, 1978), Table 7; DES, *Aspects of Secondary Education in England*, A Survey by HM Inspectors of Schools (HMSO, 1979), Table 4c (headteachers added, makes total 102 per cent).

sample schools were graduates, and that a smaller proportion were above scale 1, and particularly on scales 3/4/senior teacher. This was only partially offset by a higher proportion of heads and deputies. The full comparison is shown in Table 4:2.

Salary costs per primary pupil are considerably lower. In 1978/79 they were £254, compared with £365 per secondary pupil (DES, *Statistics of Education*, 1978). Many of the factors mentioned for secondary schools still cause differences for the salary costs of schools of comparable size.

1 The Burnham group of a school affects the salaries of head and deputy head(s). One deputy head is required for schools with unit total over 151 (76 pupils), two in mixed schools in group 7 (500 pupils).
2 LEA option to extend a school's total responsibility allowances. A school's unit total places it within a points score range. Although the total points are obviously smaller for the lower groups in which primary schools fall, yet the actual percentage variation within a group is much greater than for secondary schools. For example, in group 4 the maximum number of points is three times the minimum number; in groups 6 to 8 it is just under two; in group 10 to 13 the maximum ranges from 1.3 to 1.1 times the minimum. Thus this LEA policy option has more effect on salary costs in smaller schools.
3 LEA policies on pupil–teacher ratio for larger primary schools, say 250 and above. Pupil–teacher ratios vary considerably between LEAs, as the published league tables reveal. It is worth noting from Table 4:3 that the salary bill for a primary school of 300 in Newcastle with staff on the average pupil–teacher ratio would cost £27,300 more than its counterpart in Bolton; and one in Bedfordshire £11,900 more than its counterpart in Somerset

**Table 4:3** Variations between LEAs – in pupil-teacher ratio (PTR) for primary schools

| *LEA* | *Primary PTR* | *Staffing at this PTR for a school of 300* |
|---|---|---|
| Newcastle | 18·6 | 16·1 |
| Barnsley | 22·9 | 13·1 |
| Bolton | 24·5 | 12·2 |
| Bedfordshire | 21·7 | 13·8 |
| Shropshire | 23·1 | 12·9 |
| Somerset | 24·7 | 12·1 |

*Source:* DES pupil – teacher ratios from form 7, based on actual teachers employed in schools January 1980, quoted by the NUT Research Unit.

per annum). Within LEAs there is much less variation, as primary schools are staffed on a standard scale. There is some deviation for special circumstances, or for catchment area and intake. This variation is probably rather less than for secondary schools, where the specialist nature of staff creates disparities, particularly in reorganization and falling roll situations.

4 LEA policies on pupil - teacher ratio for small schools. The problem with primary staffing is that schools are usually organized on a class basis. It is difficult to create a 'gradient' pupil - teacher ratio scale, because an establishment of, say, 3·7 teachers for 111 pupils still does not allow four classes to be created for the whole week. So 'stepped' scales are commonly used, where schools receive an additional teacher as soon as their numbers reach a particular step. This protects the smaller schools, but leads to much sharper variations in the salary costs of schools of almost equal size.

5 LEA policies about headteachers' teaching and administrative loads. All LEAs have to decide the point at which they will not expect heads to take full-time charge of a class. Commonly this is for schools with about 150 pupils. Below that they need to decide what additional staffing they will provide to free the head for some part of the week from his class teaching duties. Again, there is considerable variation between authorities, although within them the policy is reasonably standard.

### Supply teachers' salaries

Absences through illness normally have to be covered by a supply teacher in primary schools because of the devastating effect of an absent class teacher. Such absence can be cushioned to some degree in larger primary schools, where there is a non-teaching head, much less so in smaller ones. Probably supply teachers' salaries are proportional to a school's numbers of teachers, other things being equal, but slightly greater for smaller schools. However, LEA policy on covering absence for courses and encouraging absence on courses varies considerably.

### Salaries: non-teaching support

Undoubtedly there are considerable variations between LEAs. Within LEAs provision is probably more uniform than for secondary schools. Technicians, librarians, etc., are very rare, whereas classroom assistants for infants' classes are common. In 1980/81, educational support salaries in primary schools totalled 2.8 per cent of net expenditure, compared with 2.3 per cent in secondary schools.

*Expenditure on books, stationery, furniture and equipment*
This varies slightly more from LEA to LEA proportionately for primary schools than it does for secondary. However, it is quite likely that within LEAs the variation will be rather less because there is a tendency to allocate central funds more to secondary schools than primary, and to allocate primary schools more on a per capita basis. However, most LEAs make special allowance for the problems of very small schools.

*Postage and telephones*
Probably they form a higher proportion of the costs of smaller schools.

*Premises and grounds costs*
The impact of these are again underestimated, because they are split up under a number of headings. Proportionately, total premises costs are a slightly higher percentage of primary net expenditure than of secondary. However, as the average unit costs are lower the actual expenditure per pupil on premises must be lower in primary schools. Little is known of the relative effect of school size, area of buildings, age or type of buildings, etc.

Salaries
Primary schools' establishment of caretaking and cleaning staff is established on a similar regional formula to secondary schools.

Grounds
Grounds can be kept by part-time groundsmen. There is an increasing tendency for primary-school grounds to be looked after by group teams.

Rates
Rateable values of primary schools are established on a similar system to that described for secondary schools in Chapter 3.

Maintenance of premises
It is likely that there is considerable variation in schools of comparable size because of the greater impact on small schools of local circumstances. Governors of a voluntary aided school are responsible for external repairs and for school buildings (but they receive 85 per cent of the cost from the DES). The LEA is responsible for internal repairs and for maintenance of playing fields.

Heating and lighting
Costs of heating probably vary widely in primary schools, according to volume, insulation, number of entrances, etc. Electricity is not normally on a maximum demand meter, but on a flat-rate tariff.

*Assistance to pupils*

Free meals
The proportion of pupils consuming a free meal is generally higher in primary schools than in secondary, mainly because a higher proportion of children in primary schools stay to lunch. A minor factor also is that for borderline families, where only one child is entitled to a free meal, the youngest is commonly selected.

Uniform grants
These are not usually paid for primary-school children.

*School meals*
In general the take-up for school meals is higher for primary children.

*Donations*
Primary schools tend to raise larger funds per pupil than secondary schools. This is probably because they are smaller and more local, and because parents identify with them more strongly. Also the children themselves are more naturally enthusiastic about collective endeavours. On the other hand, it is less common for parents to contribute for specific items for their children, such as textbooks, games equipment, etc. However, on balance it is still likely that donations in primary schools are relatively more important. They are certainly more important if taken as a proportion of the school's capitation allowance.

## *What does it all mean?*

It means that we do not know very much about primary-school costs at all. We know much less about the cost structure of primary schools in England than we do about those in Nigeria or Indonesia. We know really very little indeed about how and why costs vary between different types and sizes of primary schools, and how they can be altered and influenced. We spend on English and Welsh primary schools about £2,000 million annually – yet we know less about their costs than we know about the costs of our fish-and-chip shops. And we call ourselves professionals?

# 5 The Cost of the Curriculum

How much does a lesson of English cost, compared with a lesson of cookery? How do costs per lesson or per pupil vary from one subject to another? How much could we save if we took one subject off the timetable and replaced it by another?

## *The cost of the curriculum in one school*

Once the total costs of a school have been established, it is obviously possible to derive unit costs for subject areas. Subject costs have been produced for Holyrood School for the financial year 1975/76. These were again based on the 'chalk-face principle', that as the school's main aim was to provide education, subject unit costs should be 'total unit costs', based on appropriate proportions of the school's total expenditure, including all servicing activities and overheads. Pastoral activities were treated as quasi-curricular and so equivalent to a subject area. It could be argued that meals and transport have little to do with French; but equally, that the latter could not exist without the former. The proportion for each subject was worked out in considerable detail (see B.A.A. Knight, *The Cost of Running a School* (1977), Appendix B). Wherever possible realistic figures were used – for example, basic salaries according to subject-periods taught; special allowances according to responsibilities; capitation and examination fees by actual expenditure; non-teaching support by duties in subject areas; premises costs in proportion to the area of subject rooms used; and central and school administrative, meals and transport costs in proportion to the subjects' 'pupil-periods'.

Figure 5:1 shows the comparative totals of the subject areas, and subject unit costs per pupil period/year. This suggests that there were considerable variations between subject areas, with a maximum difference of over 50 per cent. The reasons for the differences are fairly clear (and can be explored in detail in the Appendix mentioned above):

1 Design and remedial were high because of lower class size
2 Design and science were high because of technician's costs, larger

**Fig. 5:1** Subject/activity costs, Holyrood School, 1975/76 (a) Totals (b) Per pupil period

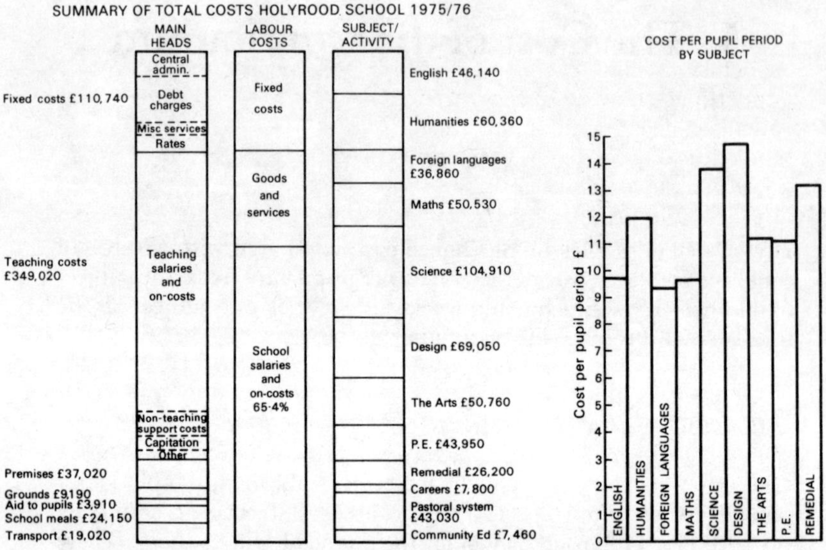


area of subject rooms, and expensive equipment

3 Science and humanities were inflated because of a historical concentration of allowances or older teachers within their faculties.

## *The cost of the curriculum nationwide*

P. K. Pearson has used a different approach. In *Costs of Education in the United Kingdom* (1977), Chapter 7, he sought to establish *marginal* unit costs. He argued that these were more useful for predicting 'the effect on total costs of changes in the volume of cost-related quantities'. He therefore only included teachers' salaries, the salaries of direct support staff such as technicians, and the cost of books and equipment. Pearson only dealt with classroom subjects, as these were more useful for the comparisons he was trying to make with computer-based learning, although he accepted that craft and vocational subjects would have a relatively high cost per student hour because of small class sizes. Using data from 1974/75, updated by one year, he concluded that costs per student hour in secondary schools were:

| | Forms 1 to 5 | Form 6 |
|---|---|---|
| Arts subjects | £0.22 | £0.53 |
| Science subjects | £0.24 | £0.58 |

Pearson made a number of sweeping assumptions, and some of his conclusions have received criticism. However, his conclusions underlined 'how dominant a factor is class size'. He estimated that ancillary help added about 10 per cent to the science costs, but that the effect of books and equipment could be ignored.

Much more detailed studies on curricular costs were carried out by C. E. Cumming (1971). He, too, only included teacher salaries, and non-teaching salaries and supplies 'which could be allocated unambiguously to a particular subject'. His approach was followed and extended by Ilett in his study of three Walsall schools (1981). Both suggested that there is considerable variation, both within and between schools, in the distribution of resources between subjects, year groups, ability groups, etc. The arguments and calculations are complicated - so much so that they can hardly be used as a management tool - and personally I find some of the assumptions difficult to accept.

Currently some LEAs are showing interest in what are called 'curricular costs', particularly those highlighted in small sixth forms. However, this is a loose use of the term, for LEAs are not really concerned with the comparative cost of individual subjects but rather with the costs of different size teaching groups and particularly teachers' salary costs. The Arthur Young study on costing 16 to 19 provision shows clearer reasoning when it first considers the curriculum analysis for a particular educational scheme, and then derives teaching-staff costs. Clearly such a study is not really concerned with the differential costs of teaching subjects per se.

A different attempt to establish subject-based costs has been made in the United States. Robert M. Anthony and Regina E. Herzlinger, *Management Control in Non-profit-making Organisations*, (1975), described the application of 'program accounting' to education. Program accounting rose out of the program budgets which were an essential element in the PPBS (planning-programing-budget system) approach so popular in the 1960s and 1970s. It classified operating costs by programmes, related to objectives and outputs in contrast to the traditional 'line item' accounts which classify costs by types of expenditure, for example, salaries, textbooks, supplies, and so on.

Under this system, a school district would adopt an accounts structure based on programmes as follows:

1 Pre-elementary school education
2 Elementary education
3 Junior high school education, etc.

The junior high school education programme would be broken up into sub-categories. For example:

1 Regular instruction
2 Supplementary instruction
3 Instruction support (libraries, resource centres, etc.)
4 Pupil support services
5 Other support services, for example, food and transport
6 Premises
7 Administration, general

For our purposes, the interesting feature is that the first sub-category, regular instruction, is broken up into the following elements:

1 English language
2 Foreign languages
3 Social sciences/social studies
4 Sciences
5 Mathematics
6 Cultural
7 Occupational
8 Physical education
9 Other

PPBS enjoyed a cult following in the early 1970s in the USA, and in a more restrained form in the UK. Los Angeles adopted it for education. The State of Indiana has directed all public school districts to adopt it. But it has often been over-sold, over-complicated. The central problem has proved to be defining the programmes and preventing overlap and duplication. (Information from the US Department of Education; two handbooks on PPBS, by Furno, Collins & Brain and from the Research Corporation of the Association of School Business Officials of US and Canada, are listed in the Bibliography.)

## *Where does it lead?*

It is rapidly becoming clear that subject costs are not a very profitable area for investigation. First, we have the theological question to resolve. Do we believe in total unit costs or marginal? The former are time-consuming and complicated, involve many subjective judgements, are difficult to use for comparisons between schools. The latter tend to leave out relevant costs (for example, premises), and blur actual differences between school and school. Both approaches emphasize the obvious, that the main factor in subject costs is class size. So subject cost analysis does not tell us much more than we can read off the school's curriculum analysis in five minutes; the allocation of staff per subject per pupil. Not only do the two approaches look unhelpful; in a sense they are unreal.

For the real marginal cost of a lesson of English or mathematics or any other subject is . . . nothing! Or next to nothing. For a school's curriculum is a self-balancing cost system. The school is allocated its resources from external sources, its teaching and non-teaching staffing, its capitation, premises, and so on. Within that global sum the school's management then takes decisions about curriculum. One subject grows more popular, additional students join its classes. The additional cost to the ratepayer is nil, because such increases only arise by reduced student demand elsewhere. The process is familiar to any school timetabler. He knows only too well that if a certain subject spawns another fourth or sixth-form group, for example, it has to be offset by some comparable reduction. While the school's staffing establishment is fixed, the number of teaching periods available will be fixed - and so will its costs. As long as the present conventions of compulsory education, of the normal school year, school week and school timetable, and the traditional system of financing schools remain, then any change between subjects can neither appreciably increase nor decrease demand on resources. There are some exceptions. Obviously if the proportion of design subjects falls, there could be some reduction in electricity consumption and in technician salaries. A growth in science would often lead to a higher proportion of more expensive teacher salaries, and could lead to increased technician and equipment costs. But the overall effect of such a shift would be very small, and often imperceptible. Unless, of course, we embark on the extravaganza of 'curricular staffing'. But that needs much fuller examination and is dealt with in Chapter 10.

In any case, are subjects on the timetable 'the curriculum'? Is curriculum the label on the class - or what the pupils carry from it? For five chapters we have been solemnly costing inputs. Can we ignore outcomes any longer? We are into the quicksand . . .

# 6 Efficiency, Effectiveness and Productivity

This is the most difficult aspect of school costs. Some teachers will find parts of the chapter unacceptable. After all, notions of efficiency and productivity sit uneasily upon a school. We normally talk about a good school, not about an efficient or productive one. And this is very proper – 'efficiency' has mechanistic overtones. Yet any serious discussion of resource allocation and costs must ultimately rest upon such considerations.

## *The importance of measuring output*

So far all the costs discussed have been costs of inputs. Yet any commercial organization would relate these firmly to output. In the commercial world, input costs unrelated to output are largely valueless.

> *Example.* Sausage factory A has lower input costs than factory B. It could be that factory A has more modern machinery; or better sausage makers; it could be simply that it produces fewer sausages; or that its sausages are inferior or inedible.

In the commercial field, costs are related as far as possible to finished products. Sometimes the nature of the organization and the cost information prevents this, and only 'process costing' can be achieved – the cost of putting a number of units of production through a particular process. However, it is much more desirable to achieve 'job costing' where the complete cost of producing a batch of articles can be found.

The importance of assessing school outputs can be seen very easily. If two pupils of equal ability study French for five years, each at a cost of, say, £400, and one gains a grade A pass at GCE O level, and the other a convincing 'ungraded' in the CSE, then the input costs are the same, but the output costs per unit of acquired skill in French are rather different. A grade A pass is more 'valuable', and so any department which produces more of these from the same resources must be producing them more cheaply. To give an absurd example, if a hundred pupils took O level after a five-year course and a hundred passed, the average cost would be £400 per pass; if only one passed, and the rest retained nothing from the course whatsoever, the cost of that O level pass would be £40,000! Let no one deride the word 'cheaper'. There is no advantage in a process being more expensive than it has to be. If it is, the only result is to block the opportunity costs that would have been freed by a cheaper, comparable process.

While teachers and administrators may be a little coy about assessing a school's outputs, our clients are a little more candid. Pupils are very concerned to enrol on courses which have a good chance of success. They are suspicious of teachers, courses, or schools which have a poor reputation. Parents have a similar approach. They are not too impressed with inputs of a school, with fine buildings, impressive equipment, new textbooks. In the last resort, parents are only really interested in what a school achieves for the children that pass through it. Parents who opt out of the state system actually place a cash value on their chosen school and its likely output in terms of their particular child.

Production of output costs can be thought-provoking. Rather like cost allocation, it can bring new insights and lead us to think of alternative and possibly cheaper ways of producing the same results. It will become more important as new technology makes its impact on schools. If it could be shown, for example, that the cost of bringing a particular class to a certain standard is less if computerized learning is used rather than a conventional system, then the whole question of methods would be thrown into very high relief. Already there are straws in the wind. The considerably lower cost of obtaining a degree by the Open University seems to have been a factor in encouraging government support for it. Conversely, the original experimental work with computers in education – before the microchip – faded when it was realized that output costs were higher. The final *Report of the National Development Programme in Computer Assisted Learning*, (Council for Educational Technology 1977) wrote its epitaph: 'There is little doubt that in most Computer Assisted Learning educational projects the total cost is much higher than for conventional instruction and that none of the early claims for realizable savings of staff time or cash can be supported'.

## *The difficulties in measuring school outputs*

While output costs are much more important, measurement of them is much more difficult, for various reasons.

First, there is only a limited range of arithmetical measures of educational output available. Examples would be:

Number of examination passes
Improvements in reading ages

Numbers of pupils learning to swim
Numbers of pupils playing musical instruments at various grades.

However, even these simple measures are not so simple to use. There are often various grades of performance, and so some sort of weighting system is needed. Taking examination passes, for example, one can argue that an A-grade pass is more valuable than a C-grade pass. If a weighting system were used, so that one O level grade A pass is given say 9 points, a grade 4 CSE pass 5 points, and a 'dropped the course in third or fourth year' pupil, 1 point, it would be possible to calculate the cost of a point, and so the cost of one grade A or C pass, etc. (See Knight, 1977, Appendix C.) This sort of weighting would show the higher grade pass cheaper in a successful examination passing school or department than in a less successful one (the greater number of points aggregated by the department, the lower the average point cost, so the lower the cost per pass). Since there are sometimes very considerable variations between individual schools and individual departments, this approach would highlight the cost implications of inefficiency. H. R. Thomas in 'Educational Administration', May 1981, has developed this approach much more fully, using cost effectiveness analysis to assess the comparative efficiency of teaching A level economics in a comprehensive school and three sixth-form colleges 1974–76. He relates the educational inputs expressed in financial terms to academic outputs in weighted A level passes, but related to the variation in student material measured by weighted O level scores. He uses established techniques of economic analysis and includes within his costs students' earnings foregone. Thomas' conclusions are clear although it is likely that he heavily underestimates the non-teaching costs involved. Although Thomas actually compared different institutions, he points out that in practice this is quite difficult, because the data belongs to different sub-systems, and suggests that it is much more easily done within a single institution. The trouble here however is that it is still a time consuming business. Although it gives insights, it isn't yet a very practical management tool for regular use.

The second difficulty in the way of measuring a school's output is more fundamental. Much of the valuable output of a school cannot be measured quantitatively.

How do you measure quality of design? Artistic achievement? Moral education? Awareness of careers opportunities? Enthusiasm for reading? Curiosity? Confidence? . . .

The third is equally intractable. The human material with which schools deal varies considerably from catchment area to catchment area, so while two schools with the same input costs and the same results in a particular subject can be said to have similar output costs, yet if one school has a worse catchment than the other, it could be said to be more efficient. We are not just trying to measure the final output, but rather the 'value added'. But comparison of school intakes is very difficult. It is certainly difficult to quantify, though measures have been used for this, for example, in identifying educational priority area schools.

There may be other constraints, of buildings or staffing, which may inevitably restrict a school's efficiency, and which it has no way of overcoming. For example, a severe shortage of science laboratories, or a lack of science teachers, would have obvious effects on the learning of science in a school.

## *Some possible approaches to measuring outputs*

### *The quantitative approach*

The New York City school system measured output in each school by a combination of

Attendance figures
Extra-curricular participation
Number of diplomas awarded
Number of scholarships gained
Percentage of students with five or more major subjects
Percentage of students with 85 per cent grade A standard test scores
Number of pupils 'discharged'.

Michael Rutter and his team in *Fifteen Thousand Hours* (1979) used a similar approach. They chose five measures of outcome:

Attendance
Academic attainment in public examinations
Pupil behaviour
Delinquency
Employment.

Rutter justified the choice:

> Obviously, these five measures do not reflect the whole range of aims and objectives of schooling. Nevertheless, they do provide important indicators of some crucial aspects of the outcome of the educational process. Also, they reflect areas in which some degree of success is necessary if less tangible aims are to be achieved. Thus, while we have not been able to tap many vital aspects of personality development it would seem unlikely that a school was being successful in meeting objectives of this kind if absenteeism and delinquency rates were high and if attainments and behaviour were poor. Similarly, children can be successful and show achievement in many different skills and many different facets of life, but examination

success and job satisfaction are two useful indicators of attainment in areas of particular importance in the educational process.

Unfortunately the last three items involve data which is not kept systematically in schools. Indeed much of this material was collected by the Rutter research team itself (that on employment was deferred from the report), and so would not be available for easy costing of outcomes. The first two are certainly accessible, however. One can imagine a certain revision to an LEA's league tables if school A had results 10 per cent better than school B, and costs 30 per cent higher! Clearly these two items alone are too narrow – but given the precision and advances achieved by the Rutter approach, it might be possible to develop a 'multi-factor success index' for costing.

*The qualitative approach*

Coombs and Hallak (1972) underlined the problem: 'Wherever human activity cannot be measured precisely, there is all the more need to approach it with a systematic method of analysis which will focus attention upon, and invite careful judgments about, the critical issues and relationships, in lieu of precise measurements.' It is likely that with the current concern about standards, assessment, monitoring and evaluation, this approach will become steadily easier. Perhaps this refining of qualitative judgement is better suited to costing a process like education. It is not necessary to prove that school A's outputs are cheaper than school B's; it is sufficient to show that school A's outputs are better for the same costs, or the same for less cost.

*Adjusting for intake*

The Rutter team went to great trouble to adjust their school outcome differences for variations in intake. They measured these mainly through verbal reasoning scores, parental occupations, and children's scores on a teachers' behaviour questionnaire. The first could certainly be used, and the second possibly, to assist in, or at least qualify, costing of outputs.

*The prospects for output costing*

We should not underestimate the possibilities. Research could well develop practical procedures for costing outputs. But the dangers are obvious. It is a very complex field. Errors in statistical methods could mislead. So could errors in data. Any system would need to be reliable, valid, simple to operate, and worth the trouble. Almost certainly both quantitative and qualitative approaches will need to be combined – *and* a sense of balance and humane values retained. Who relishes the brave new world of the multi-factor success index?! Perhaps the problem needs approaching from a different angle.

## *The alternative approach: costing in time*

*Speeding of processes*

Other service organizations have achieved considerable improvements in efficiency and productivity by reducing the time spent on each process. A good example is the hospital service, which has achieved a remarkable increase in efficiency by shortening the stay of patients in hospital. The patients do not always appreciate their speedy ejection! But it certainly achieves a quicker turnover. The long stay of the appendix patient may have been humane and considerate, but it was also an expensive luxury, and it masked the opportunity costs which could be tapped if that patient could be passed out earlier.

*'Seat-time'*

In our schools, no such progress is possible. 'Seat-time' blocks it. Seat-time is a basic feature of our school economy – as characteristic and as obstructive of change as slavery or strip-farming in other economies. Seat-time decrees that all students of the same age shall sit in their places for the same amount of time, whether they need it or not, whether they benefit or not, whether they progress or not. A student may be doing no more than keeping his/her seat warm. He/she may even suffer frustration and alienation. He/she may obstruct or even damage the working of the school. But he/she still has to be provided with his/her daily dose of seat-time. And the dose is a fixed ration. Students must not have less – but like Oliver Twist, they cannot have more. It is obvious that in most classes different pupils work at different rates, and need different amounts of time to reach the same standard. So, for example, in a physics class, one may find some who could cover the course comfortably on less time; others who need all the time available; and others who have no hope of passing, who are doomed to failure from an early stage, although if they had more time they could probably reach the required standard. Are courses to be norm-referenced (geared to the norm that a particular class *on average* can be expected to achieve), or criterion-referenced, enabling each student to meet the agreed criteria? After all, when we take driving lessons, the time for instruction is not related to some norm, but to the criterion of whether we are ready to be tested.

This is a restatement of the input versus output costs argument. Are we interested in the input of a given dose of teaching, or are we interested in the output and the final standard achieved? If the latter, then the idea of a fixed ration of time is anathema. Yet it is universal. In almost every secondary maintained school and in most independent schools, seat-time rules. Of course it is not quite so black and white. There is a little flexibility – a squeezed lunch-hour lesson here, some extra coaching there – but not very much. It can be argued that seat-time is a product of the system – of compulsory education, of school transport, of the timetable and organization. But the French find ways round it. Seat-time is neither cost-effective nor cost-efficient. It is high time that we analysed the historical traditions and the regulations that have created it, and devised a more productive system (see Chapter 12).

*Costing outputs per hour*

The real key to costing outputs lies in the unit of measurement. Time is a more natural currency for schools than money. Technical colleges commonly use it, to state the duration of a course or to assess fees by lecturer-hours or student hours. The City and Guilds Institute use it for course description, including the Foundation Courses now coming into schools. Pearson (1977) used it to establish the cost of lessons (see Chapter 5). But normally schools do not.

Time as a unit can be introduced in three stages:

Stage 1 Measurement of inputs in hours

*Examples*

(i) City and Guild Foundation Course (Construction)

| | |
|---|---|
| Industrial and environmental studies | (about 200 hours) |
| Industrial skills and practice | ( ” ” ” ) |
| Construction Technology | ( ” ” ” ) |
| Communication studies | ( ” ” ” ) |
| Optional activities | ( ” 100 ” ) |

(ii) Extract from pupils' option booklet: 'Two-year Physics course. Objective GCE O level pass. Duration: 190 hours.'

(iii) Extract from Special Activities prospectus: 'English skills unit: basic punctuation. Duration: 10 hours.'

Stage 2 Measurement of outputs in hours

(a) For quantitative objectives, this can be established by simple formula:

$$\text{Cost of objective, in class-hours} = \frac{\text{input of class-hours}}{\text{number of objectives achieved}}$$

Examples

(i) 30 students take computer studies, $2\frac{1}{2}$ hours weekly for two years (200 hours); 22 pass GCE O level.

$$\text{Cost of one GCE pass} = \frac{200}{22} = 9 \cdot 1 \text{ class-hours}$$

(The more students in the class that pass, or the shorter the course, the lower the cost).

(ii) 14 pupils receive remedial teaching for 3 hours weekly for one year; raise reading age by average of 10 months.
Cost of raising reading age by one month =

$$\frac{120 \text{ (class-hours)}}{14 \text{ (pupils)} \times 10 \text{ RA months}} = 0.86 \text{ class hours}$$

(iii) A class with 20 non-swimmers has 12 periods of 35-minutes in a pool;
14 learn to swim.
Cost of one pupil learning to swim

$$= \frac{12 \times 35 \text{ minutes}}{14 \text{ pupils}} = \frac{7}{14} = 0.5 \text{ class-hours}$$

(b) For qualitative objectives, this can be established by comparison if *either* outputs are equal:
*Example.* Two careers programmes are evaluated and thought to be of approximately equal quality. Programme A required 120 hours, B 60. Clearly B is twice the value, or half the cost, of A.
*or* inputs are equal:
*Example.* Two sex education courses require the same time allocation. Course A seems much more effective than Course B. Clearly Course A is much better value for money (this last type is identical to the evaluation normally used in schools).

Stage 3 Conversion of output/hour units to output/money units
This can be done easily by using the schools unit costs per hour.

*Example.* If we use Holyrood School's class costs from Chapter 2, adapted from 35 minutes to 1 hour units, we can convert the examples above

2(a)(i) One GCE pass in computer studies costs $9 \cdot 1 \times £20 \cdot 6 = £187 \cdot 5$
2(a)(ii) Raising of reading age by one month costs $0 \cdot 86 \times £20 \cdot 6 = £17 \cdot 7$
2(a)(iii) Teaching one pupil to swim costs $0 \cdot 5 \times £20 \cdot 6 = £10 \cdot 3$.

This approach has some clear advantages. Course duration is easily calculated from the existing timetable; it is a relatively simple system; it can be introduced in stages; it makes possible easy comparisons across schools and over time. Obviously there are limitations. It only works for discrete courses or elements, so it is not suitable for primary education. It still fits much more easily with quantifiable objectives. Differences in intake material still have to be allowed for.

So time-costing is not a panacea. But it is a step forward. It emphasizes the importance of time, and so leads our gaze towards efficiency. It tempts us to consider alternative approaches, and so leads to productivity.

Above all, it emphasizes the idiocy of seat-time and opens up scope for effectiveness.

## *Increasing educational efficiency*

With present technology, almost the entire classroom process is controlled and affected by teachers. Their salaries make up over half of the costs of a secondary school. So consideration of efficiency must begin by considering improving the effectiveness of the teaching force.

The ratio of teachers' salaries to the cost of in-service education to improve their effectiveness is very low. There is a strong argument for trying to improve it. Resources for secondments, sabbatical terms or years, should be increased. The recommendations of the James Committee (DES 1972) in regard to commencing teachers and established teachers could be implemented. Yet increased attendance at in-service education could, if it followed the present pattern, simply lead to greater teacher absence from school. It might become a classic example of cost ineffectiveness, if the value of the courses was less than the disruption caused. However, it might be possible to relate in-service provision to teachers' conditions of service. Or it might be worth considering adapting the school year, or school week.

> *Example.* If the school year was reduced by two days, savings of transport, meals, lighting, heating and cleaning, would probably be sufficient to provide reasonable in-service education for the whole of the teaching force. Children would lose 1 per cent of their school year. But if one could achieve more than a 1 per cent increase in the efficiency of their learning, then the measure would be worth while.

Capitation allowances are another area where the ratio with teachers' salaries is crucial. At the present time, with cuts and inflation, capitation allowances have become eroded. Yet the skill and the cost of the teacher is only translated into the actual educational process through the use of capitation. Cutting it can be a classic mis-saving which reduces the efficiency of the expensive teaching force.

It can be argued that another important factor in efficiency is the pupil–teacher ratio. But the research results are equivocal. There is little solid evidence to show that a better pupil–teacher ratio (smaller classes) actually leads to greater teacher efficiency. Conversely, there is little evidence that local authorities that have poor pupil–teacher ratios gain worse results than others. However, parents who opt for independent schools because of their smaller classes certainly think that it is important. But looking at the opportunity costs involved, it is quite arguable that instead of a better ratio, it might be more productive to put the money into improved capitation, in-service education and training, and other developments.

Finally, no discussion of efficiency in education can ignore the motivation of the students, and the attitude of their parents towards their education. Both are widely accepted as crucial factors. Yet schools spend little time and even less money on improving either. There have been a few encouraging examples of home tutors or home visitors attached to schools. It is obviously expensive in financial terms, but it could prove a very good investment. So could much more educational counselling for students and parents.

Because schools are so labour intensive, and because so much of their costs arises from teachers' salaries, the failure to increase those other items which would make that initial expenditure more effective is deplorable. Obviously, in hard financial times, it is difficult to see how this can be achieved in the short term. But in the long term, as I shall try to explore in Part III, there are several strategies available which could make such spending for efficiency possible.

# 7 Attitudes, Policies and Regulations

The cost structures of our schools and local authorities are shaped by attitudes, policies and regulations. Of these, by far the most important is attitudes.

Attitudes are intangible and elusive. Any description of them has to be subjective, impressionistic and anecdotal. Yet despite the difficulties, the attempt is necessary.

Our attitudes are shaped by many forces: our training, at college or university, or on-job; our experience in education, and contact with others in the same field; the tradition and history of the field in which we work; the influence of wider ideas; our current role and function in the educational system; our proximity to or distance from the actual classroom encounter.

## *General attitudes*

Despite this range of influences, and despite the range of educational environments, we can begin with three generalizations.

*People in education do not take school costs seriously*

School costs are not thought to merit serious study; they do not deserve academic research, discussion in depth, or training.

These assertions can be substantiated very easily. Simply look at the HMSO publications in education, and try to find just one dealing with school costs. Or search the DES list of short courses. Or comb the DES recent primary or secondary surveys. Look at the MacFarlane Committee which had to sponsor a review of 16 to 19 costs *after* it had reported on 16 to 19 education! Try to find just one Schools Council project or report on school finance!

At local authority level, look for a department for school costs of the same importance and size as that for buildings, staffing – usually in vain. Look for LEA in-service training on school costing. Scan the pages of the *Times Educational Supplement* for articles in this field. At school level ask any comprehensive headteacher for his or her examination results, timetable analysis, points structure, first XI record, and face a deluge of statistics. Ask him or her what the school costs to run, and meet an embarrassed silence. Look at the agendas of school staff meetings. How often is there an item remotely related to school costs and finance? Any teacher could name a handful of writers who have influenced his or her work on the curriculum or on methodology. But on school costs. . .?

What other major industry with a share of the gross national product or a labour force comparable to education would dream of existing without analysing intently and professionally its cost structures? If a contracting industry like steel had produced a report totally ignoring the financial aspects of contraction – as did the DES-sponsored Briault report on falling rolls – it would be laughed to scorn. That it could occur in private industry would be incredulous; even in public sector areas like the armed forces, the health service, the water boards, it would be unthinkable.

This strange attitude may arise because school costs lie at the interface of several disciplines – of economics and accountancy, of management and education. It is rare for someone with actual experience or qualifications in accounting, particularly cost and management accounting, to work in a school or education department – and even rarer for them to work in a position where such expertise is of direct value. If they do, they are isolated and ignored. There is, of course, plenty of accounting expertise in the county treasurers' departments, but until recently the barriers between these and education departments were fairly strong. In any case, theirs is a tradition of financial, not cost and management accountancy.

However, this factor is not a sufficient explanation. After all, education has borrowed extensively from other disciplines in recent years, for example, for curricular theory, group relations, pastoral skills. Perhaps the striking example of such borrowing is the whole development of educational management theory and practice in the last twenty years. It sprang from nothing, and now is academically respectable, with a good corpus of research and theory and burgeoning qualifications and courses. Yet, significantly, even educational management has the same deficiency. Theory and practice help us to manage all aspects of education except finance!

*The study of school costs is seen as at best negative and routine and at worst base and ignoble*

Circumstances may force us to pursue it, but only as an unpleasant necessity. Unforced interest, and worse, enthusiasm, suggests sordid perversion. For the study of school costs can never compare in idealism and nobility to the study of curriculum and educational methods, with their utopian possibilities of human improvement. Rarely is it seen for what it should be – an opportunity to make the best use of the resources available, and to create better conditions within which education may flourish and develop.

*It is often assumed that educational factors must always have priority*
At first sight, a fine idealistic attitude. The interests of our children should have right of way over money considerations. But this view can only be relative, never absolute. If scheme A is somewhat better educationally than scheme B, and is only very marginally more costly, then we should prefer A. But if it is massively more expensive? The danger is that we slide into believing that financial factors do not really matter.

> *Example*: 'The Education Committee Chairman . . . stressed that the 11–16 schools chosen were on sites that would provide six forms entry and that financial considerations had played very little part in the joint committee's considerations.' (*Education*, 29 May 1981; concerning Croydon Borough's plans for an 11 to 16 tertiary system.)

This short report may not do full justice to the discussion of the committee. But many readers could relate examples where financial considerations have been under-weighted, with serious long-term results.

## Group attitudes

Although the attitudes above are general to most who work in education, each group has its own attitudes arising from its viewpoint and function.

*Teachers*
Teachers hold a set of trusting naive beliefs:

'*It all comes from heaven.*' This is the belief that in the universe there is some celestial cow from whose heavenly udder life-giving nourishment descends. Occasionally, the flow splutters; and they must reach up and tweak until the flow is restored. Admittedly of late years there have been signs of heavenly drought, but this has not fundamentally affected the cosmological view. It is a very comforting belief.

'*It's all right, it's his money*!' His money, you see, is different from my money. My money has to be guarded, watched, weighed. But his money is a different currency. It should always be spent, never saved. Normal restraints, doubts and alternative priorities do not apply.

'*The bottomless pocket.*' A subtle development of the 'his money' idea. My pocket has a bottom to it; turn it out – it is empty. His pocket cannot have a bottom. He must have some more tucked away somewhere.

'*The magic wand.*' 'What do you mean there is no money! Surely you can find some, somewhere. We only need a little.' This particular belief can be very flattering. It endows the wand-holder –

the head, county or 'the office' – with magical powers. Unfortunately, if he or she cannot work magic, disenchantment is that much the stronger.

'*It's their fault.*' The further distant they are, the more their fault it is. So the principal culprits are usually 'the treasurers' or 'the politicians' with the 'DES' or 'the office' in a supporting role. 'They don't understand us', 'We're a special case', 'They've no idea how a school works', 'We're sacrificing education for administration'. . .

*Headteachers*

Headteachers, Janus-like, face both ways. They share many of their working colleagues' beliefs. Their faith in the working of magic is tempered by their experience of management problems. The underlying tenets, however, still show through. Just two examples from recent memory:

1 A working group of headteachers discussing with officers how educational cuts can be made . . . and five minutes later pressing for expansion of a particular service.
2 Talk with a colleague about week-end courses for talented children. A discussion of possible charges, including an element for heating and lighting. 'I don't see the need for that – the facilities are already there.'

Heads, however, have buttressed declining beliefs in magic with more realistic defences;

'*It's not my business.* I'm an educationist, not an accountant. My job is to look after the education and personal development of my pupils, not to worry about the resources. That's somebody else's job.'

'*I'm not paid for this.* I'm not trained to keep accounts! (Admittedly, I have had to train to be the manager of a large institution, a senior social worker and a personnel manager . . . but you can't expect me to train as an accountant!)'

'*Of course, you can't compare us with others.* We're different – and probably unique – certainly a special case.'

'*I'm not selling the pass.* The cost information could be dangerous in the wrong hands. Keep 'em in the dark. Let them do their own dirty work.'

*Advisers and inspectors*

Although based on the education office, they are close to schools and detached from the main budget-making process, so they share some of the magical beliefs of their school colleagues. In some ways their attitude is not dissimilar from school heads of departments. For example:

'*There's no subject like my subject.* You don't understand the importance of my subject, starving it of funds/staffing/time . . .'

*LEA administrators*

LEA administrators do not believe in magic. They are practical people, although with a hankering for idealism.

'*You can't beat the good old Muddleshire system.*' Each LEA has its own home-grown systems, painstakingly developed to solve practical problems as they arrive. There is remarkably little exchange of information between LEAs about different administrative procedures. Each LEA is an island of its own, so this leads naturally to. . .

'*It's never been done before.*' (or '*We mustn't set a precedent.*') A good administrator is suspicious of a new procedure unless the existing procedure is clearly defective. He or she does not mean to be unkind, but what is well tried and well tested should not be lightly discarded. In the last resort, he or she may be driven to extremes – 'It can't be done.'

'*Simple and quick is beautiful.*' Time is at a premium in administration. New procedures which need a lot of studying, thinking out and preparation, and which are complicated to use, are suspect.

'*You can't use that – that's the wrong pot.*' Money in LEAs is kept in separate purses and pots under the bed. It is very difficult to persuade the housekeepers that spare money from one pot should be used to fill an empty purse elsewhere.

'*Don't reveal all – you'll excite them too much.*' Information arouses people. Too much encourages groping for more. Particularly susceptible are politicians and the press. Comparative information is especially titillating. It should be concealed at all costs. Also information provokes queries, and uncovers embarrassing slips, and it all creates work for hard-pressed people.

'*The branch manager at Curry's.*' That is what the headteacher is, or should be. Send the orders down the line, and the head jumps, delivers the goods, sends back returns. To be fair, many administrators reject this view. Many of them believe that 'heads are managers and paid to manage'. But all administrators are ambivalent to some extent about this. After all, the more heads manage, the less there is to be administered.

'*They couldn't run a whelk stall.*' The Friday afternoon view, when the havoc created by the accident prone and the administratively tone-deaf out in the schools builds up. It is natural to blame the many for the few.

'*They should do it for love.*' There should not be incentives to make savings on heating – they should do it just for love. Out of sheer professionalism.

*The treasurer's department*

A cloistered and sometimes unloved group. They tend to be rather insular. Treasurers seem to gain more promotion internally within a local authority, compared with education officers. Treasurer's staff do not seem to go to so many national conferences, do not have such good information links with their counterparts in other authorities.

Treasurers spring from a fiduciary tradition, protecting the public purse against embezzlement, incompetence and overspending. There is no real cost accountant tradition in the treasurer's department, such as one would find in the financial departments of large private firms. So they share attitudes such as:

'*Beat the crooks.*' There have to be checks and counterchecks, even if this makes the system cumbersome and resistant to change. Not a penny of public money must be misspent.

'*Balance the books.*' Once the budget has been fixed, the treasurers' main concern is that the budget will be observed. Overspending is the worst of crimes, more serious than unwise buying. So treasurers are more concerned with the supply of money than with its control and management. An important distinction.

'*Keep to the rules.*' Treasurers have a set of hallowed conventions, which they are reluctant to discard: conventions such as a rigid distinction between capital and revenue; a dislike of switching funds from one budget heading to another – it is almost immoral or illegal to spend money for one purpose when it has been voted for another; a respect for the strict limits of the financial year.

'*Education's not our business.*' Very commendable too. The treasurers are often very modest about this. They do not want to interfere in educational matters. As a result, they help to create the present dichotomy where the treasurers administer and control, but the educational administrators manage.

*Local politicians*

Obviously politicians have party and personal views. But whatever party, they share certain attitudes:

'*Spending on my patch is different.*' However parsimonious politicians may be, they will back expenditure for their own area or interests.

'*Back our committee.*' Councillors soon gain a very proper loyalty for their own committees, and tend on the whole to protect them if they can.

'*If it makes good publicity.*' Politicians prefer to support or be associated with schemes which are new and prestigious. There is not much publicity or praise for getting involved with the workaday and the humdrum.

*DES officials*

Although their attitudes are shrouded in mystery, they seem to be similar in relation to LEAs to the views of local administrators about schools. There is the same irritation with the incompetence of the few, the same aspersions about whelk stalls; the same compartmentalizing and traditional thinking. There is also insular thinking, and too little importing of new procedures from abroad or from private industry. They are even more protective of information than their local counterparts. It is there for those who inquire, and inquirers get a very good service indeed, but it is not much publicized. However, the coming of open government has begun to alter this. The DES publishes relatively little in the way of financial statistics, it is almost all at macro level, and often some years out of date. One feature of the DES that needs understanding arises from their distance from the schools themselves. They have little personal contact with schools except through the eyes of the Inspectorate, and the Inspectorate has no real specialists on school costs and finance. So there is a tendency for the DES to make piecemeal regulations through circulars which consider national cost considerations, but with little idea of the impact that these will make on school costs at the local level.

Finally, I cannot resist referring to the delightful account of budget game tactics in Anthony and Herzlinger (1975):

*Introducing new programmes*

1 Foot in the door (thin end of the wedge)
2 Hidden ball (smuggle under another heading)
3 Divide and conquer
4 It's free! (ignore hidden costs)
5 Top level support
6 Nothing too good for our people
7 'Keep up with the Jones'
8 We must be up to date
9 If we don't, someone else will
10 Give a rose another name
11 Call in the outside experts.

*Maintaining or increasing programmes*

1 Razzle dazzle (blind 'em with science)
2 Reverence for past heroes
3 'Sprinkling' (adding a few per cent here and there throughout the estimates).

*To resist cuts*

1 Let's make a study (set up a working party to waste time)
2 Cut out the gold watches (All we've left to cut is the gold watches for old retainers!)
3 Witches and goblins (warnings of ruin and disaster)
4 We're the experts
5 Agreement in principle (wriggle through the loopholes in the details).

## *Policies and Regulations*

Obviously these are so numerous that there is no point in describing them in detail. What is more important is to look for some of the main features at each level.

*School policies*

Actually, schools do not really have a policy relating to their own costs and finance. At least, they certainly do not have a well developed set of policies, as they do, for example, in relation to examinations, discipline or pastoral care. All they have are a few policies mainly revolving around capitation, for example, for allocation, placing of orders, purchasing, storage, inventory control, with perhaps some exhortation about general economies.

Perhaps this is partly because schools consider school costs of little importance, not really their business. But it is also because they do not ask the right questions. They ask questions about their pastoral care system for example, or about their examinations policy and what sort of outcomes they should expect. But some of the obvious questions about school costs never even get asked, let alone answered. For example, can we make economies in the total running cost of the school? Can we get better value for money within the total costs of the school? Is the balance of the cost structure right? What constraints could be modified to make better use of our financial resources?

*Local authorities*

No lack of policies and regulations here. But they tend to be tactical rather than strategic. They develop as a response to new crises, rather than from deliberate planning of a campaign. As a result, policies often develop piecemeal and without realization of the side issues. They tend to be continued until there is a positive need to repeal them, which may mean that they outlive their usefulness. For these reasons, and because of pressure of time, there is reluctance in local authorities to look for alternative strategies.

> *Example.* Present new strategies on school meals have only come in response to acute financial pressure. There is no reason why local authorities should not have got together ten years ago and lobbied ministers into changing legislation affecting school meals. In fact, little was done in this area, and much of the pressure came from teachers' unions.

This is an excellent example of a strategy which was developed piecemeal and late, which could have been developed much earlier had authorities been better equipped for taking the long view.

Another feature of LEA policies is their diversity. In the summer of 1981 I conducted a survey of a balanced 20 per cent sample of LEAs. Of twenty-two authorities, eleven included cleaning materials in their general school allowances; nine included postage, eight included telephone charges, five included telephone rentals, three included light bulbs and tubes. Thirteen of the LEAs allowed crediting of income to school allowances; eleven allowed carry forward of balances; about half kept individual allowances entirely watertight.

A marked feature of LEA current policies is that they fail to produce an adequate data base. LEAs at the present time just do not have correct and usable information on their schools, comparable to the sort of information that any respectable industrial concern of that size would expect. Hough has put it nicely: 'Many LEAs just do not know how much one of their schools costs to run: this is, apparently, not something that interests them.'

*National*

Policies and regulations of the DES, together with national legislation, adopt the same piecemeal tactical response to a situation which is a feature of the local level. For example, since the 1944 Education Act, legislation really has been a series of postscripts. Schools' Regulations in particular need a thorough overhaul. In the non-financial field, the disparity between schools and further education regulations for the 16 to 19s is a considerable embarrassment. But it is not always realized that Schools' Regulations create a set of constraints which are hardly questioned, like the ill-fitting pair of shoes which the wearer comes to love. Good examples are those relating to the school day and school year, taken up in Chapter 12. Other examples are those relating to payment of charges, examination and other fees, meals, transport. Of course the DES is in a strange position, since it has little executive control over LEA expenditure on education. The Treasury holds the reins; the DES gives instructions; but the LEA rides the horse.

# PART TWO

# Controlling the Present

# 8 Making a School's Money Go Round

State schools, unlike independent schools, actually control very little of their own finance. Yet the small amount they do control includes the vital element of capitation. Success or failure in getting value for money from this and augmenting it can make a difference to a school's performance out of all proportion to its share in the school's total costs. Equally, saving of money from the main costs for which a maintained school is not normally responsible can make money available for its chalk-face operations.

## Allocating capitation

### *The problem*

Although the total amount of capitation for one school is not a huge sum by commercial standards, it is very important for the performance of the school. Most schools seem to have disparities between departments in the adequacy of provision for books, equipment, etc., almost similar to disparities between schools within a single LEA. Capitation is a microcosm of the problems of financial allocation in education, whether in a school, in an LEA, or across the country. One still needs to ask the same questions:

What is the present state of provision?
Which areas are well provided, and which poorly?
What does each department need?
What system of priorities should be established if the total need is greater than the resources available? – which it always will be!

### *Possible approaches*

There seem to be four main strategies:

1 *Benevolent despotism*. This assumes that capitation is best allocated by a central arbiter, usually the head, sometimes the bursar. He or she attempts to assess how well last year's monies were used, He or she discusses with heads of departments the needs of the coming year, matching one against another, and one year against the next.

Properly administered, this procedure can be quite effective. It can be gratifying to the participants. It involves some crude evaluation of cost-effectiveness. But it is time-consuming and is very much open to prejudice on the part of the arbiter, or special pleading and lobbying on behalf of the recipients.

2 *Open market*. Each department is invited to produce estimates for the coming year, both for ongoing expenditure and for any new items. Estimates can be requested under various headings, and/or in order of priority. Each department may and perhaps should be required to justify its requests. The problem, however, is that this approach encourages departments to inflate their estimates and to include hopeful as well as vital items; it tends to undervalue the modest and realistic departments against the pushy and wily ones; and it still leaves unsolved the problem of the final decision. Sometimes this is still taken by the head or bursar, sometimes by the heads of departments collectively. In either case again it tends to be a very time-consuming business, because the total estimates will always considerably exceed the capitation available. Paring them down can be harrowing and difficult, and is often on a broad proportional basis.

3 *Creeping incrementalism*. This assesses the percentage increase available, and then raises last year's quota for each department by that proportion. It has the advantage of being simple and time-saving. However, it only perpetuates historical situations; it does not make allowance for special needs; and it does not reflect any changes in the relative importance of departments.

4 *Formula*. The needs of departments are determined by two factors: the number of weekly pupil-periods that they teach, and the level of expenditure they need for each pupil-period. The first is logical. If a department has 10 per cent more pupil-periods, then it has a prima facie case for a 10 per cent increase in capitation. This automatically makes allowance for any change in the position of faculties. However, it is still necessary to introduce a weighting factor to allow for the greater cost per pupil-period of design compared with, say, French.

A department's actual allowance is easily calculated, as follows:

Step 1. Department initial allowance = weekly pupil-periods × weighting factor (in pence)

Step 2. Department's final allowance =

$$\frac{\text{Department's initial allowance}}{\text{total of all departments' initial allowances}} \times \text{total sum available for distribution}$$

*Differential between subjects*

This is at the heart of argument about capitation. How much more expensive is one subject than another? Obviously there is no simple answer. Needs will vary between school and school. In a school a particular subject may for historical reasons be under-resourced, and therefore need supplementing. The subject may be limited by accommodation or facilities, and so not need a normal allocation. In another school it may be saddled with equipment which is particularly expensive to maintain. Sometimes a department may be unenterprising and static and may need - or deserve - less for that reason. Comparisons between two similar departments in different schools will often be misleading, perhaps because one department's allowance has to pay for stationery and the other not; because one of the departments may have to pay for particular items like cookers or transport for school matches, and the other not; or possibly one may be assisted from central capitation funds - 'special estimates', or whatever they may be called - or special LEA grants, or LEA replacement of equipment, or PTA or unofficial funds. So comparisons will never be easy. It is unfortunate that there seems to be no research on this contentious subject and no generally available parameters for one subject area compared with another. HMI almost certainly have the facility to produce this but have not yet done so.

A rationale can be constructed for variations between subjects, according to whether they have large demands for stationery, text-books, other learning resources, materials not paid from income and equipment. But measuring the variations has to remain subjective at present. However it is a useful exercise for a school to take the total allowances of each subject, divide it by the subjects' current pupil-periods . . . and compare! Often this actual variation between subjects will look unbalanced or unjustifiable.

*The best method*

The most commonly used system at the present time is benevolent despotism, with varying degrees of benevolence. It is quite common for schools to use two or more strategies, for example, benevolent despotism for the departmental allowances and open market for large development items. The formula method is only used at present by a minority of schools, but having seen all four approaches at work I am personally convinced that it is the best by some margin. It has a number of virtues. It is very time-saving. It is simple to operate. Departments know where they stand, and can project what they are likely to get each year, and plan accordingly. It devolves responsibility to faculties and departments, and so involves staff more in decision-making. It is not so open to pressure from particular individuals or the bias of the despot. It is particularly suited to larger schools and schools running a faculty or large department system. It does have some weaknesses. First, the weighting factor is crucial. It is not actually any more important under this system than any other, but it seems more important because it is highlighted. In my own school, we currently use the following factor: foreign languages, English, mathematics, humanities 20; P.E., science, arts 22; design 25. This works tolerably well in this school, although currently design is becoming under-resourced. But as mentioned above, such figures will only make sense within a particular school; it is difficult to translate them elsewhere. Second, it doesn't allow for major needs, e.g., replacement of a lathe, purchase of an offset printer. For these central grants will be necessary. Third, although the system leads to better resource planning at the chalk-face, it tends to be conservative and perpetuate the historical distribution.

*Allocation of resources review*

Whichever strategy is used, a thorough review needs to be made every few years. A useful starting-point is a matrix, with vertical columns for books, stationery, materials, minor equipment and major equipment; horizontal columns for year groups/courses; and a scale for assessment, such as:

| | |
|---|---|
| 5 very good | (all essential items provided in good condition and most of the inessential) |
| 4 good | (all essential items provided in reasonable condition, and good range of inessential) |
| 3 adequate | (all essential items provided, although some in poor condition or tight in numbers; some inessential items) |
| 2 inadequate | (insufficient textbooks to issue one for each pupil; insufficient equipment to allow necessary class activities; few inessential items) |
| 1 very poor | (essential textbooks and other major items not available). |

Departments can complete this initially as a basis for the review. It highlights areas which are badly resourced.

*Central items*

All schools retain some capitation to be spent centrally. The smaller this sum is, the better. A good example is stationery. Some schools still allocate stationery centrally. But there is little doubt that teachers do not look after stationery well, or think so carefully about ordering, if 'someone else' is paying. Finances for stationery should always be included within departments' allowances. Central expenditure should only include the minimum necessary for office stationery and expenses, and other miscellaneous central items, plus any special grants to departments of the sort described above.

*Managing a department's capitation*

Good heads of department should obviously control this allowance carefully. Ideally it should be spent as early in the year as possible to offset inflation. However, this is not always possible, because they need to be quite certain that they are buying what is needed. Textbooks in particular can be very expensive, and it is unwise to invest heavily in a textbook until it has been fully tested with one class. Capitation should be planned not just for the year, but over the succeeding years. Good heads of department should have a reasonable idea of what their needs are going to be the next year, and to some extent the year after.

It is also important that they analyse the department's expenditure at the year's end. This can be done quite simply and quickly. The ideal method is to use the list of expenditures to construct a bar chart on squared paper. This can be for types of expenditure. For example, a design department's analysis could be broken down under textbooks; hand-tools and minor attachments; new or replacement equipment; repairs and maintenance; materials (net of income, if appropriate); stationery; audio-visual aids; visits; miscellaneous. These bar charts do not have to be works of art. It does not matter if some items cannot easily be classified, and obviously figures should be rounded off. But the chart is illuminating, and like all analyses, gives cause for thought. Not only can it be quite rough and ready, it does not necessarily have to be done every year, since in some departments it will be similar from one year to another. Similar bar charts can be useful under different categories, for example, expenditure allocated by year groups; expenditure allocated across the ability range, for the most able, the average, the less able.

Heads of department also need to be conscious of value for money, and ready to shop around for 'best buys'. Discounts can be substantial. VAT is reclaimable on educational purchases, but for cash purchases a VAT voucher must be obtained. Secondhand purchases can be useful, including buying up items no longer needed by other schools. These will be more plentiful as rolls fall.

## *Financial flexibility*

Allocating capitation is one thing; increasing it is another. However fair the division, the size of the cake remains fixed. If flexibility is possible, the effective total available to the school can be enlarged, and better value gained. There are several possible approaches.

*Carrying balances forward*

Incredibly, many LEAs still do not allow schools to carry forward unspent capitation allowances from one year to another. Any head or governing body suffering from this medieval practice should complain bitterly. An increasing number of local authorities do allow schools to carry balances forward, so clearly it can be done. The procedure is simple. Any unspent capitation is carried on to the next year and credited to the school's account; any overspending is carried forward as a deficit to be paid off. Obviously, extremes of underspending and overspending are not welcomed by treasurers, but within reasonable parameters, it is quite acceptable.

The advantages of carrying forward for the school and for individual departments are threefold:

1 Departments can plan their expenditures if necessary outside the limits of one financial year, and without being forced to spend at artificial intervals. Many purchases of books and equipment are made in the spring and early summer for the following September, and an end of March deadline is a definite nuisance.
2 There is no rush to use unspent allowances in February/March, a process which often leads to expenditure on less essential items, or to stocking up with stationery.
3 Schools spend less time on administration, because there is no longer any need to balance expenditure exactly against allowances. Time is also saved in LEA offices for similar reasons.

It should be noted that in many schools, carrying forward tends to build up a balance by the end of the year, because the pressure to spend by 31 March is now gone. To offset this, a school should plan to overshoot by the same amount as this underspending, so that this credit balance is offset. In the example below, the John Spendwell Comprehensive spent £3,000 less than its Jack Holdtite counterpart in 1980/81 – so needs to plan to spend £3,000 more in 1981/82 to catch up. No school should carry a large credit balance at the end of each financial year – this is plain bad management. Nor should a department, because the balance erodes with inflation – although its underspending does allow a corresponding increase in capitation for other departments!

| | *John Spendwell Comprehensive (allowed to c/f allowances)* | | *Jack Holdtite Comprehensive (no c/f allowances allowed)* |
|---|---|---|---|
| | *External a/c with LEA* | *Internal a/c* | *External and internal a/c* |
| *April 1 1980* | | | |
| New capitation allowance | £30,000 | | £30,000 |
| *April 1 1981* | | | |
| Total spent 1980/81 | 27,000 | | 30,000 |
| B/F unspent balances | 3,000 | 3,000 | |
| Less owing to departments | | – 3,000 | |
| New capitation allowance | 30,000 | 30,000 | 30,000 |
| Anticipated underspending for 1981/82 | | + 3,000 | |
| Total available for new capitation | 33,000 | 33,000 | 30,000 |
| *April 1 1982* | | | |
| Total spent 1981/82 | 33,000 | 33,000 | 30,000 |
| B/F unspent balances | – | – | – |
| Less owing to departments | | – 3,000 | |
| New capitation allowance | 30,000 | 30,000 | 30,000 |
| Anticipated underspending | | + 3,000 | 30,000 |
| Total available for new capitation | £30,000 | £30,000 | £30,000 |

*Virement*

Virement is the deliberate decision to switch funds allocated under one central heading for expenditure under another. The practice has long been enjoyed by technical colleges, who have normally been able to switch expenditures under headings within certain defined areas, although not between the areas. It is relatively new to schools. The best developed scheme is the AUR scheme (alternative use of resources) operated for some years by the Inner London Education Authority (ILEA, 1980/1981). The scheme has been very well thought out, and is worth quoting in detail:

> *Objective*
>
> The Authority determines the resources that can be made available. The AUR scheme is designed to allow the schools themselves to have a major say in how the money should be used.
>
> *Main essentials*
>
> Each school is notified of the resources it will have for the following school year. The information is given in two parts:
>
> 1. Main staffing (both teaching and non-teaching). Schools may not reduce their staff, but may add to it.

2. Money resources, quoted under sub-heads:
   (a) School allowance
   (b) Additional resources
   Subject to certain limitations, schools may choose to spend any of the resources 2a and 2b on
   additional teachers
   additional non-teaching staff
   school allowance (books, equipment, educational visits, etc.)
   minor works

The school allowance (2a) is determined on a per capita basis; the additional resources allowance (2b) is related both to the school's roll and to its position on the LEA's own index of educational need. The scheme applies equally to primary and secondary schools. Schools have wide discretion but may not vire their main staffing for a cash equivalent, or use more than 80 per cent of their additional resources for additional staff, or spend more than a specified sum on one minor improvement. There are also some limitations on virement of AUR posts. The sum available under the additional resources allowance is substantial, of the same order as the school allowance. Most schools seem to use it for a mixture of additional part-time teaching staff, music teachers, part-time and full-time non-teaching staff, minor works, and for supplementing capitation allowance. The scheme is well established and easily operated. It definitely brings flexibility into school expenditures, and enables capitation to be boosted if necessary. However, it should be pointed out that it is only possible in a relatively wealthy LEA, where there are, as the term suggests, additional resources available. It can therefore be adopted with advantage by some of the metropolitan authorities, but would be difficult for poorer authorities to operate.

Several other LEAs have introduced limited virement schemes. These are not on the scale of AUR, and are rather different. Whereas AUR requires every school to take a decision about its use of resources, the more limited schemes are on an opting-in basis. The facility is there if you like to use it, but you do not have to. The scheme currently operated by Somerset is quite a good example. Its objective is to give headteachers greater freedom to allocate funds in accordance with their assessment of the schools' needs. A school may submit a proposal for virement across any revenue heading providing that it:

Does not increase the total expenditure falling on the LEA
Is consistent with its educational policy
Does not conflict with national wage agreements
Does not provide commitment from capital
Has, where appropriate, the agreement of staff concerned, and where relevant the school governors;
Is made 'in respect of a deliberate intention of determining a

future requirement and is not retrospectively made to take account of past or present practices for which no prior approval has been given' (Somerset LEA document 'Virement', 1979).

Obviously, the scope for such virement is much more limited than the AUR scheme. Normally it takes the form of a short-term deferment of the appointment of a member of staff, the substitution of one type of non-teaching staff to another, the allocation of a 'point' for expenditure elsewhere, or the viring of part-time ancillary help into expenditure on equipment or material. There are obviously other restrictions in practice. The termination of employment of an existing member of staff would not normally be acceptable, so virement would commonly only arise when a place becomes vacant. Virement of capitation would be suspect because of the long-term implications, etc. There is some reluctance to vire between capital and revenue. Examples of this type of virement:

1 Virement of a part-time technician to buy expensive reprographic equipment
2 Virement of lunch-time supervisors, staff doing the lunch-time duty themselves, to provide additional capitation
3 Closure of one of a pair of kitchens. This is a more complicated example creating a 'balance sheet':

| *Saved* | *Spent* |
|---|---|
| Salaries of staff, kitchen A for two years | Some additional staff, kitchen B |
| Overheads of kitchen A | Some increase in overheads, kitchen B |
| Value of kitchen equipment replaced elsewhere | Stripping kitchen A, converting to pottery room. |

Potentially the most radical scheme has been that introduced by the Solihull LEA in April 1981. This gave three pilot schools financial autonomy with complete virement, subject to statutory obligations, LEA policy and governors' approval. Although this seems to have evolved in an informal and *ad hoc* manner, it appears to be having considerable impact on the schools concerned. Its aims, although not formally stated, appear to be to use scarce resources more efficiently, to direct resources to the fundamental needs of the school, to make some savings for the LEA, to observe the pressures which occur when schools have such autonomy, and involve the staff of the school more fully in financial decisions. The schools are given virement across all heads of expenditure including areas such as:

employees' salaries (teaching and all non-teaching except school meals, and including items like removal and early retirement expenses);
premises – (maintenance of buildings and grounds, cleaning, heating and lighting, etc);

supplies and services (including examination expenses);
school transport (including school vehicles);
establishment and miscellaneous expenses (including travelling expenses);
some debt management, debt charges;

plus income from community usage, lettings and rents.

Obviously 1981/82 was largely spent in examining existing expenditure and considering ways in which it could be redirected, but considerable virement did take place. It is only in subsequent years that the impact of the scheme will be seen. Staff involvement has been quite substantial. For example, in one school a deputy head was given special responsibility for finance, while the school bursar dealt with the detailed administration of the scheme. A financial sub-committee of the governors and three staff committees were set up – general purposes (building maintenance, heating and lighting), grounds, and unofficial school funds. Regular financial reports were given at staff meetings and heads of departments meetings.

Cambridgeshire introduced a similar scheme into six secondary schools and one primary (pilot) school in April 1982.

*Non-compartmented allowances*

Some LEAs still cling to the antique practice of keeping separate allowances such as furniture, school visits, or cleaning materials quite watertight from other allowances for capitation. This is deplorable and indefensible. Savings which may be made in one area cannot be redeployed to another. There is little incentive to save. One is also tempted to spend on matters of low priority and starve others of higher priority. A number of authorities, however, follow a more liberal approach. Even if money is allocated under different heads, and even on different formulas, it is rolled together in one general allowance. Some authorities call this 'virement', although this is really too grandiose for a simple procedure. Advantages of such 'rolled-together' allowances are:

1 Time is saved on administration, both in schools and LEA offices, because accounts do not need to be kept under sub-heads (although there will still need to be some coding system to meet DES requirements for information)
2 There is an incentive for schools to save in the non-chalk-face areas such as postage, cleaning materials, and add savings to capitation.

There is, however, one danger: if the inflation increment awarded by the LEA for the non-chalk-face elements is not adequate, then schools can find their capitation bled. (See Chapter 10, page 155.)

*Crediting of income*

Many LEAs allow schools to retain income collected for sales of materials for practical subjects. This may also include additional elements in payment for visits to drama performances, etc., and matches for school teams. Undoubtedly schools which are allowed to credit income in this way to capitation are much more careful in collecting it. The income is credited internally direct to the departments concerned, and can easily add 10 per cent to the school's total capitation. It seems quite indefensible that this should not be universal among local authorities. Where they cannot afford to sacrifice the loss of income from their budgets, it would be worthwhile for schools to encourage them to reduce capitation by the equivalent amount of income received, and then allow it to be credited.

*Direct and free ordering*

Better LEAs allow their schools to order direct, and to choose their own suppliers, and to order items of any value (sometimes with purchases, say, over £500 to be approved by governors). Other LEAs require schools to route requisitions via the local office, specify contract suppliers, and require consent for individual items (sometimes as small as £50!). Such practices seem counter-productive. They create delays and cause much unnecessary double-checking, queries and correspondence. Contract suppliers do not need complete protection. Schools will normally order from them, but if they can find cheaper alternative suppliers they should be allowed to use them.

*Imprest accounts*

Imprest accounts are simply a device to give schools a sum of petty cash and replace this at intervals, debiting the capitation allowance where necessary. It is important that the actual size of the imprest is adequate. It does allow for local purchasing which can be much more economical for small items, particularly with the growing policy of suppliers to add a heavy surcharge for single item orders.

*School bank accounts*

Hertfordshire pioneered school bank accounts as early as 1950. The school account is fed by the county treasurer at intervals from the school's capitation allowance (a combined allowance for books, stationery, materials, minor equipment, repairs, cleaning materials, first aid, educational visits and postage). The school's income monies are also paid in. A balance on the school's current account can be transferred to a deposit account, the interest on which is credited to the school. The school orders capitation supplies and services direct from any source it wishes, and pays by cheque. Petty cash can be drawn from the account, although it is kept to a minimum. Overdrafts are not allowed, but balances can be carried forward into the new financial year. No bank charges are made. The unofficial 'school fund' bank account is kept separate.

It can be seen that the scheme incorporates most of the flexible features described earlier - carrying balances forward, non-compartmented allowances, crediting of income, direct and free ordering, an imprest account (in effect). The bank account feature brings some additional advantages:

Speeding up of payments - gaining all discounts, avoiding some price-rises
Flexible purchasing - to take advantage of special or local offers, etc.
Prompt management information - the school or department knows today what it has spent; the LEA can plan its cash flow
Elimination of considerable administrative work - for example, LEA checking of school invoices, keeping of school accounts; school checking of LEA statements of its accounts; and most school-LEA queries.

There are some disadvantages:

The school has some additional administration (record of bank transactions, reconciliation of statements, reclaiming of VAT)
There are extra postage costs at the school end and some loss of interest overall (schools need to tie up some money in current accounts, command less favourable short-term interest rates).
The LEA needs to establish firm audit controls

The Hertfordshire Scheme has been slow to catch on. It has been viewed with suspicion by LEAs (risks and problems?) and schools (extra work with no extra help?). It can be argued that the LEA is already the school's banker. Some LEAs would claim equal flexibility can be obtained without it, certainly if a bank account is used in a restricted form as a sort of extended imprest. Recently (1981) two LEAs have adopted it in this form. Another, Northamptonshire, has adopted the full scheme in five pilot schools, and has even extended its range to include furniture, cleaning equipment, telephones, fuel and electricity. It also includes travelling expenses and some ancillary staff salaries, although those are paid centrally and debited to the school's account.

Perhaps the importance of a school bank account is symbolic as much as real. It is a symbol of local independence, pointing towards the further devolvement discussed in Chapters 9 and 13, although not essential for it. The spread of microcomputers in school administration is likely to encourage it. The more progressive LEAs could adopt the system easily. Those which still operate archaic and rigid practices would find the change more difficult, although it would encourage them to modernize at a stroke.

*Crediting of donations*

Procedures should exist to enable schools to pay in donations and credit them to their capitation allowances. In this way the money can be spent as for any other school expenditure, and since it is now clearly an LEA expenditure VAT is not payable. It obviously leads to a saving of some 15 per cent. It need not apply simply to capital items. It can apply also to expendables, such as mini-bus petrol, books, minor equipment.

*Unofficial funds*
There is a tendency for schools to proliferate separate unofficial funds for particular purposes, kept in different accounts and sometimes in different banks. It is a very wasteful arrangement. It is much more efficient to hold one unofficial fund with a series of accounts within it, each relating to a particular activity. The fund can then hold its balances in two accounts in the same bank, one current and one deposit. As it will be found that many of the accounts within the current account carry a balance for a large part of the year, and that these aggregate into a substantial current account balance, this can then be transferred to a deposit account and adjusted at weekly or monthly intervals. The amount of interest earned in this way can be substantial.

## *Costing major projects*

We have all suffered from projects which have thrown up hidden costs at a later date. In some cases the projects should not have been started in the first place. More commonly they were worth introducing, but the cost should have been analysed more carefully so that proper provision could have been made.

> *Example.* Nuffield Science GCE O-level courses were commendable for their content and worth introducing, but: the heavy emphasis on practical work had implications for technician time; there is a great deal of practical apparatus required (what are the replacement implications?); the textbooks are expensive (if they are revised, one would be obliged to buy new copies – what are the implications for capitation?); there are also timetable implications in the amount of time required, possibly slightly more than conventional science O levels.

It is therefore important that any new project should be properly costed before it is begun. The best introduction to this field is J. Fielden and P. K. Pearson *Costing Educational Practice* (1978). While they deal mainly with projects much larger than those relevant to a single school, they do deal very thoroughly with most of the principles involved, and the following section owes a great deal to their thinking.

For many innovations objective cost measurement will be impossible and precise measurement difficult. But even a crude attempt at 'profit-and-loss' will enable hidden and future costs to be identified, suggest alternative approaches, and reassure (or disconcert!) all concerned.

The following crude check-list is sufficient. Costs or gains can be entered in 'natural' units – £s, hours, periods, etc. Because of these mixed units one cannot do a straight debit-credit sum, but one can try to make an overall judgement.

*Costing the setting-up stage*

| *Item* | *Cost* | | *Gain* | |
|---|---|---|---|---|
| *People* | | | | |
| Staff, teaching: timetabled time diverted | | .. periods p.w. | | ........................ periods p.w. |
| Staff, teaching: non-timetabled time | | ........ hrs p.w. | | |
| Staff, non-teaching: increase or decrease in establishment | | ........ hrs p.w. | | ................................ hrs p.w. |
| Staff, non-teaching: time to be diverted | | ........ hrs p.w. | | ................................ hrs p.w. |
| *Space* | *Capitation* | *Non-capitation* | *Capitation* | *Non-capitation* |
| Rooms or facilities: increase or decrease in area | £..........p.a. | £.............p.a. | £..........p.a. | £.............p.a. |
| Rooms or facilities: space to be diverted | | square metres or other units | | square metres or other units |
| Rooms and fittings, modifications necessary | £............... | £ .................. | | |
| Running costs: | | | | |
| heating | | £............. p.a. | | £............. p.a. |
| lighting | | £............. p.a. | | £............. p.a. |
| power | | £............. p.a. | | £............. p.a. |
| postage/ telephone | £..........p.a. | £............. p.a. | £..........p.a. | £............. p.a. |
| *Equipment* | | | | |
| Teaching | £..........p.a. | | £..........p.a. | |
| Other | £..........p.a. | £............. p.a. | £..........p.a. | £............. p.a. |
| *Materials* | | | | |
| Books and printed resources | £..........p.a. | | £..........p.a. | |
| Stationery | £..........p.a. | | £..........p.a. | |
| Other materials | £..........p.a. | £............. p.a. | £..........p.a. | £............. p.a. |
| *Educational effects* (brief assessments, not in units) | | | | |
| *Non-educational effects* (brief assessments, not in units) | | | | |

N.B. Remember virement. Saving under one item may pay for another.

*Costing the 'steady-state' stage*
Repeat as above, omitting initial purchases and costs, but looking especially at replacement, depreciation and maintenance.

Crude assessment like that above need not be very time-consuming. The figures do not have to be worked out with precision. Intelligent guesses may be sufficient. Examples of projects which could easily have hidden costs and so which would deserve this sort of treatment would be: setting up a specialist pottery room; introduction of extensive microcomputer facilities; setting up a major reprographics unit; building a school swimming-pool.

## *Financing a project*

*Sources of finance*
When the total costs of a project are known, they can often be daunting. However, it is worth systematically thinking of all possible sources of finance. It may well be possible to tap several sources and so make up a package. It is common to find that a project which will be quite impossible for a school to finance from one source is quite attainable if the costing can be broken down. A check-list of possible sources of finance would be:

Capitation from department's own allowance
Capitation from central items or special estimates
LEA central funds of various types (various funds could possibly be tapped for a particular project)
Money to be raised by pupils – sponsored walk, raffle, etc.
Unofficial funds
Staff sponsored fund-raising event, for example, a fête
PTA funds
Local councils
Local employers and firms
Local authority county architects/estates department/area building surveyor (sometimes alterations to premises can be financed in this way)
Local and national trusts and charities
Appeals to parents or to the community
Sponsorship by a bank or local firm
Donations from individuals.

*Making a bid (or Machiavelli made easy)*
We all make 'bids' for additional or alternative resources – to colleagues, heads, Chief Education Officers, outside bodies. The following check-list may speed success.

*What exactly are we bidding for?* We may need to distinguish between what is ideal, what is reasonable, and the bare minimum. Which do we settle for?

*Who has their hand on the jackpot lever*? Colleagues? Head? Governors? Advisers, or others at county hall? Outsiders? Often more than one group. Does anyone else have influence or veto?

*What are the main arguments in favour of our bid*? These should be presented in logical order, and concisely – not more than one sheet of paper. Additional information can be added in appendices. Which will most impress the people who hold the jackpot lever (put these first?).

*What will be the costs*? Are there any savings, or special benefits, to offset these?

*What are the odds of success*? The longer the odds, the more care and the more lobbying needed.

*Is there a special time for the decision on the bid to be taken*? For example, annual county or school estimates; meeting of governors, council, etc. If so, how much in advance of this should the bid be made? A moderate bid at the right time is better than a good bid at the wrong time.

## *Good housekeeping*

Good housekeeping is unfortunately very dull, unexciting, and time-consuming. But it does save money.

*Inventories and stocktaking*

Most local authorities normally require proper inventories to be kept for all expensive items. This is commonly all durable items costing more than £50 each, or others less valuable if portable and attractive. Such inventories usually have to be completed at the end of the financial year and to show write-offs and new acquisitions. But in fact many of the items on this list are not items likely to disappear. Chairs do not often walk or lathes move! The only items that are really at risk from damage or theft are small and attractive items, perhaps in the practical workshops or science laboratories.

Local authorities do not always require schools to keep inventories for expendable or minor items, for example, textbooks, or minor hand equipment. These are things which are in much more heavy use, much more portable, and much more easily lost, damaged or stolen. Schools should always require departments to keep reasonably full inventories of all their textbooks and other books, minor equipment, and so on, but excluding the totally consumable items such as stationery, art materials, chemicals, etc. Undoubtedly such inventories involve time-consuming stock-taking, but they prevent a great deal of loss.

Simple procedures within the school can also do a great deal to prevent loss of items: proper labelling; insisting that all textbooks are numbered before issue, and the number recorded; covering textbooks; shadow boards for design shops, art rooms, etc. In departments short of textbooks, lending out a set of books for one homework is a sure recipe for waste of time and books. If books are in short supply, it is much better for one book to be issued among a pair of students and homework to be set over a longer period. Proper issuing systems for departments and libraries are essential, as are systems for the handing in of books by any student leaving. Books lost or damaged should be paid for by the pupil concerned, and the funds credited to the department's capitation.

*Postage and telephones*

Any large organization will find its postage and telephones used to some extent for private use. However, this can be reduced to reasonable levels by keeping an eye on outward postage, and by restricting the number of 'phoning out points, and insisting that calls are made after 1.00 p.m. whenever possible. Some schools claim that franking machines reduce their postage bills.

*Cleaning materials*

Considerable economies are possible here.

*Heating and lighting*

Simple measures can effect considerable economies, such as encouraging staff and pupils to switch off; discouraging doors being left open; ensuring that doors close effectively; excluding draughts; control of thermostats; removal of obstructions from windows which reduce light, etc.

*Maintenance of premises*

Accidental damage and vandalism vary a great deal from school to school, but obviously they cost money. They can be reduced by internal arrangements. Self-help can be important – pupils reporting damage to premises and defects, and swift repair and painting over of minor blemishes. Sometimes a school may have its own handyman or caretaker who can do minor repairs at a very much reduced cost.

Much of this good housekeeping is very worthy. It undoubtedly saves money, which is then available for other purposes. But apart from being dull and routine, it suffers from one other disadvantage. In the main, it is saving 'their' money, not 'my money'. Perhaps schools would be much keener on good housekeeping if they were able to share in the benefits.

# 9 Schools as Cost Centres

In management accounting, responsibility centres have a high place. Under this approach a large organization divides up its areas of responsibility and traces all costs and revenues to the individual managers responsible. Charles T. Horngren (1977), in a standard textbook on cost accounting, sums this up:

> Ideally, revenues and costs are recorded and automatically traced to the individual at the lowest level of the organisation who shoulders primary day to day decision responsibility for the item. He is in the best position to evaluate and to influence a situation – and to implement decisions.

Responsibility centres come in various shades: profit centres, which hardly apply to state schools; revenue centres – again barely applicable at present; mission centres (centres directly related to the organization's objectives); service centres (subsidiary to the main objectives); and finally, cost centres, for example, non-profit-making centres, like schools (or as one LEA wag suggested, 'loss centres').

It is strange that this recognized accounting concept sits so uneasily upon our shoulders. We do not think naturally of a school as a separate or autonomous cost centre. Yet we should think it very strange if Clarks' Shoes or Bowyer's Sausages or Halfords tried to manage their organizations with only aggregated costs, without a break-down for their local shops or factories.

Good management relies upon effective information – information presented at the right time and in the right form. Without such information rational decisions just cannot be made.

> *Example.* What is your attitude towards the dripping urinals in your institution? It will entirely depend upon the size of your water bill. If it is £20,000 p.a., you will want the washers changed tomorrow; if it is £20 they can play like the fountains at Versailles.

Most managers in the education service do not know, and are not presented with, the detailed costs of their institution or department, and indeed do not think them important. Yet cost information could be readily available. All expenditures go through the LEA computer, and therefore can be extracted with a suitable program. Obviously a full-scale system of management information cannot be set up at a stroke, but it can be provided in several easy steps.

## *Step 1 An annual print-out of each institution's costs*

One full print-out per year is sufficient as most school costs are not readily controllable during the school year itself. The print-out should arrive as soon after 31 March as possible, however. Monthly print-outs are only needed for the controllable items – for example, capitation, heat, light, water, postage and telephones, etc.

Ideally all expenditures should be debited to an institution. In practice, this will certainly not be the case initially. However, in the long run there is no reason at all why every expenditure should not be coded through a school or college to a head of expenditure. Initially, only direct costs will be included, but eventually the aim should be to include the school's appropriation of all indirect costs as well.

The raw information will be very indigestible. Ideally it needs grouping under appropriate headings, with a key to explain treasurer's jargon. In addition, back-up information will be useful, for example, to explain how tariffs operate and how other costs are made up. This information on the unsolicited computer tabs will be complicated and off-putting to the average busy head. Initially it will be incorrect and defective. It is not likely to be put to much use unless we take step 2.

## *Step 2 An annual cost audit*

Each institution should be asked to collate the information on the annual print-out in a 'cost audit'. A suggested outline for this audit is given in Appendix C. It would be helpful if a national manual could be produced for this, as it would make the introduction of cost audits easier and assist inter-authority comparisons. The audit is really a rearrangement of the print-out data under standardized cost headings. Initially probably not all items will be complete. The finished audit will be free-standing for its particular school, and will resemble a simplified version of the costs for Holyrood School given in Chapter 2. Some items will raise queries and so monthly non-capitation computer tabs would now become useful, to sort out queries at the time they arise.

## *Step 3 Making comparisons*

The simple audit above is useful in making the staff of an institution aware of costs and encouraging them to act in areas where economies are possible. But it is of limited value in isolation. Cost audits come into their own when they make possible comparisons between similar 'peer-group' institutions. Each cost audit should be compared with those of similar institutions. These comparisons should be done by computer. A number of LEAs are beginning to put in computerized financial information systems, with which these would fit easily. Initially comparisons may need to be done manually, although this creates work for LEA offices and means that comparative audits will be delayed. Such cost information cannot easily be compared in raw form, largely because differences in numbers of pupils, for example, can mask differences in costs. So comparisons will need to be made on a per pupil basis. For certain items, sixth-form pupils will need to be weighted at 1.6:1. Figures should not be rounded too coarsely. For example, total heating and lighting will perhaps be in the order of, say, £15 per pupil, and so needs one decimal place.

Apart from straight comparisons, school A with school B, it is also essential that we should be able to compare school A with both school A and school B of the year before. Otherwise, it is not possible for us to make full sense of the cost data.

> *Example.* Permafrost Comprehensive School finds that its electricity bill has gone up 16 per cent, from last year. Is this because (a) it has been a severe winter, (b) the number of pupils has increased, (c) charges have gone up, (d) pattern of use has altered, (e) energy saving has slipped? However, if Permafrost staff knew their electricity had gone up by 16 per cent per pupil in twelve months, and their sister schools had gone up by only 10 per cent, then much firmer deductions can be drawn. It is probably not (a), (b) or (c).

The six columns shown in the sample in Appendix C are designed to build up such comparative information between schools and over time.

## *Step 4 Asking for action*

Comparative cost information can be interesting to managers, but they do not have to use it. Nor does anyone else. So it is important that this information is actually put to use. The simplest way to achieve this is to ask heads of institutions to present the annual cost audit to full meetings of governors and staff, and to ask for their recommendations to be made to the LEA. This would only need a simple return as follows:

__________ School,

Cost Audit 198__

I have presented the cost audit for this year to the governing body.
They wish to make the following recommendations:

Proposals for economies
Proposals for obtaining better value for money
Proposals for virement
Proposals for more efficient financial procedures
Other suggestions.

Signed____________Headteacher

(Similar, for report from the staff.)

The advantage of a system like this is that it is very simple to operate, and it does require heads to present the information they have accumulated to the two groups of people apart from themselves who are best able to do something with it. It could, and should, lead to a flow of constructive suggestions to the LEA.

Heads, governors and staffs are not the only possible users. LEAs themselves could well put the information to good use. This would be particularly true if it were computerized, so that it could be easily reclassified under heads of expenditure as well as under local centres. Equally, LEAs could use it to establish school unit costs, monitoring the effect on these of fluctuations in school rolls, and also possibly comparing them to standard unit cost established by Grant Related Expenditure, as discussed in Chapter 3, page 52.

## *Step 5 Devolving responsibility to local centres*

So far the steps suggested have given schools information and involvement but no real responsibility. However, once schools have an ordered set of annual costs, it is only a small step to take responsibility and control for many of those items. The advantages in devolving financial responsibility to an institution are threefold:

1 It tends to look after 'its' resources more carefully than 'theirs', because it knows it can spend anything it has saved
2 It is more likely to look at the whole of its budget in a flexible manner, transferring expenditure from one heading to another
3 It is more likely to think radically about its cost structure and its cost effectiveness and to search for new strategies.

The tradition of devolvement is, of course, well established in technical colleges and in independent schools, but it is relatively new to maintained schools.

Since most LEAs have not yet gone far along the road, they would find it easiest to proceed in stages. The first stage would be to allocate to schools *under one allowance* all those items which are at present covered under the broad heading of capitation in many authorities:

Books – textbooks, library books, hymnals and Bibles
Stationery – classroom and office, reports, registers, order books, office sundries, printing
Classroom materials
Equipment, both teaching and office
Repairs to equipment – P.E., musical instruments, workshops and other practical rooms, audio-visual aids, etc., together with repair contracts
Furniture and fittings, including blackout, blinds
Prizes and hospitality.

Next there are items which could be added to the general allowance, either one at a time, or in groups

Educational visits, courses, and other activities off the school campus
Lectures and visiting theatre and music groups
Television licence and rental
Minibus or similar insurance and tax
Hire charges for home economics equipment
First aid, replacement of fire-fighting equipment, doormats, protective clothing
Postage costs, including postage for school examinations; telephone charges and telephone rental
Cleaning equipment and materials; school meals cleaning equipment and materials; light bulbs and tubes; swimming-pool chemicals
Travelling expenses and subsistence allowances paid to teaching and non-teaching staff.

In addition, there are some items which are not normally seen as ideal for devolvement.

Examination fees
Water (water should be an easy item to devolve as it is largely related to pupil numbers and numbers of school meals)
Heat and light: most authorities have found this process difficult and they are tending to come at it through their fuel efficiency officer setting targets
Minor advertisements expenses, and interview expenses
In-service education (it would be very easy to allocate schools all INSET funds and allow them to spend their appropriate share).

## *Step 6 Cost reapportionment*

Cost reapportionment is a further refinement to the cost-centre approach. It is often assumed that local cost centres should only deal with controllable costs – those items which are subject to the local manager's control. However, in practice, controllability is all a matter of degree. It is tempting to think that it is mainly the variable costs which are controllable, and fixed costs which are not. However, as the first chapter made clear, there is no black-and-white division between one and the other.

Undue concentration on variable and controllable costs means that a large part of the educational budget is excluded from local cost centres. In the short run this is sense, but in the long run it is short-sighted, because (a) it is still important that managers should be aware of *all* their costs; (b) by being aware of costs that they cannot control they may wish to put pressure on managers elsewhere to reduce them; and (c) because in the longer term many apparently uncontrollable costs can be altered.

Cost reapportionment has several purposes:

It establishes the true costs of a service
It can be used to increase motivation and efficiency
It is useful in predicting the effects of planning decisions.

*Examples*

(a) An area psychologist is asked to identify what percentage of his/her time is spent with FE/secondary/primary and 'no school' pupils. The cost of his/her salary with on-costs and administrative support is then allocated to those sectors, and then proportionately to schools. He/she may identify a fifth area of activity, namely central services such as advising the local authority over policy, and running courses. This proportion should be apportioned to those particular services and then reallocated to schools via them.
(b) An area team is responsible for maintenance of school grounds. First its total costs are established, salaries, premises, equipment, running costs, etc., and its appropriate share of central administrative costs. Then it is asked to establish its approximate annual share of time in each school, and its costs are allocated accordingly.
(c) A residential centre. The total annual costs of the centre are established and divided by its total number of bed-nights. The costs for the bed-nights is then allocated to schools using the centre.

Some of the principles of cost reapportionment are already appearing. First, it will be necessary for some costs to be allocated from one centre or service to another and from there to the chalk-face centres. It is therefore necessary to use a step-down method of allocation, rather like the pyramid suggested in Chapter 1, page 8. One should start first with the most distant and central costs, for example, LEA administration, and allocate a share of these to specialist services, and then allocate the services themselves to the schools and colleges. The second principle is that wherever possible reapportionment should be based on the actual service itself, rather like an internal price. It is particularly useful for items such as residential centres, in-service education. Where this is not possible, however, then reapportionment has to be done on a subjective assessment of the time devoted to each sector and then to each school as in the examples (a) and (b) above. Thirdly, the system needs to be 'tied in', so that *all* central and service costs have to be reapportioned – and so that it is not possible for any of them to be counted twice.

The path of cost reapportionment is not an easy one. It needs careful planning and implementation. If the reapportionment is too finicky, it can be very time-consuming and frustrating for those who have to account for their time and allocate their services. If it is too crude, and the service in question is a major one, then a relatively minor change in notional allocation can distort the cost picture. As the system becomes established it is open to intellectual dishonesty. For example, the psychologist in the example above may attempt to play down the total costs of his section or may apportion an undue part to a sector which is unlikely to complain. There is a risk that the process can be seen as a time-consuming, unrealistic, unusable paper exercise. There is little doubt that attempts to introduce cost reapportionment for local cost centres would be strongly resisted by central service agencies for many of the above reasons. Treasurers and administrators tend to be sceptical of its value, even though they already operate a similar system for the school meals service.

The problems are obvious. However, the advantages are such that cost reapportionment could be well worth adopting. The system does not need to be over-elaborate. The apportionment only needs to be done once a year, and in many cases once factors for allocation are established, they would not need to be reassessed annually. The great virtues of cost apportionment are, first, that it gives a realistic breakdown of central costs at the local level, and so gets questions asked from both ends. Are the costs of the educational psychologist, or the equipment repair depot, or the grounds team broadly reasonable in terms of the services they provide or not? This question was explored earlier in Chapter 1 (pages 7–9). Secondly, cost reapportionment paves the way for the much bigger step of recharging, and so to the establishment of schools as autonomous financial centres responsible for their own total budgets, on the public school model. This is a much more fundamental change than the cost-centre approach, and is discussed in Chapter 13.

## *Are cost centres worthwhile?*

It would be idle to pretend that the cost-centre approach does not involve risks.

*Problems and dangers*

1 The information base has got to be sound. If the information supplied to cost centres is seriously defective, then the LEA's credibility will be weakened, friction created, and incorrect conclusions drawn.

2 The administration of a cost-centre approach needs to be efficient. It needs testing on a few pilot schools. If procedures are cumbersome, time-consuming, and difficult to follow, then a potentially useful approach will be harmed.

3 Cost centres tend to draw administrative work from the centre to the periphery. This may lead to pressure on heads, bursars, and office staff and slack in divisional or central offices which is not necessarily taken up. This again stresses the need for simple procedures. In practice, steps 1 to 4 involve schools in relatively little work, and even step 5 should be manageable if there is reasonable time to adjust.

4 The fifth step – devolvement – brings a special set of problems:

(a) Accurate information here is particularly important. For example, if there is not correct information on how much schools spent individually on swimming-pool chemicals last year, then any attempt to add that to the capitation grant is likely to create problems.

(b) Formulas need to be right. For many of the devolved items, a straight per capita allocation will probably suffice. However, for some, different bases for allocation will be necessary. For example, telephone rentals are probably better related to the existing telephone installation in the school; swimming-pool chemicals to the size of the pool. The more separate formulas there are, the more complicated the scheme becomes, and the more time-consuming for the LEA – but the fairer for the schools. Formulas, however, do tend to discourage schools from rationalizing facilities. For example, home economics hire charges could be allocated on a per cooker basis. However, this does remove any incentive for schools to reassess expenditures.

(c) Some safeguards may be necessary. For example, the LEA may wish to earmark particular funds for one purpose only. In-service education would be a good example (to discourage schools spending the funds on textbooks). On the other hand, schools may want some sort of safety valve, for example, for heating and lighting costs – otherwise a severe winter could drain away the textbook fund. To some extent the more items are included in the devolved allowances, the fewer safeguards and the fewer separate formulas will be needed.

(d) Inflation increments must be realistic. Otherwise some areas of devolved expenditure which are under-financed, say postage, will drain away the resources from other areas more important for the school's function. This is quite crucial, and is dealt with in Chapter 10.

(e) Neglect or stagnation could possibly result. At present all the pressure is on the central administration to maintain and improve the standard of the service. The pressure comes from school staffs, parents, governors, advisers, inspectors and from the central government. Devolving of items which are at present handled centrally to schools could lead to a more negative and parsimonious attitude towards schools, with less awareness of needs.

5 Attitudes are crucial. Where there is reasonable trust and respect between treasurers and administrators and between both and the schools, then the cost-centre approach is likely to succeed. Where there is mutual distrust or contempt it is probably doomed to failure, and best not attempted.

*Advantages*

1 Cost centres look right. They are a well-tried approach in industry and commerce, which is generally accepted as being much more cost-efficient than the public sector. If one detaches oneself from one's personal position as a head or administrator, then the approach seems logical, sensible, and is well-tried elsewhere.

2 At a time of financial restraint and even contraction, savings and better value for money have got to be found. A cost-centre approach is relatively inexpensive to introduce and promises to produce more constructive suggestions from the schools for improving procedures. It also would highlight areas of unduly high cost, and would give schools much more flexibility.

3 It keeps a good balance between schools and local authorities. A number of local authorities are now beginning to experiment with financial information systems, and it is quite likely that these will expand rapidly. There is a serious risk that they could be operated in a mechanical and centralized manner which would allow schools very little scope for development.

4 A cost-centre approach does look to the future. It opens up further possibilities, for example, for the development of autonomous school budgets as discussed in Chapter 13. It could also ease the technological changes which will transform schools in the future.

## *Current developments*

A few local authorities are beginning to show interest in the cost-centre approach. Cheshire, for example, has run a trial scheme for two of its districts which is being extended to the whole county in September 1983. While it does not adopt the comprehensive approach suggested earlier in this chapter, it is clearly an advance. Expenditure and income items are divided into school controlled and central or district controlled. Each school is required to produce estimates for the forthcoming year for its responsibilities and to submit these for approval. The actual range of items within its control is not at present significantly different from that operating in many other authorities which don't actually use the term 'cost centre', but there are discussions going on for other categories such as fuel to be included. At present the scheme is limited, and is mainly a pyramid system for budget construction, with decisions limited at each level. However it does advance administrative decentralization and provide schools with much fuller financial information. It has provided some degree of virement and increased powers of local purchasing, and could easily become the basis for greater cost-centre autonomy.

Cambridgeshire, which already had an impressive amount of cost information available for invididual schools, now seems to be taking up the cost-centre approach very actively. Its three-year feasibility scheme, introduced April 1982, allows Governors 'to control their own budgets within a total cash limit' (Cambridgeshire, 1982). It includes: teaching salaries and expenses; non-teaching salaries, other than meals and grounds; rates, heat and light; examination fees; cleaning, furniture, postage, telephones, capitation expenditure; income; and possibly community education, maintenance and repairs, and some aspects of school meals. The Solihull scheme referred to on page 125 is even broader. Both show many of the characteristics of a cost-centre scheme, although not called such. Because they are pilot schemes, they have not extended steps 1–4 above to all schools. They have leapfrogged direct to step 5, and indeed are bordering on the autonomous budgets envisaged in Chapter 13.

Clearly the term 'cost centre' is coming into educational use. It already masks variations in practice. There are stages of development for cost centres which can be identified by questions such as:

> Are *all* costs allocated to the cost centre, including costs which it cannot itself control, and in particular the reapportionment of central costs?
>
> Is the cost centre able to compare its performance with similar cost centres?
>
> Which of the expenditure and income items can the cost centre control itself?
>
> How much virement is permitted within budget headings, and across them?

# 10 The Ugly Three: Cuts, Inflation and Falling Rolls

We have all learned to live with cuts the last few years. Inflation is a fact of daily life. Falling rolls have hit or will hit most schools in the country. All these things are familiar, but seldom analysed or studied. It would help if our working vocabulary was more precise, and if we distinguished between:

Economies: doing what we do now, at less cost
Cuts: cutting out some of the things we do now
Transfers of expenditures: persuading someone else to pay for things the education department pays for now.

## *Economies*

### *The problem*

Economies are very commendable. But they are also hard to make – much harder than shrugging off costs on to other people, or cutting out services that people need. On the face of it, the prospects are daunting.

As over 50 per cent of a school's costs comes from teachers' salaries, the obvious economy is to shed teachers. But any reduction makes the pupil–teacher ratio worse than it would have been. Admittedly there is little research to prove that a worse pupil–teacher ratio leads to lower standards of performance. But it is true that the appeal of independent schools often lies in their promise of smaller classes. And reducing teachers does not really alter the main unit-cost determinant – each pupil still has to be taught and supervised every hour and every day of his or her compulsory schooling. This is the crux of school costs. Expenditure is hitched to the treadmill of compulsory education, five and a half hours a day or so, for 190 to 200 days a year, from the age of 5 to 16. Most items of school expenditure are related to this commitment – capitation allowances, examination fees, upkeep of premises and grounds, assistance to pupils, ancillary staff, meals and transport.

*The possibilities*

Yet there are some consolations. First, 1 per cent is a lot. Even saving 1 per cent of the cost of a school or an authority is very substantial. Secondly, substantial economies have been made already, where it was often said that none could be found. Many people in the education service would secretly accept that some of these economies, despite the kicking and screaming, have been long overdue. Thirdly, falling rolls do offer considerable scope for economies in total expenditure without worsening the service, despite the impossibility of reducing staffing or closing buildings exactly in line with the fall in numbers. Fourthly, as earlier chapters have shown, there are enormous differences of provision between one authority and another. Even allowing for geographical differences, this does suggest that if two authorities provide a similar service at differing costs, then the higher cost authority has potential economies. This argument was developed powerfully by Ian Coutts, Chairman of the Association of County Councils' local government finance committee, in an article in *County Councils' Gazette* in 1979. He pointed out 'a dispassionate examination of the figures that are available would appear to indicate that if all local authorities could deliver their services at the same unit cost as those who do it most cheaply, then many could make savings of not 2½ per cent, nor 5 per cent, nor 7½ per cent, but approaching 20 per cent.' Coutts made allowance for geographical factors and social background, and accepted that the best available statistics were not always reliable, but he pressed home his argument that

> in any commercial organisation operating on a national scale in providing services and faced with the necessity to reduce expenditure, a look would be taken at the different cost centres or point of delivery of the service. Where the unit costs differed an enquiry would be mounted as to the reason for the difference, and in most cases the managers of the expensive centres would be given a few months to bring their costs into line with the more efficient of their colleagues. Failure to do so would mean their departure from the company.

Coutts suggested that there are four necessary moves for reducing costs:

1. CIPFA must be encouraged to present its statistics to show more unit costs
2. LEAs must look at reasons why there is so much difference between unit costs in comparable establishments
3. Multi-professional teams should be sent into low unit-costs areas to ascertain why their costs are lower
4. Central government should encourage authorities which are cost conscious with financial incentives.

*Cost reduction*

Cost reduction, meaning the planned and systematic attempt to reduce the cost of services, became one of the buzzwords of the 1970s. CIPFA set up a study group whose report *Cost Reduction in Public Authorities* (1979) explored the approach fully. 'The study group believe that *the* way ahead is for authorities to introduce a Cost Reduction mentality into their decision-taking and operating methods.' However, while the idea may have been buzzing around the local government stratosphere, it has not often descended to the lower levels of school administration. Most schools and LEAs have only reduced costs under pressure in a reactive way, not in the positive and planned approach suggested. Most senior staff in schools and many officers in LEAs are not familiar with either the jargon or the thinking behind it.

The CIPFA study group defined cost reduction as 'systems, activities and ideas which aim to assist in the more economic and efficient provision of services. In plain English it is the search for value for money.' It saw two approaches: the pragmatic (immediate, short-term measures leading to common sense economies), and the systematic (longer-term strategies).

The pragmatic approach

The group recognized that it was unprofitable to tilt at the windmills of policies and 'major methods' which were unlikely to be altered, however strong the arguments. So the first step should be to identify profitable areas for inquiry. They saw little value in a special panel of members, or even officers, as attempts to impose change from above or outside often provoke resistance. Rather they saw a role for local authority accountants as missionaries in spreading the good news. 'The ultimate aim is for Cost Reduction to become a way of life for professional disciplines in the same fashion as Budgetary Control has now largely managed to do.' Elsewhere cost reduction is referred to as 'largely an attitude of mind'. 'The practical reality is how to introduce a continuing sensitivity to potential cost-reducing measures into the workaday methods of all.'

The zeal is fine, but perhaps misplaced. It is not easy for accountants to enthuse others. They are often too remote from the actual cost centres to be able to tease out economies. And the necessary information is often lacking. The study errs when it suggests 'The Pragmatic Approach to Cost Reduction requires common sense interpretation of the facts and figures which in the public sector are already available in large measure through existing Management Information Systems.' The earlier part of this book has argued exactly the opposite. Finally, there is often a gulf between the accountants and the administrators at the centre and the local managers, which makes effective cost reduction almost impossible. One group holds the information, such as it is – the other group has the local knowledge which can make sense of it, and can effect changes. Cost reduction will make little progress until there is a much closer partnership between the two groups, much more openness, more exchange of information and views, and full acceptance that cost reduction brings mutual benefits, or at least avoids mutual discomfort. Indeed, cost reduction will spread more quickly if the local participants share in some of the savings, along the lines suggested in Chapter 9.

The CIPFA group made a number of practical proposals, such as:

More flexible staff deployment
Plant-intensive approaches
Cheaper in-house training
Scrutiny of the non-productive tail
Rationalizing of buildings, and rejection of the 'What we have we hold' philosophy
Disposal of surplus land, equipment, vehicles
Increased local responsibility for premises maintenance
Greater flexibility in central 'planned maintenance'
Fuel and electricity saving measures
Technical recommendations concerning debt charges and cash-flow management.

The proposals are by no means exhaustive, and some are general or not very relevant to schools. But they make a useful starting-point, and can be extended from cost breakdowns such as those in Chapters 2 to 4.

The systematic approach

The study suggested setting up systems to question the content of budgets and to measure achievements against money spent. The examples given were outside education, and the approach exposed the problems of output measurement discussed in Chapter 6. It probably has little to offer education unless new technology and more flexible use of school time make 'performance-measures' possible.

*Zero-based budgeting*

This concept, much beloved by Jimmy Carter, is an alternative approach to cost reduction. Public services are very resistant to economy drives, because for every employee seeking to reduce costs there is another hundred trying to maintain or increase them. J. L. Neuman put it nicely (*Harvard Business Review*, 1975): 'A reduction in service is almost never in the receivers' interests, particularly if they are not charged for services. Nor will the suppliers normally be happy to see demand for their services reduced.' Zero-based budgeting in essence requires that budgets must be justified from the ground up, instead of the normal approach where they are accepted in principle and only considered at the margin. Under this system, the LEA in the case of its budget, or the head in the case of a school budget, starts from the premise that none of the services have to be provided in their present form. The slate is clean. Each section manager has to make a case and justify his or her budget, This poses fundamental questions:

Should the function be performed at all?
What should the quality levels be?
Should it be performed in this way?
How much should it cost?

The process is time-consuming; it is not always appreciated by the recipients; it can only be done practicably every few years.

## *Transfers of expenditure*

These open a tempting vista – to transfer some of our costs so that someone else pays for them – but they are not always so tempting. 'He who pays the piper plays the tune.' Transferring expenditure to other departments or to parents may transfer control. And we should not fool ourselves that in any sense this is an increase in productivity. The actual costs remain the same. It is just the paymaster who alters. However, having said that, it is an area which is being increasingly explored.

### *Transfers to central government*

The most obvious candidate is teachers' salaries. Periodically a lobby among teachers' unions suggests that teachers and parents would be better off if these were paid centrally. Somehow this would make it easier to finance schools. Others join in, who are anxious to level out the variations in expenditure so starkly revealed in Chapters 3 and 4. But it is a very dangerous game. It is incomprehensible that such a shift could take place without the DES becoming the major controller of the education system instead of a sideline spectator. There also seems no strong reason why there should be more money available for teachers' salaries just because this is paid directly by the central government instead of indirectly through LEAs.

Another possible transfer is the actual administration of schools by LEAs. The birds of woe croak at intervals that the system is breaking down, and that we would have a more effective and generous system if it was centrally provided. Personally I find it difficult to imagine that we would be any better served with the educational equivalent of a Regional Health Authority or that the system would be any cheaper to run.

### *Transfers to other local authority departments*

The prime target here has been social expenditure – school meals, uniform and other grants, and free meals. These, it is said, are social and not educational benefits, and therefore should be administered and paid for by the social services department or the DHHS. There is a certain logic, but it certainly would throw up problems if the social services department provided meals on premises and to clients in the domain of the education department. Other possible transfers are transport to highways, and buildings and grounds to the estates/public works/architect's department. Some of these transfers have already taken place, a sort of shot-gun marriage under corporate management, and many of them have produced some unattractive and ill-disciplined offspring.

*Transfers to parents*

This has proved the most attractive. Other departments have not always welcomed the attempt to shuffle expenditure on to them, whereas parents have not been in a very strong position to resist. Various strategies have been adopted, often reactive to financial problems rather than planned.

Charging for 'frills' has always been a grey area. Some activities were always considered as legitimately chargeable to parents. The most obvious were visits abroad, even in school time. Almost as well accepted were school journeys and educational visits, full or part payment. The proportion charged for visits, camps and journeys has tended to rise, and in many cases is now the full cost. Charging for music lessons and for musical instruments has been a new and increasingly widespread feature for an expensive service, and no doubt the temporary setback of a court judgement that such charges are illegal is likely to be reversed by legislation. Similarly, charges have been levied for swimming in public baths. There is also an increasing tendency to maximize income from materials.

Another strategy has been to invite parents to provide textbooks, stationery and items like files, small equipment for technical drawing, and so on. This often begins in an ad hoc way with a department very short of books or equipment and in despair asking parents to help. But it then tends to develop its own momentum. Admittedly, we are one of the few countries that provides free stationery for students, and a number of countries do charge for textbooks, the United States being an example. Another strategy has been to charge parents for examination fees. This began originally with a quite reasonable charge for double entries, was then extended in some cases to entries against school recommendations, and has gone further with LEAs declining to pay for more than eight or seven subject entries.

One school of thought holds that this growth of ad hoc payments would be better rationalized. Why not be honest and actually make parents a standard charge, say, £20 per year? The arguments against this, however, seem very strong. It would probably need to be a uniform national arrangement. If it were not uniform, it would then be based upon the spending power of the catchment area, and would widen the gap between rich and poor schools. If it was a standard charge authorized by legislation, without doubt this would soon be offset by an equivalent reduction in national expenditure. It would in effect become an educational tax on parents, and so not a useful device to finance schools, but simply an alternative and regressive form of taxation.

A more profitable approach would be to pass legislation to allow charges for services beyond a general and basic education. The latter would need to be defined (with difficulty?) and would then be safeguarded as the free service. This would mean that instead of parents being taxed for a state education, they would receive their child's main education free, but would be entitled to pay for extras. There is considerable evidence that parents would be quite willing to do this if it meant an enhanced service for their child. They do at the moment contribute very generously for expensive items such as visits abroad or computers at home - or even educational Christmas presents! Admittedly this approach appears to work against children from poor or working-class families. But perhaps we need to accept that the ideal of universal education, universally free, is no longer realistic. If we take the Vaizey view that 'the level of the national income, over a period, and its rate of change, are closely associated with changes in the outlay on education' (Vaizey and Sheahan, *Resources for Education*, 1968, page 128), then the cessation of growth in national income will lead (is leading!) to a permanent blocking off in resources for education. Indeed, since 1973 education's share of the national income has slowly fallen. In this situation do we just rely on central and local authority funding - accepting that it will shrink, that standards of provision will fall, that universal education will become impoverished? Or do we attempt to supplement it from parents' disposable incomes? The parents of a school of 1,000 pupils will commonly have a total post-tax income in the order of at least £5 million per annum. If they can be persuaded to spend just 1 per cent on extras for their children's education, this would provide £50,000 a year. Taking the school illustrated in Chapter 2, it would more than double the capitation allowance, or provide six extra teachers. Surely schools are almost in a commercial situation where their traditional 'market' is shrinking and they need to use new methods to restore their market share.

There is a useful parallel in the health service from which we can learn. Launched in 1948 on an entirely free basis, three forms of payment have crept in. First, those charges which recoup money for the government, in effect a health tax, and which also have some deterrent effect to reduce demand, for example, prescription charges, dental charges. Secondly, payments which do not reduce demand and which do not improve facilities, but allow special treatment for the privileged, for example, private payment of specialists. The third area is where private payments have actually enhanced the total of medical facilities in the country – subscription to private medical schemes which have led to the growth of private hospitals. Of these three, the last seems by far the most promising.

## *Cuts*

It is very difficult for inside observers to give an objective view of cuts in their own authority or their own school. Undoubtedly cuts have led to a worsening of provision in a number of areas. On the other hand, the consequences have not always been as dire as the critics have suggested. This seems to be partly because people always exaggerate the dangers, both as a defence mechanism and because they are genuinely worried. There also seems to be an important settling down factor. Although cuts may be potentially serious, the system shakes itself down and accommodates them to some extent. But the process cannot continue indefinitely without serious damage being done.

There are some principles:

1 Across-the-board cuts are often inequitable. They affect schools unequally. Ill-equipped and ill-staffed schools suffer most. Unfortunately, making cuts with discrimination is administratively more difficult, and requires a good information system.
2 Cuts should be planned against a set of priorities. Highest priority should go to items closest to the chalk-face – teachers, capitation, ancillary support and premises, usually in that order.
3 Cuts require a good information base. Otherwise they may not realize the amount expected, or may have effects which have not been anticipated.
4 Cuts in capitation allowances are easiest to make, but pound-for-pound the most damaging. They cause no redundancies, they are immediate and easily made. They have the added attraction that the pain is delayed. It will only be towards the end of the financial year that the effect is felt. Even here it is deadened. For if we assume that the total stock of goods and services bought by capitation is replaced on average every five years (stationery in less than a year, but many books and pieces of equipment in ten years), then a 10 per cent cut in capitation for one year only reduces the *total* stock by 2 per cent. But the pain is only deferred. For if a 10 per cent cut is made in April 1981 and not replaced, by April 1984 a *44 per cent increase* will be needed to restore the stock of capitation goods to its original level.

   *Example.* Trimshire LEA give a capitation allowance of £20 per pupil (in real 'no inflation' terms). In April 1981 it cuts this by 10 per cent. The cumulative situation, assuming a five-year average turnover of capitation items, is as follows:

| | *Capitation allowances per pupil* The original policy | The 'cuts' policy |
|---|---|---|
| April 1980 | £20 | £20 |
| April 1981 | £20 | £18 |
| April 1982 | £20 | £18 |
| April 1983 | £20 | £18 |
| April 1984 | £20 | £18 |
| Total stock of capitation goods and services, per pupil | £100 | £92 |

So the LEA needs to increase its £18 allowance by £8 (44 per cent) to restore the original position

5 Crisis cuts are worst. It is difficult to implement cuts reasonably without plenty of time for study and consultation. If the crisis is outside the normal budget-making time of autumn and early spring it is worse still. Worst of all are cuts in the summer, as timetables have already been made and orders placed. Disruption is out of all proportion to the money saved.

6 Smuggled cuts are insidious and destructive. Insidious because the damage is not fully realized and because legitimate objections or alternatives are not considered. Destructive because they destroy confidence in the LEA, and because they are more difficult to restore.

*Example*. An actual quotation from a headmaster in the north of England, June 1981: 'The LEA transferred the payment of telephone bills to capitation last year. In the first year of operation, the extra monies allocated were just sufficient to cover costs. Subsequently, capitation has gone up by a fraction of the rate of inflation, whereas telephone charges have gone up much faster . . . Personally I feel that this has been a retrograde step, not in principle, but because the LEA has used it only to cut costs, and has not given the schools enough time to begin to think of "virement" in the proper sense.'

## *Inflation*

Inflation operates separately from cuts, at least in theory, and can be totally offset by an adequate inflation increment. In practice the separation is not so simple. It is not easy to devise an accurate inflation increment when one is dealing with compound costs, each element of which has inflation at different rates. The complexity of the problem can be seen in the following calculations made by the

Somerset County Treasurers' Department for 1981/82.

| | % | | % |
|---|---|---|---|
| Gas | 50 | Electricity 1.4.80 | 10½ |
| | | 1.8.80 | 3½ |
| Solid fuel | 25 | Oil | 29½ |
| Water | 14½ | Cleaning materials | 26 |
| Furniture | 15 | Rates | 19·55 |
| Books | 15 | Educational equipment | 15 |
| PE equipment | 15 | Cleaning equipment | 26 |
| Administration equipment | 7½ | School stationery | 20 |
| Medical requisites | 27 | Crockery | 23 |
| Food | 11 | Protective clothing | 7½ |
| Laundry | 14 | Petrol | 17 |
| Tyres | 13 | Road fund licence | 20 |
| Vehicle maintenance and repair | 14½ | Advertising | 20 |
| Travel allowance | 24 | Subsistence | 22½ |
| Coach hire | 21 | Rail fares | 20 |
| Bus fares | 15 | | |

Obviously the increment hinges upon the increases for each item being assessed accurately, but also on accurate knowledge of the proportion of each within the LEA's total budget.

Central government alleges that it makes allowance for inflation in its expenditure targets and its rate support grant. Its increment is based upon the inflation it expects during the next twelve months. However, such estimates tend to err on the side of optimism – and in recent years the government has hardly even kept up the pretence of allowing adequately for inflation. Indeed, current cash limits clearly do not allow sufficient, and use inflation to press the LEAs into making cuts. The government does issue a price index of education expenditure in its annual statistics for education, and rather more up-to-date information in the DES *Handbook of Unit Costs*.

Local authorities are more realistic. They base their inflation increment for capitation on their actual assessment for the twelve months ending November before the new financial year. There are no national guidelines, though obviously there is national data which can be drawn upon. Because of this November base, the increment is in effect seventeen months in arrears – inflation for the year beginning November 1980 determines the increment paid for the year beginning April 1982. As a result, at a time of rising inflation schools suffer quite considerably, and at a time of falling inflation they catch up. On other items such as pay, prices for heating, lighting, transport, meals, etc., the LEA has to make intelligent guesses and estimate ahead.

So each local authority works out its own sums. No doubt each treasurer's department is influenced by the optimism or pessimism of its staff, and also by its sympathy with the education service. The accuracy of its forecasting, and its foresight, will be important, though to some extent errors in one year can be corrected in the next. There may also be a political factor – an element of conscious or unconscious evasion in the inflation increment, either smuggling a cut or flinching from recognizing the true situation. LEA attitudes towards inflation increments are affected by the simple question of 'Who pays?' If the LEA pays centrally, it will obviously make sure there is sufficient money in the budget. It would be very embarrassed if it did not provide enough to cover inflation for employees' expenses, premises and transport expenses. It would not be able to shrug off the blame on to anyone else. But with expenditures which are mainly made by schools or for schools, for example, capitation allowances, cleaning expenses, postage and telephones, equipment repairs, etc., there is a temptation for the LEA to be less realistic.

For all these reasons the impact of inflation varies considerably from LEA to LEA and from year to year. A report from the Educational Publishers Council (1981) studied five home counties. It showed that there was substantial variation in the increments they allowed for inflation in each of the three years studied. Similarly, in the 1981 sample used in Chapter 7 (page 113), three LEAs allowed 8 per cent, 11 per cent and 17·24 per cent as inflation increases to capitation allowances in 1981/82.

B. E. Day, Deputy Chief Education Officer of Oxfordshire, has explained the 'shopping basket' system used in his authority (*Education*, 25 September 1981), and asserted that this has maintained schools' purchasing power in real terms (apart from a 2½ per cent reduction, a relic of past cuts). He has kindly provided the figures shown in Table 10:1.

**Table 10:1** Inflation indexing of capitation allowances in Oxfordshire, 1974–82

| | PRIMARY SCHOOLS' CAPITATION | | SECONDARY SCHOOLS' CAPITATION | | RETAIL PRICE INDEX (RPI) | |
|---|---|---|---|---|---|---|
| | *Index** | *% increase* | *Index** | *% increase* | *Index* | *% increase* |
| 1974/75 | 100 | – | 100 | – | 100 | – |
| 1975/76 | 122 | 22 | 126 | 26 | 115 | 15 |
| 1976/77 | 153 | 25 | 157 | 25 | 146 | 27 |
| 1977/78 | 178 | 17 | 178 | 13 | 166 | 14 |
| 1978/79 | 201 | 13 | 195 | 10 | 193 | 16 |
| 1979/80 | 211 | 5 | 211 | 8 | 208 | 8 |
| 1980/81 | 219 | 4 | 214 | 2 | 235 | 13 |
| 1981/82 | 259 | 18 | 248 | 16 | 273 | 16 |

* In constant terms, ignoring cuts 1977–1982.

He feels that the RPI is not a realistic monitor of school capitation, and that successful value-for-money contracts by the LEA justify the recent lower capitation index.

Apart from the immediate problem caused by inadequate inflation increments, the less obvious but more serious problem is rectification. If the shortfall is allowed to continue, it builds up on a compound interest principle.

> *Example.* Lagshire LEA allows 5 per cent inflation for 1981/82, inflation running at 10 per cent per annum. By April 1984 the capitation index will stand at 146 (April 1980 = 100), but actual capitation at only 121·5. The cumulative loss to capitation can only be put right by an inflation increment for 1984/85 of 39 per cent.

The other effect is long term. Unless inflation increments can be hitched to the wholesale price index or an equally reliable educational spending index, many attempts to introduce better financial practices will abort. For most improved procedures involve devolving responsibility for expenditure in one way or another to schools. This can only work if a proper allowance for inflation is made. The point was made graphically by a head in an authority which has recently extended virement. He wrote, 'Virement in "hard times" does not count as an advantage'. There is a serious risk that promising moves to develop schools as cost centres and later as responsibility centres will fail over this issue.

Finally, we should remember that inflation increments only restore the status quo. What if the status quo is unsatisfactory?

## *Falling rolls*

### *The problem*

The theory of educational costs under falling rolls is simple enough. It is an equation comprising fixed costs and variable costs, as in Figure 10:1 below. If *all* costs are variable, costs will fall exactly in step with pupil numbers, as in line *AB*. If a proportion are fixed, so in that proportion will costs fail to fall. In practice the situation is more complex, because many costs are partially variable. Even fixed costs are only fixed for a given period of time. Disposal of premises, for example, can certainly lead to a dramatic drop in costs. So total costs for falling rolls are more likely to show a curve as in Figure 10:1, smooth as in *X* or more likely irregular as *Y*.

The theoretical effect of fixed costs on *total* costs when rolls fall can be calculated by formula:

Let $C_1$, $C_2$ = total costs at present, future point, etc.
Let R = percentage reduction in student numbers (e.g. 20, for 20%)
Let V = variable costs, as a percentage of total costs (e.g. 75, for 75%)

Then $C_2 = C_1 \dfrac{(10{,}000 - VR)}{10{,}000}$

*Example*
Let R = 30 (average national percentage fall in rolls)
Let V = 75 (taking only premises costs as fixed, excluding rates, i.e., 25% of total school costs as in Table 10:2)

Then $C_2 = C_1 \dfrac{10{,}000 - 2250}{10{,}000} = \dfrac{77{\cdot}5}{100}\, C_1$

So if rolls fall by 30% with 25% fixed costs, total costs fall by 22·5%.

**Fig. 10:1** Models for school costs with falling rolls

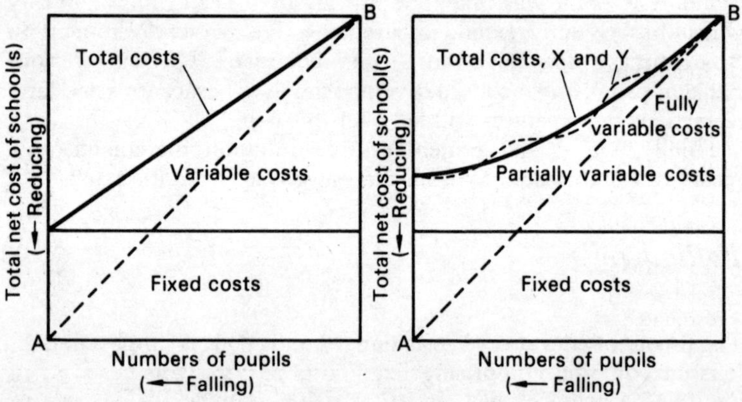


Graph 1: Total, fixed and variable school costs, simple model

Graph 2: Total, fixed and variable school costs, alternative models

Note: Proportions of fixed/variable costs are for illustration only.

Note that the above only takes premises as a fixed cost. It makes no allowance for other fixed costs, lower pupil-teacher ratios, etc. Of course premises costs are not 100 per cent fixed. If pupil numbers fall there will be some reduction in heating and lighting, water and soap, etc., but the overall effect is only marginal. Rates, however, do fall broadly in line with rolls (see page 60).

**Table 10:2** Premises-related expenditure, England and Wales, 1980/81

| | PRIMARY SCHOOLS | | | SECONDARY SCHOOLS | | |
|---|---|---|---|---|---|---|
| | *Estimated expenditure in £000s* | *Per cent of total primary school premises-related expenditure* | *Per cent of total net primary school expenditure* | *Estimated expenditure in £000s* | *Per cent of total secondary schools premises-related expenditure* | *Per cent of total net secondary school expenditure* |
| 1 Premises-related staff salaries and on-costs | 129,459 | 22·1 | 6·2 | 145,653 | 17·9 | 5·0 |
| 2 Repairs, alterations and maintenance | 117,393 | 20·0 | 5·6 | 131,908 | 16·2 | 4·5 |
| 3 Fuel, light, cleaning materials and water | 91,123 | 15·6 | 4·4 | 114,727 | 14·1 | 3·9 |
| 4 Furniture and fittings | 6,738 | 1·1 | 0·3 | 9,093 | 1·1 | 0·3 |
| 5 Rent and rates | 53,562 | 9·8 | 2·8 | 97,715 | 12·0 | 3·3 |
| 6 Total, above items | 398,275 | 68·6 | 19·3 | 499,096 | 61·4 | 17·1 |
| 7 Debt charges | 175,233 | 29·9 | 8·4 | 297,894 | 36·7 | 10·2 |
| 8 Revenue contributions to capital outlay | 9,196 | 1·6 | 0·4 | 15,634 | 1·9 | 0·5 |
| Total premises-related estimated expenditure | 586,704 | 100·0 | 28·1 | 812,624 | 100·0 | 27·8 |

*Source:* CIPFA, *Education Statistics,* 1980/81 Estimates. Net expenditure + 27·5 per cent (primary) and 46·6 per cent (secondary) total debt charges and RCCO (percentages from DES revenue expenditure statistics).

Similarly, another formula will calculate the effect of fixed costs on *unit* costs when rolls fall:

Let R and V be as above
The percentage increase in unit costs from fixed costs

$$= \frac{10{,}000 - VR}{100 - R} - 100$$

*Example*. The percentage increase in unit costs from a 30% drop in rolls,
with 25% fixed costs $= \frac{10{,}000 - VR}{100 - R} - 100$

$$= \frac{10{,}000 - (75 \times 30)}{100 - 30} - 100$$

$$= \frac{7750}{70} - 100 \quad = 10{\cdot}7\%$$

This formula can be used to plot a graph (Figure 10:2).

**Fig. 10:2** Rise in unit costs per pupil caused by fixed premises costs

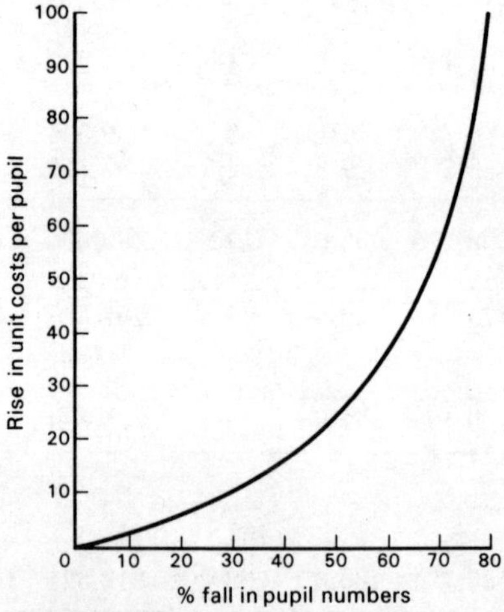


*Individual cost factors*

While the theoretical model may be simple, practice is complex. We cannot produce a realistic model for a school or an authority unless we can feed in sophisticated data for the various cost elements. The Briault report (1980), although excellent in other respects, suffered seriously in its failure to deal with cost implications. However, it did outline very clearly a whole range of strategies applicable to local authorities, each of which will have an effect upon costs.

Admissions policies
Briault examined these fully and brought out the implications in

terms of under-occupancy of premises and lower pupil–teacher ratio. 'The issue may be simply stated: are parents to choose the schools they prefer or is contraction to be planned, controlled and managed at the expense of parents' freedom of choice?' Clearly a cost figure could be put on that parental choice in terms of lower pupil–teacher ratios, additional premises costs, and so on, to the tune of £*X* per parental choice. A sobering thought.

Staffing policies

The tendency for staffing in falling roll areas to lag behind theoretical establishments because of difficulties in redeploying specialist teachers is well known. The actual financial difference between one policy and another is much less known. A planned lag in staffing – the new 'curricular staffing' – is such a major issue that it is dealt with separately on page 162.

Policies on early retirement have substantial cost implications too, though they may well be necessary for the greater efficiency of the service. Linked with this is the serious financial effect of the aging of the teaching force. The salary pyramid is steadily narrowing and salary drift has now become a considerable cost factor.

Premises costs

If premises costs include debt charges, etc., then about 28 per cent of both primary and secondary school net expenditure is incurred for premises. Full details are given in Table 10:2. Rates broadly fall in line with pupil numbers, and water if it is metered; fuel, light and cleaning materials, and some minor costs will be affected by changes in pupil numbers, but only marginally. Niki Bartman and Tom Carden, from the DES Architects and Buildings Branch, in an important article 'Falling rolls and building costs' (*Education*, 16 October 1981) remark, 'Premises-related costs depend almost entirely on the number and size of the buildings and sites being used and are only marginally affected by the number of pupils using them.'

The DES has certainly realized that premises costs are at the centre of the financial implications of falling rolls. Hence its pronouncements to local authorities to 'take surplus places out of use'. Circular 2/81 considered that 1·3 million surplus places should be taken out of use by 1986, two-fifths of the total surplus, but that progress towards this was lagging badly. It estimated that by March 1982 only 230,000 places would have been taken out – 'fewer than 1 in 8 of the places then expected to be surplus nationally'.

Much depends on the LEA's policy about disposing of assets. Most simply cling to their outposts of empire, just changing the flag. This may reduce premises costs slightly, but by nothing like the fullest amount. A glance at Table 10:2 will show that most premises costs continue while the premises are still LEA property. Only by sale or leasing may substantial reductions be made. Obviously, market values of premises will vary considerably across place and time. Planning permission for alternative use is crucial in the sale value of redundant premises.

Equally crucial are LEA policies towards the proceeds of any sale. Are sales to be used totally or largely towards paying off loans and so reducing revenue demands on the education department? If so, they will commonly pay off three or four times the loan charges attributable to a particular school. For example, one Somerset school 25 years old was valued recently at £750,000. As it had an outstanding loan of approximately £200,000, requiring debt charges of approximately £40,000 per annum, the sale would reduce debt charges by almost four times the amount needed for that school. Or will such receipts be paid into a capital receipts fund, maybe to avoid future borrowing, maybe to make possible borderline projects (and so adding to the LEA's premises costs). The latter is a common practice, and a strong disincentive to departments divesting themselves of surplus plant. If the education department can recycle all the proceeds from the sale of school premises within its budget, it will be much more eager to dispose of them.

Figure 10:3 shows two possible extremes. The model simulates 5,000 pupils in five schools, averaging 1,000 pupils each, in an urban area where rolls drop steadily (shown by lines *AS, CT*). 'Slowshire' LEA does not sell or lease any premises, No doubt some of them are used for new purposes, or even mothballed, but all remain a charge on the rates. So premises costs AB remain fixed apart from rates and a small reduction in fuel, light etc. 'Hastyham' LEA sells school premises at the earliest possible moment (at *X, Y, Z*). The complete sale proceeds are used to reduce loan charges – so that each sale not only removes the costs for that building, but reduces the costs of the remaining premises. Premises costs *CD* fall faster than numbers. Obviously, no LEA could act as hastily as Hastyham. However, some look uncommonly like

**Fig. 10:3** Effects of different LEA policies on premises costs with falling rolls

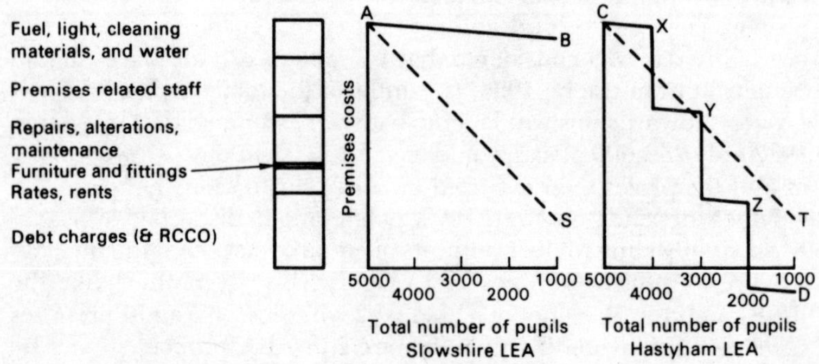

Slowshire. And it is worth noticing that if Hastyham had deferred sale *X* by 12 months, *it would have failed to save over £300,000* (25 per cent of the average annual cost of such a school, plus reduction in debt charges from sale proceeds).

Each LEA needs a policy on premises costs and premises contraction. It needs to survey its stock of buildings, schools and other, in the light of falling rolls. It needs to plan the early disposal of those which it does not need and which can realize a good value. The Education Department needs to negotiate with other departments so that it can retain all, or the major part, of the realized cash value. If it does not have such a policy, not only will it fail to realize the opportunity costs involved, but the rift between the LEA and the central government over expenditure targets will grow even wider. Bartman and Carden have shown in considerable detail where savings can be found.

It would be folly to pretend that sale or leasing of school premises is an easy answer to the rising unit costs of falling rolls. Even the DES has come to accept some of the practical and political difficulties involved. Obviously there will often be strong social and community factors. Local community opposition may be unpleasantly and often justifiably strong. A powerful local politician may be sufficient to block an individual closure. Even the disposal of temporary accommodation faces the same problem. If the accommodation is movable, it simply shifts elsewhere with no reduction in costs (in fact the move actually increases them). If it is 'permanent' temporary accommodation, destroying it seems an act of vandalism. In rural areas, closure may not be possible at all – or may be partially offset by transport costs. The work of Coles (1980) suggested that the concentration of rural primary schools has a cost ceiling. Of course, local authorities have to be cautious and safeguard surplus accommodation against any possible upturn in school rolls. They and the local interests will clutch at such straws, even if they are insubstantial. It would be interesting to know how many urban schools that have been closed, particularly secondary schools, have had their premises sold. Very few I suspect. Usually as a school closes the vultures are circling, and barely have the children moved out than other branches of the service or other departments have moved in.

### Non-teaching salaries

The Briault report looked at staffing policies for non-teaching support staff in times of falling rolls. Clearly this has cost implications. So do equivalent policies and agreements relating to caretaking and cleaning staff. As for central LEA costs, to what extent should central or divisional offices or the advisory services be expected to reduce? To what extent should the psychological service shrink in proportion to the contraction of its clients? Or the careers service in relation to the contraction of a fifth year and sixth year?

Unless these central costs are closely analysed, there is little doubt that they will lag badly behind.

*Comparison of alternatives*

The Arthur Young study on the costing of 16–19 provision sets out a method to cost alternative schemes. It is not confined to a falling roll situation, but is particularly relevant to it. The merit of the study lies in its rational approach and its careful setting out of a logical method for assessing alternative costs (although designed for 16–19 costing, it can be easily used for 11–16 or other age ranges). It emphasizes that 'since the objective is to assist in choosing between options, it is not necessary to get accurate estimates of costs which do not differ between options' (page 11). It is not intended to produce universal conclusions about costs of particular types of organizations since costs of options will vary considerably from one situation to another. Instead it provides a framework for an LEA to apply in an area. It is at this stage that the problem which has been stressed so often in this book appears. When it comes to practical as opposed to theoretical costing, many LEAs do not have the detailed information which is necessary, and such information as there is will often be misleading. The accurate costing of options is fraught with difficulties, and great care needs to be exercised. A costing exercise may produce figures which look very positive but which in fact may be completely overturned by alteration of one factor. This was powerfully illustrated by Peter Newsam, Education Officer of ILEA (*Guardian*, 2 March 1982), when he showed that in one of the two extended examples given in the Arthur Young study the conclusion that a particular option would lead to a saving of £120,000 was misleading, since it would in fact involve the LEA in expenditure of an extra £120,000 above another option which had not been considered!

*Curricular staffing*

Staffing a school according to its curriculum, rather than on a straight pupil–teacher ratio, is increasingly seen as the answer to the problems of falling rolls. It may well be the answer to the problems of maintaining the curriculum in small schools. Indeed it has a lot to commend it, but the financial implications have to be accepted. It is quite useless to embark on a policy of curricular staffing without recognizing that it is going to be considerably more expensive, make unit costs higher and reduce or remove the pressure to rationalize the school system.

The theory of curricular staffing is simple enough. One establishes the minimum reasonable curriculum for a pupil at a given age. One then takes the numbers of pupils in that particular year group and calculates by formula the number of staff required to mount that curriculum. Obviously, although there is a broad general principle, in practice there is considerable variation over the model curriculum proposed and the formulas used. Whatever the variations, the effect will always be to provide more generous staffing and preserve smaller schools. The Briault report quoted (page 87) some data from the Sparsely Populated Areas project, and using this we can calculate that, if we take one teacher's annual salary with on-costs as £8,000, it would cost £56,000 more per annum for teaching salary costs to provide the same curriculum for 900 pupils in two three-form entry 11 to 16 schools as in one six-form entry school. These price tags on policies make our choice more realistic and underline the alternatives. Even the Briault report hinted at this. 'The dilemma . . . will become more common: at the expense of which other school or schools is this or that curriculum being protected?' There was a time when falling rolls were seen as a golden age in which pupil-teacher ratios would fall, quality of non-teaching support would improve, and there would be an enhancement of the service, side by side with economies for the public purse. Daily this prospect becomes less and less real. We may embark on curricular staffing, but is it always the wisest policy? Is it always the best use of the money available, taking the best advantage of the opportunity costs? As long as the supply of finance for education remains limited and finite, taking up the policy option of curricular staffing closes options elsewhere. One school's gain will inevitably be another's loss. After all, small village primary schools enjoyed curricular staffing. Is it realistic to embark on curricular staffing in the secondary field when we have been steadily cutting it back in the primary?

# PART THREE

# Managing the Future

# 11 What Sort of Future?

It is difficult to foresee the future for school finance unless we have some idea of the future for schools themselves.

## *The scale of educational change*

Futurology is a hazardous pursuit. This chapter rests upon one main assumption – that schools will undergo more fundamental changes in the next twenty years than in the last hundred. The argument can be simply stated. The schools we now have are the final flowering of the schools of the Industrial Revolution. Consider their prevailing features:

Compulsory free education
Concentration on the 5 to 16 age-range
Little adult education
A limited school day and school year, with little use of buildings outside this
The annual timetable and curriculum, derived as much from the historical development of knowledge as from projection of future needs
Teacher-centred, large-class, book-based learning
Education by age-cohorts
Seclusion from the community, with principal service to full-time students.

All these are the product of, and the response to, the Industrial Revolution. Will they still be relevant to the second Industrial Revolution, the 'Information Revolution' and the post-industrial society? At some time ahead, five years, maybe ten or more, the new educational technology will burst upon us. Home learning will be facilitated, individual learning transformed. At the same time new forces in the economy and in society will make new educational demands. Can the schools of one era serve another unaltered?

For, paradoxically, schools have not yet passed through an Industrial Revolution themselves. The typical school classroom of the 1980s is still functionally and even visually the direct descendant of the Victorian schoolroom. There have been false dawns of a technological transformation – audio-visual aids, programmed learning, educational television – but education has remained one of the last of the handicraft industries. But for how long?

So despite the risks, we need to peer ahead to identify likely trends and assess their financial implications. For the technological changes, when they come, are likely to come quickly – at least this has been the experience of other industries. But schools change very slowly, and are set in a firm mould of custom and tradition. Unless we can think ahead, develop new approaches and loosen constraints, we shall find ourselves trying to finance a new system with the policies and procedures of the old.

## *The schools of the future*

### *The nature of the information revolution*

It is difficult for people in the middle of change to see it in perspective.

> Two cautions are necessary. First, even in a time of revolutionary change, many things remain much as they always were. Second, we cannot be at all clear about the speed at which changes will come about, though discounting both those who preach instant science fiction transformations and those who are confident that the world they are accustomed to will see their time out. (Council for Educational Technology, *Microelectronics: their Implications for Education and Training*, 1978).

Yet already some of the main features of the Information Revolution are becoming apparent. Information itself is becoming the most important factor of production – above land, labour or capital. Information is expanding exponentially, and yet is increasingly accessible. In a few years it will be commonplace for a person in his own home to command a pool of knowledge far greater than any single person commands today. Information will be instantly available, and transferable, worldwide. The trend for activities to be home-centred will increase. Already television has made much entertainment, political discussion, and even religion 'home-based'. This is likely to extend to jobs being carried out at home, to shopping, private banking and commercial transactions, and to other aspects of life. The extension of home entertainment, with games and with satellite born entertainment, will be rapid. Knowledge-based industries – electronics, computers, chemicals – are likely to grow fast. But within the manufacturing sector technological change, usually based around electronic information systems, will steadily reduce the numbers employed. Although service industries may continue to grow, the total pool of labour required will shrink steadily. Hours will shorten, retirement advance and studenthood extend. Unemployment and redundancy may persist or grow. Opportunities and demand for leisure will increase steadily. Adults will need to change jobs, or to retrain, ever more frequently.

There is scope for disagreement over details of this post-industrial society, but it is becoming clear that some of the bench-marks of our present economic and social system are being swept away. So what of the schools?

*Changes in school functions*

We can begin to speculate about some of the likely characteristics of schools in the future:

1 They will continue to provide substantial education on a teacher-and-class basis. This will be particularly important in the primary and lower secondary years, with their heavy emphasis on basic skills and on socialization.
2 A period of education is still likely to remain compulsory because of the importance of some of its functions. But some flexibility may be possible – part-time attendance, deferral of attendance or even deferrable vouchers. This would be particularly likely if education became more criterion-referenced (see page 101).
3 Individualized learning systems, both inside and outside schools, will increase and learning will be more individual-centred – there will be a growing tendency for the learner to select his own programmes.
4 Schools will act as a learning centre for the community, with teacher-advisers, technical assistants, and sophisticated resources and equipment providing a guidance and feedback service not easily rendered at home. They will also serve as a social centre and hub-of-network for learners. Human beings are social animals, and learning is easier if it is not entirely solitary. It is likely that a higher proportion of students will be adults and part-time.
5 There will be more 'distance-learning' – learning at home.
6 School premises and sites will be much more fully utilized, with more flexible and extended hours, both to accommodate the functions above, and to make the premises available to the community for leisure and recreational pursuits.

It is obvious that these features will change schools considerably, though the degree of change is still uncertain. Much will depend on society's answer to that most taunting of educational questions . . .

*Is a school a factory – or a shop?*

Is a school a factory, processing its products, or a shop, from which the customers take the things they need for life? This polarization has underlain much of the past debates on the purpose of education, and the curriculum that should be created for it. Few people would answer the raw question by simply accepting one of the extremes, but the problem still remains – where on the continuum do you stand? In a new era the question thrusts again. And it has very important implications for the school curriculum and school organization, and so for school costs. It could be argued that schools will tend more towards the factory model, because of the tendency to extend the years of education and to defer specialization, and because it seems likely that man's social and political problems are more intractable than the technological, and so require extended socialization within schools. However, historically, the trend has been more towards the shop model, reflecting the more complex content of education, the pressures of the bulging curriculum, the more active role of students, the greater awareness and sophistication of both students and parents. It can also be argued strongly that the individualized nature of the new learning technology will encourage the trend.

Personally I feel the latter arguments are stronger, and that schools will become more shop-like, certainly secondary schools and possibly, to a small degree, primary schools. This will be important because the factory and shop models have different cost structures. However, the question of degree is still important, and this hinges upon the curriculum.

*Changes in the school curriculum in the post-industrial society*

1 Basic communication skills will be even more important – oracy, literacy, numeracy, graphical communication. Teletext has no compassion for the weak reader!
2 New skills will be needed relating to information technology – retrieving, processing, computing, keyboard.
3 Learning skills and attitudes – 'the most important task of the schools will be to instil in young people a general curiosity and a pleasure in learning. In their adult lives it may be very desirable for learning to play a continuing part, as vocational retraining, as a worthwhile activity replacing work, and to maintain self-esteem. The worst damage that could be done to young people would be for their schooling to leave them with a distaste, or an incapacity, for learning. More positively, there is a need for a deliberate emphasis on developing study skills, particularly those related to independent learning which is likely to play a major part in the schemes of recurrent and continuing education.' (CET, 1978)
4 Knowledge and understanding will still be very important. But the knowledge explosion and the more rapid obsolescence of

knowledge will make principles of selection even more important, perhaps:
(a) core knowledge for all, related to aspects of the physical world which are likely to be useful and which are not likely to alter (for example, scientific, geographical)
(b) 'growth-points', on to which later learning can easily be grafted (for example, key concepts across a broad range of disciplines)
(c) advanced knowledge for future technicians, technologists and managers.

5 Physical skills in design crafts and technology, arts and physical education, both as a base for leisure activities and for vocational skills.
6 Careers guidance and careers education.

So far, so good. Each of these aspects has financial implications. Some will be amenable to individualized learning, and others can be acquired quickly in an efficient institution. Others, however, will still be very labour-intensive. But the most contentious areas of the curriculum await decision:

7 Social education - development of social skills and personal qualities.
8 Development of moral and political understanding and values.
9 Transmission of our cultural, historical and religious heritage.
10 Support for children with personal and family problems.

This second group will pose a much greater problem. These areas are less easy to evaluate, less amenable to use of new technology and more cost-efficient methods. They represent the classic problem of costly inputs and intangible outputs. They are mostly processing functions on the factory model.

## *The future for school finance*

If we accept that schools will alter substantially in the foreseeable future, then we must accept that school costs will alter too. Obviously it is not possible to be precise or to attach financial values, but at least we can see the directions in which cost factors will probably move.

*Changes in the educational costs system*

School costs are a delicate eco-system where each element interacts upon others, and where the whole seeks to achieve a precarious equilibrium. Changes in the nature of education and the function of schools will apply pressures at different points in the system which will go juddering from one element to another. To take one

**Fig. 11:1** Possible changes in the educational cost system as a result of the Information Revolution

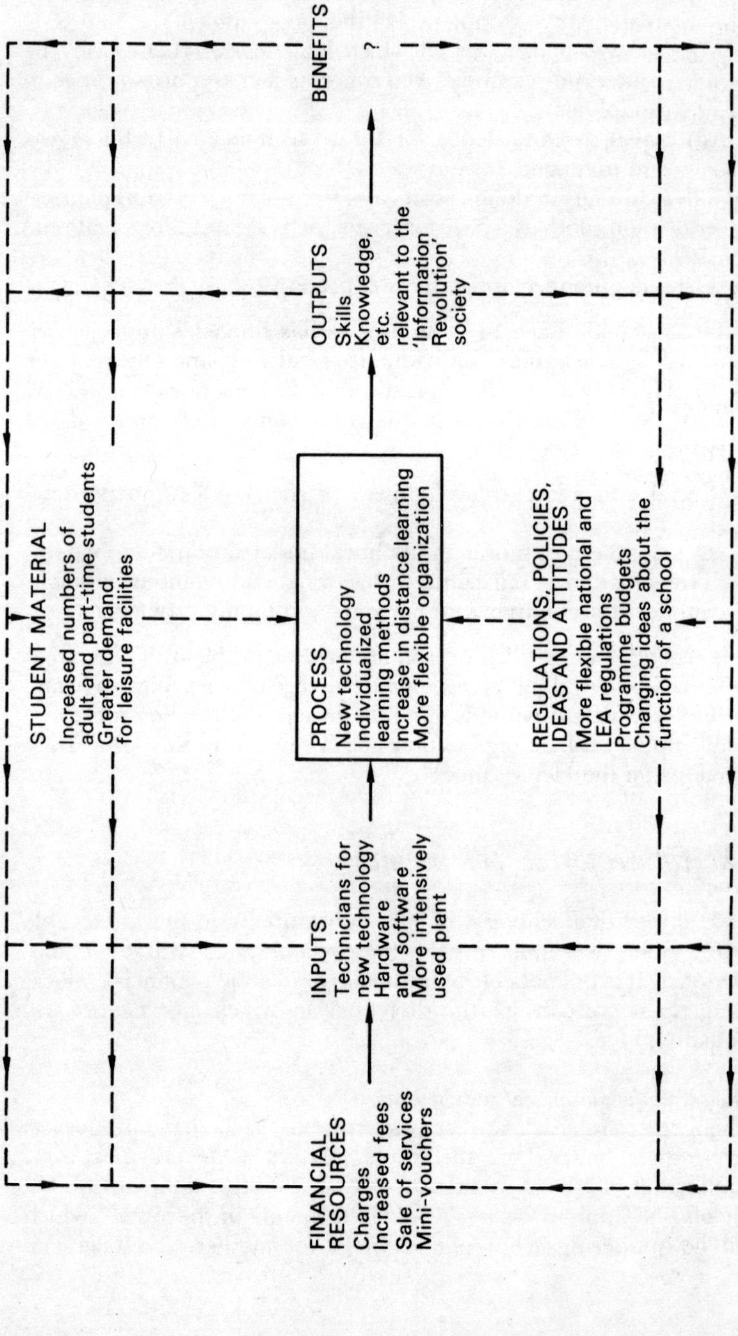


*Note.* This diagram is intended as an overlay to Figure 1.4 to show only the changes which seem likely in the present system.

example: the mere introduction of a large amount of electronic technology into school will affect non-teaching technician costs and the costs of equipment provision and maintenance. Because it is relatively more expensive than paper and blackboard, it will encourage more intensive plant utilization. This will then lead on the one hand to greater caretaking and heating costs and on the other to more flexible regulations about school use and school attendance. This in turn will encourage greater use of schools by adults and by part-time students, and so affect the character of the schools themselves and the community's attitudes towards them. The curriculum itself will change in response to the needs of the Information Revolution, and this will trigger a similar series of reactions in learning methods and school organization which again might have financial implications for perhaps teachers' salaries or for clerical support. Any change in the system will wind its way back to the base of the cost chain, namely the actual provision of financial resources to mount the whole operation. Figure 11:1 attempts to present such possible changes in the cost system.

*Changes for an individual school*
The simplest approach is to take the costs of one secondary school presented in Table 2:1 (page 25) and to consider how these would probably be affected by changes in cost factors (at constant 1979/80 prices).

*LEA overheads*. Little change in most items. However at a time of methodological change, it would be important to increase expenditure on in-service education, say . . . + £2,000
It is also likely that the LEA would develop a central information and advisory resource facility, an extension of the library and museum service, say . . . + £1,000
Possibly some LEA administrative functions might be devolved to the school, but any reduction in LEA overheads would probably be offset by increased school-based costs.

*Teaching costs*
*Teachers' salaries*. It is very difficult to guess whether this account would grow or shrink. Much would depend on changes in regulations and organization such as those explored in Chapter 12.
Overall, as always, this would be the crucial factor.

*Non-teaching salaries*. These are likely to increase, for: technician assistance for the increased hardware and software, with on-costs, say, minimum of . . . + £6,500

| | | |
|---|---|---|
| some increased clerical support to service a more complex organization . . . | | + £500 |
| *Books, stationery, materials and equipment* | | |
| Possibly some reduction in books, | – £1,000 | |
| but heavily offset by purchases of electronic equipment and software | £10,000 | + £9,000 |
| *Postage and telephones*. Increased on-line telephone charges; possibly some reduction in postage, say . . . | | + £500 |
| *Premises costs* | | |
| Caretaking, for extended hours | | + £1,500 |
| Heating and lighting, for extended hours | | + £2,000 |
| Modifications to buildings – adaptations, wiring systems | | + £1,000 |
| Assistance to pupils, School transport, School meals – not affected | | |
| *Community education*. Increased salaries | £1,000 | |
| less increased fees | £2,000 | – £1,000 |
| | | £23,000 |

*Sources of additional finance*

These projected changes in the costs of one particular secondary school can be read in two different ways. On the one hand it can be argued that the increased costs of £23,000 on Holyrood School's total costs of £868,000 are only marginal, a mere 2·8 per cent increase. This is the sort of increase that any industrial or commercial organization would normally take in its stride when considering a change to a new system of working to meet new conditions. On the other hand, much of the earlier part of the book has argued that the school cost system is in fact very rigid and that finding such a marginal increase is in practice very difficult. It is extremely difficult to find it from within the system itself unless some way can be found to alter the proportion taken up by teachers' salaries. It is sometimes suggested that more individualized learning will make possible a higher pupil–teacher ratio, and so make this redeployment of finance possible. In fact this is most unlikely, for various reasons. First much teaching will still continue on a full-class basis; secondly, individualized learning still involves considerable interaction between learner and teacher, queries, problems over equipment or programmes, advice, discussion, and so on, and it is very doubtful whether larger classes will in fact be workable; thirdly, because a higher pupil – teacher ratio makes schools more impersonal and reduces social control. It is significant that modes of learning which use booths, for example, language laboratories and programmed learning centres, have found difficulty in functioning with groups larger than thirty. Visions of one teacher and fifty students toiling at their terminal seem unlikely. Also, the difficulty of financing a 'marginal' 2·8 per cent increase is underlined when we remember that this is equivalent to a 70 per cent increase in the school's capitation allowance – an increase for which it would be very difficult to gain approval.

Therefore, if our assumption is correct that schools of the Information Revolution will be more expensive to run, then such changes can only be financed in one of the following ways:

1 Central and local government reversing the current trend and increasing education's share of the national income.
2 Recycling the savings of falling rolls. Unfortunately at the present time this seems most unlikely and it is more likely that falling rolls will require a real reduction in the service.
3 Sharply reducing the quality of other aspects of the education service.
4 The introduction of educational charges and fees of various kinds (discussed in Chapter 10, pp. 149–51). The present tendency to charge for an increasing number of fringe items on an ad hoc basis would not provide a solid enough base for increased expenditure. An actual per capita charge, perhaps to cover stationery and books, would be self-defeating because it would only lead to a reduction in central government support. However, the last suggestion in that section is more profitable, namely that the state could agree that a defined general education should be free, but that items additional to that should be paid for. Obviously, all would hinge upon the definition of the free area, but it might be easier to define such a core curriculum of skills and knowledge under the new conditions of the Information Revolution. This would then leave freedom for individuals to pay for topping-up items. There would be pressure upon the schools from the consumers to make the provision of this additional education as cheap and as effective as possible. Or, perhaps more reasonable and more likely, the government could finance a certain amount of the fringe items as well as the core, and leave a smaller range of additional items for parents.
5 Increased sale of services to adult students and members of the community. If these were properly marketed at full cost or market prices, enhanced income from fees would be attained. After all, adult students, part-time students and employers now pay quite considerable fees for courses, seminars, leisure week-ends and special services, etc., to commercial organizations. In the past LEA fees have often been unrealistically low, and have failed to recover the full cost of the service. Of course, it may still remain policy to charge some services at less than cost.

6 Mini-vouchers. The full voucher scheme seems to have run into considerable difficulties, principally because it is an all-or-nothing affair, where the voucher is for a whole year's education. Provision of mini-vouchers might be much more feasible. These could be for say, units of twenty hours instruction, or time for access to the educational hardware or software, or they could even be on a subscription basis. Vouchers could be provided free to pupils of school age and could if necessary be deferrable. They could also be provided to selected groups of adults, for example, the unemployed, and could then be redeemed for cash from the Department of Health and Social Security or the Department of Employment. One advantage of such mini-vouchers would be to accentuate the whole idea of cost-effectiveness, with short courses providing value for money
7 Central government accepting the implications of radical changes in educational conditions, and creating more flexible regulations and policies to allow for adjustment. Unlike the preceding alternatives, this would allow the additional finance for the likely changes to be found from within the schools without impairing the service. This new flexibility is explored in the next chapter.
8 Improved efficiency – but accepting the difficulties discussed in Chapter 6.

*PPBS born again?*

The programming – planning – budgeting system discussed on page 93 has not really caught on. Even in America it has tended to die back. The Department of Education and Science and some LEAs flirted with it, but it is now largely discredited in the UK. Recently however Paul Harling (1981) has outlined an interesting PPBS approach to resource management in primary schools. He suggests the formulation of overall aims; the establishment of a programme structure broken down with attendant objectives; selection of best-in-the-circumstances approaches to achieve these, including both activities and resource provision, and a plan for action. Harling suggests that 'fundamentally this approach offers a way of improving the ability of a school to reach its objectives within the constraints imposed by limited resources'. His approach won't appeal to everybody, but it is certainly of interest and not just in primary schools.

It seems possible that the educational demands of the future will encourage the resurgence of PPBS under another name. For if education becomes more individualized, more frequently packaged into modules and short programmes, then it could be much easier for the central government, an LEA or a school to allocate finance for programmes rather than in global amounts. The current interest in criterion-referenced courses for the 14 to 19 age-group could reinforce this. Already central government shows some distaste for indiscriminate feeding of education, and a growing interest in specific grants. The mushroom growth of the Manpower Services Commission is really PPBS under another name. At LEA level one sees this approach where, for example, specific funds are set aside for adult literacy. One could envisage programmes for, say, basic functional literacy, remedial literacy programmes, specialist skills, and so on, each of which would have funds allocated on an annual basis, obviously bearing in mind priorities and demands. Some costs could be allocated to programmes very easily, for example, teachers' salaries on a time basis. Others could be allocated per class-hour, for example, premises costs, or per student hour, for example, clerical costs. Finally, will financial information systems assist?

*Financial Information Systems*

These are beginning to spread quite rapidly. They have arisen from the expansion of computer technology and from improvements in data-handling techniques. The present financial pressures encourage their introduction. There are several systems currently available in Britain, in addition to those home-grown by local authorities.

Perhaps the best developed system is LAFIS, which is being developed by ICL in cooperation with the local authorities of Oxfordshire, Lambeth and Doncaster, and with support from the Department of the Environment. Essentially LAFIS is a software package which can be used on local authorities' own computer systems. Its core is a coding and information retrieval system. Each single item of financial information, whether payment, receipt, transfer, total, etc., receives a sophisticated code. Once the code has been attached, it can be retrieved with all other similar items.

> *Example.* A St Trinian's primary-school electricity bill, once it is coded, can be retrieved as part of the electricity costs, heating and lighting costs, premises costs, unit costs, committed costs, total costs, or any other cost feature for St Trinians, for schools of its size, for all primary schools, for all schools . . . or in any other aggregation that we require.

LAFIS has an interrogation and command system. The user can ask questions, including 'What if . . .' questions, and can command tabulations, reports, etc., as required. It has been designed for people who are not computer specialists. It can produce information by batch processing, for example, tabulations for all secondary schools on a fixed date, or on line, for example, tabulations requested by individual schools on a particular day and inquiries about specific items. LAFIS is flexible in that it is adapted to the existing systems and particular needs of each local authority. Besides the core, it contains eight modules, and an authority can select any of these, depending on its priorities. It is intended for use by all local authority departments, including treasurers, highways, social services, as well as education. However, there are obviously particular implications for local education authorities and schools.

A system such as LAFIS is a very powerful management tool. It is not just an information storage system. It could be better described as a financial information management system, because it is the dynamic management applications which are likely to have the greatest long-term effect.

At the LEA centre such a system will obviously be of great value for:

Capital planning (not that there is too much of that nowadays!)
Forecasting and modelling (likely to be particularly important with falling rolls and with changing government policies)
Budget preparation (at present a major exercise which takes up a good part of the autumn)
Calculation of inflation increments
Comparisons, on a historic basis over a period of years, or between authorities, or against national averages
Financial control (including exception reporting, see below)
Unit costing
Recharging
Statistical returns.

There will probably be some unplanned effects. Because LAFIS is designed for local authorities which are basically similar, it is likely that it will gradually have the effect of standardizing their procedures, codings and classification of financial information. This will arise simply because authorities will find it easier to borrow systems or coding structures developed by other authorities than to invent their own, or at least to use these as a starting-point. Also they will find that it will be an advantage to be able to compare some of their cost information with other authorities and this will only be possible if similar cost analysis systems are used.

There are a similar range of possibilities in schools, particularly when they have their own administration computer connected on-line to the central county computer. LAFIS would then offer the following:

*Instant financial information*. Departments would be able to know immediately what their current balance was, on inquiry to the computer – and if schools were made responsible for payment of invoices, then departmental allowances would be automatically up-dated at the time the cheque was paid.
*Management by exception*. It would be possible for heads or bursars to instruct the computer to alert them when a particular department had exceeded certain given parameters, for example, spent more than 80 per cent of its capitation within six months of the year.

*Cost audits*. Obviously LAFIS would be ideal to implement the cost-audit system described in Chapter 9. It could print out such audits early in the new financial year, and make possible sophisticated cost comparisons with other similar institutions.

*Autonomous school budgets*. Financial information systems will make it easier for schools to handle a much larger devolved budget, including the dramatic possibilities outlined for autonomous budgets in Chapter 13.

*Measurement of outputs*. In the rather more distant future, it is conceivable that such systems could be extended to measure outputs and to relate them to expenditure along the lines suggested in Chapter 6.

*Cost analysis*. Much more sophisticated cost analyses should be possible. A very good example would be establishing charges for lettings of school premises so that they do not prohibit use, but do not encourage heavy heating and lighting costs and do recoup a proportion of these. At present the information base for this is so poor and there are so many variables that most LEAs have failed to get to grips with the problem.

*Will cost forces be centrifugal or centripetal?*

This is one of the most fascinating areas of speculation for the future. On the one hand one can argue that with computerized information systems it will be much easier for the central government to establish a tighter grip over local authorities (which indeed it is already doing for macro-economic reasons) and for local authorities to establish similar control on schools. Under this model, a school becomes a sort of educational Kentucky Fried Chicken centre, with the educational equivalent of portion control, overheads analysis, etc., and with constant central watchfulness for aberration from the norm. On the other hand it can be argued that just as the new technology makes it more easy for transactions to be carried on at home, so in exactly the same way it will be easier for education to be administered and managed at the lowest local level. It is likely that schools will rapidly acquire their own computerized information processing systems, and this would make it much easier for them to control their own budgets. Much more important, if schools become much more flexible and varied institutions, then this flexibility would have to be secured by local financial autonomy. This aspect is taken up again in Chapter 13.

There are other forces at work. The OECD report *Educational Financing and Policy Goals for Primary Schools* (1979) in a survey of ten countries, remarked

> Increased centralization and bureaucratization of educational systems, coupled with parent and student disaffection with schools' performance records, have in recent years led to demands for more local participation in

> educational decision-making . . . In response to these demands a number of countries have begun to take some cautious first steps towards decentralising educational decision making and providing for greater local discretion in the use of financial resources (p.60).

The report emphasizes that most of these developments are fairly new and somewhat modest. Yet we can see these forces for local influence and control now strongly at work in the UK. Do these not imply increased financial autonomy?

# 12 Managing School Time

All the money that we allocate to education is ultimately consumed in units of time - assembly-time, tutor-time, break-time - the timetable. So it is strange that relatively little study of school time has been made. Within a school there is considerable discussion every year on the composition of the timetable. There will periodically be discussions on the detailed timing of the school day. There will occasionally be a flurry of interest in the continental day or the four-term year. But in the main our schools roll on using a time structure which they have inherited largely unexamined from the past. Why should the school day be 9.00 a.m. to 4.00 p.m. or thereabouts? Why should schools be open from 190 to 200 days in the year? Why in most schools should all pupils receive the same allocation of time? Why should there be three terms of varying length, and three holidays of varying length? Most of our present practice in structuring school time springs from long custom. It is encased in national and local regulations, but its real foundation is in our tradition and expectations. Yet better use of time could save money or secure better value for money in our schools.

## *Existing constraints*

The English school day appears to be determined by the Schools' Regulations laid down by the Department of Education and Science. These prescribe in suitably Victorian language that schools must be open for 200 days per year (except that ten of these may be remitted as occasional days for holidays, sports days, courses, etc.) and that within each day schools must provide four hours of 'secular instruction' for pupils of 8 and over (3 hours for pupils under 8). Oddly, 'secular instruction' may include breaks but excludes registration. Odd, because break-time has no educational content, whereas registration often includes tutor-time and a certain amount of informal education. Clearly the regulations have just evolved and have not really been planned. Other regulations require that this secular instruction shall be 'divided into two sessions, one of which shall be in the morning and the other in the afternoon unless exceptional circumstances make this undesirable', and that attendance registers shall be marked 'at the commencement of each morning and afternoon session'. This requirement of four hours is very modest, and well below what is normally provided. Consequently, it is topped up by additional regulations from each local authority. So the regulations for Somerset, for example, state, 'In secondary schools the normal hours are five and a half per day'. For primary schools not less than five hours is required in the autumn and spring terms, and not less than five and a half hours in the summer (but 'the school day for infant pupils should not exceed five hours throughout the year'). Similarly, LEAs make their own regulations on the ten occasional days – some allocate them all, others less.

So the regulations are not in fact very restrictive. The DES requirements allow many variations on the school day, providing there is a fairly broad interpretation of 'two session', and judicious use of a 'blind eye'. There are already some schools, for example, who do not mark attendance registers twice daily. LEA regulations are obviously under their own control.

It would be simple to amend these regulations to facilitate more effective management of school time. All that would be needed would be for the DES to replace its weekly requirement of four hours of secular instruction by an annual requirement of 800 hours. This would then allow local authorities and individual schools considerable flexibility in devising alternative patterns to meet local needs. The additional requirements about morning and afternoon sessions and registration do not justify central regulation and could be abandoned. LEAs could amend their own regulations accordingly and allow flexibility, but continue to require a greater time allocation as they do now.

People who question the present school day and school year do so for various reasons. Some seek to reduce expenditure on perhaps school meals or transport or heating, either to produce actual savings or to recycle the money for more worthwhile expenditure. The previous chapter suggested that such recycling of finance may be invaluable in the next two decades. Others may be simply attempting to create greater flexibility for the school as an institution. Again, the previous chapter suggested that flexibility will be at a premium in the future. Others are trying to promote more efficient learning. Teachers who have experienced alternative systems in the US and on the continent often suggest that children learn more effectively in the early part of the day and that an earlier finish leaves them more time for recreation and homework. Last, and certainly not least, a reform of the school day can be presented as the only means of removing 'seat-time'. As suggested in Chapter 6, 'seat-time' is a major barrier to improving efficiency and productivity in schools.

## *Continental days and four-day weeks*

*The continental day*

This is the term usually applied to a school day with a very long morning, an early start and a late finish, but with no afternoon school apart from out-of-school activities. It is actually a misnomer, because most continental countries do not in fact operate it. It ought to be called the 'German day', because it is in Germany that it is mainly to be found (although the current tendency in Germany is to fill the afternoons with organized activities, and even to provide school lunches!). If the continental day is to have as much class contact time as the present school day, it needs to run from, say, 8.00 a.m. to 1.30 p.m. In practice it will be necessary for it to be slightly longer, because a little additional circulation time will be needed.

Periodically this type of day has been urged by teachers coming back from schools in Germany. It received a fillip when the very hot summer of 1976 forced some English schools to adopt it. More recently it has come to the fore because it seemed to offer financial savings. It would reduce expenditure on school dinners. Under present regulations these do not need to be offered except to children who are allowed free meals. In any case costs would be greatly reduced because many children would go home immediately after the end of morning school. There would also be a considerable reduction in pupil and teacher free meals and in lunch-time supervisors. There would be reduction in other costs, notably heating, lighting and water. The situation over heating and lighting is not entirely clear, because the day would start in a colder and darker period, although the total extent of the day would be considerably reduced. There could possibly be a reduction in wear and tear around the school, much of which tends to occur at lunch-time. It is also suggested that children learn better in the morning rather than the afternoon, and that once staff and children are attuned to the longer morning they work well, because they know they have a refreshing afternoon in front of them. There are also some non-financial advantages which do not concern us in this context, such as the solving of the touchy problem of lunch supervision.

The continental day however has not made much headway. Both teachers and pupils have tended to flinch at the thought of a very long gruelling morning, particularly during the dark days of winter. Damage to out-of-school activities has been predicted. The largest obstacle undoubtedly has been the fear of a backlash from mothers, and particularly working mothers who would need to provide afternoon care for their children; also from families for whom the early rising and late lunching would be inconvenient; and from the community, concerned about marauding bands of youngsters with time on their hands. In 1980 the Dorset Education Authority launched a thorough study of this form of day. It avoided the now emotive term 'continental', and called it 'the restructured day'. Despite the LEA's interest in the scheme, a large petition against it helped to convince the authority that it would not be wise to proceed.

*The four-day week*

This is a much more recent proposal. It has only emerged with the pressures for financial cuts in the last five years, although it may have been assisted by the spread of a shorter working week. The four-day week shares the 'compression' approach of the continental day. It compresses the present week into four days, say, 8.00 a.m. to 4.10 p.m. each day. It offers less savings for school meals and related costs, but compensates with the prospect of reducing cleaning costs for the missing day, although this could only be achieved by a renegotiation of present agreements over caretaking and cleaning. It has a particular advantage for rural authorities, as it would cut transport by 20 per cent. It would probably cut heating, lighting and water costs. However, seasoned education officers are sceptical of some of the savings. For example, in transport, many firms make school transport the basic bread and butter of their company's operation, and since many of them enjoy semi-monopoly conditions, reducing the number of days would not lead to a proportionate reduction in costs.

The four-day week suffers from similar disadvantages to the continental day. It looks equally gruelling. It is possible that social resistance would be less, but it could still be considerable. Both versions also suffer from being open to the accusation that teachers would work even shorter hours! In fact, the amount of contact time would remain the same, but the time teachers would actually spend at school, if one includes lunch-hours, would be considerably less. Also both versions would mean a reduction of internal communication time for teachers. Personally I think it is unlikely that either variant will take root. There has been very little attempt to assess the effect on learning efficiency of such long sessions, and the social resistance will obviously be strong. The only major advantage that they offer is apparent savings, and even these would probably be less than expected. Neither of them creates a scrap more flexibility in schools; neither of them looks like producing greater efficiency,or making better use of school buildings; neither of them makes any progress towards solving the problem of 'seat-time'.

## *The flexi-day and flexi-week*

The flexi-approach is rather different. It attempts to compress the major part of the conventional day into a morning, or of the conventional week into four days – but then seeks to recycle the remainder in a much more flexible form in the afternoons or on the fifth day. If offers a little scope for redeploying finance, but its main attraction lies in its scope for variety and innovation, for more intensive use of technology and buildings, and in its more efficient use of time.

*Flexi-day*

This provides from three-quarters to nine-tenths of the present working day and the present timetable as the 'main' days, say, 8.30 a.m. to 1.00 or 1.30 p.m. or equivalent. This would be similar to the continental day, but not quite so gruelling, equivalent to a six or seven instead of an eight 35-minute period morning. This morning school would be conventional school, almost an extended core curriculum, occupying the bulk of the timetable.

The heart of the innovation is in the afternoons. Teachers would have from a quarter to a tenth of their weekly teaching commitment to give bunched in two to three afternoons or spread across the week. Pupils would be expected to attend for a fixed number of periods in the week, but would not necessarily be required to do so. There would be flexibility, and commitments could vary for older and younger pupils, or even vary for a particular pupil from one time of the year to another. Some students could top up their flexi-time quota with additional classes on modest payment, rather as students often pay for evening classes or special coaching today.

Much more variety would be possible for afternoon sessions. These would be freed from many normal constraints. A quarter to a tenth of the timetable would be spread across five afternoons. So classes could if necessary draw pupils from different year-groups, and could include adults; they need not be year-long, but could be of any desired length – thirty, twenty, ten weeks, or less, or even a single session. Some courses could be seasonal. It would be possible to provide 'supplementary studies' for poor spellers, able mathematicians, gifted children, etc., and 'keep-up' classes so that students trailing at the rear of say, an O level physics class could catch up their brighter peers – a welcome move to 'criterion-referenced' and not 'norm-referenced' education (see Chapter 6 page 101). There would be capacity available on the school premises for out-of-school activities organized by staff, parents, local volunteers and senior pupils; adult classes, with places for school pupils; consortium activities with other schools; activities for local primary pupils; experimental classes mounted by student teachers; Manpower Services Commission and Youth Service activities.

It would also be possible to put into the afternoons many of those activities that usually disrupt the timetable and impair a school's efficiency: school visits, special events, careers activities, work experience, teachers' in-service courses. Efficiency could be furthered in another way: individualized learning could be encouraged, and greater use made of the school's library, resource centre, computers and educational technology.

Obviously a new departure like this has disadvantages. It is difficult to persuade people that the untried is worth trying. It involves a substantial change, and change can be costly and wasteful. There would still be social resistance unless the additional activities and community use was sufficient to take up much of the slack and keep youngsters well occupied. The approach is less suitable for primary schools for whom flexibility and choice are not always desirable. It is much easier to adopt in an urban school, where students can more easily use the flexible afternoons, and it would be difficult for schools with a high proportion of bussed pupils. It involves changes in routine (earlier rising and later lunches), an innovative approach from teachers, and in the long term some revision of conditions of service.

But most of the problems are problems of transition, while the potential advantages look more durable:

1 There would be some reduction in school lunches and free meals, and possibly lunch-time supervision, although not as great as in the continental day. There could be some reductions in heating and lighting costs, although if the afternoons filled up heavily this would be offset. Some teachers might choose to teach for a nine-tenth week, providing their pension rights and security were safe-guarded. Such savings would only be relatively marginal, but quite enough to finance the introduction of some of the new technology.
2 More extensive use of plant, because the total time the school is in use would be extended. Also it would allow much greater use by the community of school facilities.
3 A greater range of types of courses and activities would be possible, with more scope for individualized learning.
4 A more planned, and more flexible use of time. For the afternoon sessions, seat-time would be swept away.

Finally, and perhaps most important, this type of school day fits much more closely the model of future education projected in the last chapter. If that model is a reasonably good one, then this sort of approach is likely to develop. A ten-week experiment in this type of day was operated at Holyrood School, Chard, Somerset, in 1982 and is described in a report obtainable from the school.

*The flexi-week*

The flexi-week basically adopts the same approach, but instead of providing five main mornings and five flexi-afternoons, it provides four main days, and one flexi-day. The main day would need to include nine-tenths of the present curriculum, and therefore would run from 8.30 a.m. to 4.00 p.m. or similar. The fifth day would contain the range and variety of activities described for the flexi-day afternoons. Socially this alternative would create less problems, because on four days of the week children would be fully occupied in the afternoons. In terms of organization it is less attractive because four slightly longer days are more tiring and because there is less flexi-time in one eight-hour day than in five afternoons. Initially though it offers more savings. There would probably be some reduction in lunches on the fifth day, in heating and lighting and perhaps in cleaning. Also there could be some savings in transport. In addition, it seems likely that perhaps more staff would opt for a nine-tenths week because a four-day week is perhaps more attractive than mornings only, and this would provide more funds to be recycled. Schools with heavy bussing may find this version more appropriate.

The flexi-approach needs to be worked out in great detail. Many people meeting it will be more forcibly struck by the difficulties than by the possibilities. But if they go back to first principles and accept that our present school day is largely the creation of tradition and is unlikely to serve the demands of the future sketched out in the previous chapter, then this sort of approach, even though it may be amended in detail, is likely to be the right one.

*The Stantonbury Campus Day 10*

An interesting flexi-approach, well documented and well publicized, has been the 'Day 10' operated on the Stantonbury Campus in Milton Keynes. Under this arrangement, the school follows the conventional timetable for days one to nine in a fortnightly timetable. On the tenth day, the whole timetable is stood down and a totally different timetable recreated according to the demands of the students and the inclinations and enthusiasms of the staff. It has proved very successful and is clearly an attempt to inject flexibility into the rigidity of the conventional timetable. In that sense it does attack 'seat-time', and certainly creates greater variety. It does not offer any financial savings, and probably does not offer the scope for development of the flexi approach. Its biggest disadvantage is that the day 10 timetable is rearranged at frequent intervals, and so it places heavy demands upon the enthusiasm and ingenuity of the staff. It is probably a device which is very effective for a highly innovative school, but perhaps not so easily adopted by the run-of-the-mill establishment.

## *Period patterns*

English school timetables display a great variety of period arrangements – 20 minute modules, periods of 30, 35, 40, 45, 50, 55 and 60 minutes, used in one week, six-day and ten-day timetables. One can find schools which have a different number of periods in the day for different year-groups, or less periods in one day than another. To some extent this variety is determined by conditions. Ten-day and 50-period cycles tend to appear on large campuses. However, much of it is related to the tradition of the school and the idiocyncrasies of the head and staff. Clearly such variations have implications for cost efficiency and cost effectiveness. Current thinking, for example, suggests that the frequency of weekly class contact is almost as important as its total quantity. There is not space here to explore this issue, only to note it as an area which needs extended research.

## *Modular courses*

Modules are not well established on the English school scene. They are common in further education, in TEC and BEC courses, for example, in industrial training, and in higher education. But not in schools. English school timetables do not commonly have the annual or semi-annual modules common to American and Canadian senior high schools, and to some extent to continental schools. Instead, we operate timetables and a curriculum which have prominent linear features. This seems to have arisen from our 16-plus terminal examinations. These commonly require a minimum two-year run-up, and so give the curriculum a linear coarse-grained structure. Linear, because most examined courses below 16-plus are of two years duration or more. Coarse-grained, because most examinations are whole subject, not part-subject, or multi-subject.

The linear structure of the English curriculum may seem to have a remote connection with school finance. However, it can be argued that it has a very definite relationship with cost effectiveness. It makes breadth and balance much more difficult to achieve, because fewer subjects can be included in a two-year linear curriculum than a two-year modular one. It also makes balance much more difficult to achieve across and within subjects. For example, at the present time the linear emphasis on physics, chemistry and biology causes most pupils to discard one or two after the third year and so forego any chance of a balanced science curriculum. It also ensures that any change is difficult, because a new subject can only push its way in if it pushes another out. It also makes change notoriously slow. Because any change has to work its way through a course which is at least two years long or longer, a long lead time is inevitable.

Yet there is nothing inherent in the organization of knowledge which requires a linear structure. Some subjects which depend principally on the development of skills cannot avoid it – perhaps foreign languages, English language and mathematics. There may be some sections of other subjects which require building up in a prescribed sequence. But many areas of knowledge can be regarded as self-contained modules. Indeed, modules would be particularly valuable for establishing the growth points required for the curriculum of the future discussed in the previous chapter. Modules encourage breadth and discourage narrow specialization. They also encourage stricter control over the use of school time.

There is nothing inherent in a 16-plus terminal examination to prevent at least partial adoption of a modular structure. At the time of writing, while the fusion of the GCE and CSE is still not complete, it would be quite feasible to insert a modular element in the General Certificate of Secondary Education (GCSE). Examinations could be by subject areas, such as humanities, science, arts, design and technology, etc., each comprising a number of modules. There could be conditions, for example, that some modules could not be studied with others, or would need to be studied with others. Schools and students would be able to build up courses rather like a set of building blocks. This would not directly affect school costs, but it could lead to greater cost efficiency. It could and should make a balanced curriculum easier to achieve, and facilitate change. In particular, it could allow for some of the modules to have instruction provided by the new technology. Once again, if our vision of the future is correct, a modular curriculum would seem to be much more appropriate and more friendly to it than a linear one.

## *A more rational school year*

Most readers will have experienced the present English school year in their own childhood, with its quaint features of three terms of varying length, with a shifting Easter holiday and with a long summer holiday, one of the best forgetting devices known to man. The school year created for the needs of the harvest and the Church may be traditional but it does not really stand up to logical examination.

### *The four-term year*

The four-term year has been periodically examined, but the DES and central government have never taken up the issue seriously. A pity, because there is much to commend it in terms of cost effectiveness. First, it re-shapes the present-length school year into four learning periods of equal and known length (approximately ten weeks each) and so makes course planning more efficient. It also encourages the development of semester or quarter-year modules within the timetable. An additional advantage is that it overcomes the problems of a long term. At the end of a long term pupils become very jaded, and a ten-week term is a much more effective learning unit.

This is not the place to examine the proposal in detail, but it does seem clear that a four-term year offering say a four-week holiday at Christmas (for fuel saving), a two-week holiday at Easter, a four-week holiday in June and a three-week holiday in September, with occasional days reduced to five, could be a much more attractive proposition. It would offer the advantages listed above (and it would also give a useful fillip to the tourist industry by extending the English tourist season at each end and allowing people without dependent children to take their holidays in July and August). It does require an Easter holiday independent of the calendar Easter.

*Timing of external examinations*

At present the summer term in English schools is seriously affected by external examinations, and the expensive staff resources of the school are not fully used once the examination period has begun. With the four-term year it would be possible for the school academic year to end at the end of May and for the university year to begin in October. In other words, they could be staggered. If the external examinations could be concentrated in May this would enable the marking and return of results and the processing of university applications to take place in the June to September period. There would then be none of the wastage of resources that occurs at the present time in June and July.

# 13 Autonomous School Budgets

In Chapter 11 I have argued that schools will need to develop more variety and much greater flexibility if they are to respond to the needs of the Information Revolution. Yet the new schools will be more expensive than the old, unless they can find a means of recycling finance. This need for financial flexibility can be linked with the suggestions in Chapter 9 for developing schools as cost centres with their own annual cost audits, with devolvement of an increasing range of financial responsibilities, and with reapportionment of the cost of central services. The logical step of all these trends will be to make schools financially independent with their own autonomous budgets.

The notion will jar immediately for most readers. For state secondary schools in England are not familiar with budgets. They are vaguely aware that the LEA has an annual budget system, because sometimes unpleasant consequences come from it. But they have not seen the need of an annual budget themselves, mainly because most of their finance comes 'free' and unquestioned from the centre. Indeed, schools are not familiar with financial planning, apart from that tiny sector of capitation monies and from those rare authorities which practise extensive virement. However, they are familiar with curriculum planning and with the annual cycle of time-table planning, and so the step to annual financial planning is by no means as difficult as it appears. Also doubters should pause to consider the development of independent schools and technical colleges. Both have proved extremely successful in expanding and in responding in a flexible way to the changing demands of their client groups. It could be argued quite plausibly that a major factor in their success has been the fact that both types of insitutions have autonomous budgets.

## *The function of a budget*

A budget is not a balance sheet. It is not just a statement of last year's spending and a projection for this year. It is, or should be, a planning instrument, a decision model for the management of the organization during the next financial year and beyond. 'A budget is a quantitative expression of a plan of action and an aid to coordination and implementation' (Horngren, Chapter 5). It should approximate to a formal model of the organization, stating its objectives, its inputs and its expected outputs. Obviously, in education the question of assessing outputs causes difficulties, but the principle remains.

A budget has a variety of functions. It can be used for planning, long term and medium term; for evaluating performance; for coordinating activities; for implementing long-term plans; for communicating the total plan to all parts of the organization; for motivating personnel; for giving authority for expenditures and activities. At its best a budget should:

1 Compel the management of a school to plan ahead, to formulate targets and objectives, to identify expected levels of performance and adopt appropriate strategies.
2 Provide expectations of future performance which can be used as criterion for judging actual performance.
3 Promote communication and coordination. Separate departments are forced to consider others, and to see their place in the organization. Since many school departments function apparently independently of others, this could be a substantial gain. The battle to establish English across the curriculum, for instance, is an excellent illustration of the insularity of departments. However, budgets need to be understood. The purpose behind them and the system adopted needs to be fully appreciated by all members of staff if they are to be successful.

The form of a budget is important, because the form itself will influence the effectiveness of the budget. The medium will be the message. If a school's budget is to be a planning instrument, it must reflect the organization's objectives. It should not simply be a line-by-line record of categories of expenditure past and present. It needs to reflect the functions and purposes of the school.

Rather than speculate in a general way about the implications of school budgets, it is more helpful to produce an actual example. The next section attempts to produce a secondary-school budget at the end of the 1980s. Some readers will dismiss it as a flight of fancy. But perhaps flights of fancy can help us to see the future more easily than earthy common sense.

## *Example of an autonomous school budget*

To aid comparison the school is taken to be the same as the one whose running costs for 1979/80 were analysed in Chapter 2. To create constant conditions it is assumed that numbers of pupils, the site and buildings, and price levels are unchanged. The following budget report reviews the performance of the previous year, describes the budget objectives, and comments on new features. It is followed by the budget itself, with plans for income and expenditure for 1989/90. Equivalent figures from the 1979/80 analysis are shown in the right-hand column.

HOLYROOD SCHOOL BUDGET REPORT 1989/90

*January 1989*

This report is submitted by the Budget Committee to the school governors for their final approval. It has already been approved by the academic board.

## *Performance review of 1987/88 and 1988/89*

The Performance Review for 1987/88 has already been published. This showed that Programme 1 (basic communications skills) together with Programmes 3 and 4 (core and additional knowledge areas) have seen a highly satisfactory achievement in their main detailed objectives. Programme 2 (information handling and individualized learning) exceeded its objectives within the allocated resources, and the committee were particularly impressed by the effective way in which computerized equipment was put to maximum use. The additional money voted last year to provide extra teacher tutors in the individualized learning area appears to have been repaid handsomely. Programme 5 (physical, leisure, arts and design skills) also achieved its main objectives, but the committee is concerned about its tendency to achieve this at the expense of over-spending.

The committee has still been concerned about the performance of Programme 7 (social, moral and political education) and to a lesser extent, Programme 6 (vocational education and guidance), but the committee appreciates that it is much more difficult to specify tangible objectives in these areas. However, it feels that the continued failure of the departments responsible to come to grips with this problem casts doubt on the value of the programmes.

It is obviously impossible to comment on the financial year 1988/89 because at present the fourth term of the academic year has barely started. However, all the indications are that the general position regarding performance will be similar to the previous year.

## *Financial review 1987/88 and 1988/89*

The financial review of 1987/88 has already been published. This showed that actual income and expenditure tallied very closely with the estimated totals. There was a slight tendency to underestimate the receipts from the purchase of additional lessons by pupils and the involvement of adult students. The report showed concern at a tendency in Programme 5 to overspend and Programme 7 to exercise weak financial control.

The financial year 1988/89 is only three-quarters finished, but to date projected expenditure appears to tally with the original estimates.

*Objectives*

In the main, the committee considers that the Learning Programme Objective specified in the school's education plan (1986) should be continued, with the following modifications:

Programme 1. The committee accepts the arguments that there is growing need for more demanding criteria of communications skills, and accepts the recommendation from the academic board that the Edinburgh House communications skill test level 3 should replace level 2 as the minimum acceptable level to be attained on or before the age of 16. The Budget Committee accepts the financial implications that the time allocated to this programme and its support, equipment and resources, should be enhanced, and the programme's financial quota has in fact been increased by 8 per cent.

Programme 2. The committee accepts that this programme has been of little use for increasing distance learning, particularly for home-viewed material, and accepts the modifications in the programme objectives. The suggested home-learning liaison programme to achieve this seems financially modest, but the committee is a little sceptical whether it will attain its objective and proposes to monitor it closely.

Programme 3. The academic board's recommendation that 'growth points' related to genetics, horticulture and farming should be extended in the light of the astounding recent developments in this field, to be offset by removal of the areas dealing with the internal combustion engine, has no financial cost implications.

Programme 5. The arguments for extending the objectives for leisure-oriented skills seems strong, but the committee is not convinced that these can be extended until corresponding reductions can be made in skills elsewhere. In the meantime, students will need to buy in extra courses.

Programme 7. The committee is not impressed, nor is the academic board, by the objectives set out for family education and education in family affairs and personal relationships. However, they accept the strength of the argument that experiences which are different in kind from those a student has experienced elsewhere, even though they cannot be quantified, create a prima facie case for investment. In the light of this the committee proposes a doubling in the subsidy for parties staying at residential centres.

*Income*

Most of the estimates are comparable to previous years. The committee has allowed for a small increase in income from examination fees, in the light of the stricter enforcement of the local education authority's regulations on payment, and a 50 per cent increase from 1988/89 in the purchase by pupils of additional courses. Even this may be an underestimate, as the demand for additional courses both within the flexi-afternoon and at week-ends and holiday time seems to be running very strongly. Income from vending machines is showing a 30 per cent increase, reflecting the more extensive use of school plant in flexi-time and out of school hours.

Under community education, the committee has anticipated a continued increase in fees received for classes above the income target, because of the continued buoyant demand, particularly for classes for leisure activities or with retraining value. It has also allowed for a substantial increase in the fees for use of the school's information and individualized learning systems (including Prestel), and anticipate that this source of income will continue to grow appreciably in the next few years.

*Expenditure*

LEA central services

*In-service training for teachers.* The budget has benefited from the reduced prices operated by the regional INSET consortium and there should be a £1,000 saving from the LEA grant. This should still allow for sufficient retraining to meet the needs raised under the objectives above and also to meet the continuing need to familiarise teachers with the new technology and software.

*Social worker (schools).* The committee has looked hard at this particular expenditure and in view of the pressures elsewhere feels that it is not justified in allocating so many resources to it. This year it has therefore recommended a 33 per cent cut in the time allocation recharged from the Social Services Department. In part this reflects the value of the new attendance procedures and welfare policies adopted within the school.

*Educational psychological service.* Last year's scrutiny of this area of expenditure has repaid handsomely and the committee feels justified again in recommending a more selective use of the service. The modification in *Careers service* expenditure is offset in part by increased allocation of time within the school's own teaching establishment.

Teaching costs

Salaries, teaching. The figure here masks two changes. A reduction of £5,000 on the LEA grant allocation has been achieved from teachers who opted to teach nine-tenths week under flexi-time. This has, however, been offset by £7,000 increased expenditure on staffing for flexi-time and evening courses for full-time students, which the committee felt was justified in the light of the savings in the budget elsewhere. Economy and a certain amount of self-service by the teaching staff has made possible once again an estimated saving of £1,000 on the supply teachers budget entry. The teaching support figure again substantially exceeds the LEA grant because of the provision of a full-time technician to service the new learning technology. It is likely that an additional appointment will be necessary in the future, although not in the current year. Similarly the grant for books, stationery, equipment and furniture has again substantially exceeded the LEA grant to allow the continued purchase of electronic hardware of various sorts. In this respect the LEA audio-visual and computer-assisted learning panel has given admirable advice on sensible purchasing. Examination fees are again below the county estimate because of the school's restrained policy on entering students with little hope of worthwhile achievement. Telephone expenses remain slightly high, owing to use by computer systems, but rigorous control of advertisement and interview expenses has almost offset this.

Premises

Inevitably caretaking and cleaning costs are once again above target because of the extended use created in the late afternoon and evening and on non-school days. There are similar increases in heating and lighting.

The committee is, however, concerned that the present budget system makes no allowance for debiting some of this to community education, and proposes to arrange for this in the 1990/91 budget. The committee feels if a realistic proportion of caretaking and heating costs is allocated to the community education service, its organizers will be more inclined to effect economies in their use of school premises.

The committee has been concerned for some time at the immovable millstone of rates and debt charges and in 1988/89 finally took the step of selling the annexe which was clearly surplus to requirements in the foreseeable future. This has led to a small reduction in rates but, more important, it has allowed for the sale proceeds to be offset against the school's debt charges at a net gain of £7,000 per annum.

### Assistance to pupils

Although not an intended policy, in practice free meals charges have dropped considerably because all pupils do not attend every afternoon during the flexi-time.

### School catering service

This shows similar reductions for the same reason in food, and to a lesser extent, in salaries. These are partially offset by reduced income received.

### Community education

With increasing demand the committee has felt justified in doubling the budget for postage, telephone and printing, to allow for much better publicity for the programme. The committee has felt that it needed to allow for an appreciable increase in tutor salaries for anticipated extra demand and marginal ancillary staff increases. However, as explained earlier, this will be largely offset by increased class fees and in future years may lead to a favourable financial return.

### Unit costs

The committee has been gratified to see that costs have shown a regular if slight fall for almost all programmes over the last few years. This is expected to continue in 1989/90. Undoubtedly this has arisen through the more flexible use of time and the shedding of some activities to home-learning. The committee would like to stress once again that unit costs for Programme 2 appear to be falling more rapidly than for other programmes. They feel this justifies their heavy investment in the current budget for teacher and technician support, hardware and software for that particular programme. Conversely, they remain concerned at the high unit costs of Programme 7. The programme does not have the heavy investment in equipment and technicians' support of Programmes 3 and 4, but the committee is disappointed that more resourceful means have not been adopted to reduce costs. In view of the comments made earlier about the uses and objectives of the programme and in view of these high unit costs, we would like to reiterate that because of heavy pressures of expense elsewhere we feel that next year it will be necessary to curtail this programme unless these weaknesses are remedied.

*Conclusion*

It is exactly ten years since the school embarked on a budget system, although the prototypes of the early 1980s bear little resemblance to that operated today and amount to little more than a limited cost-centre approach.

Looking back, the committee is proud of the progress that has been achieved. At first sight if one compares the budget for 1989/90 with the analysis of costs which existed for the school in 1979/80 one sees little difference. The total expenditure is the same, and the totals for main cost elements are broadly similar. However, close scrutiny shows that there has been a marginal but appreciable shift of resources away from lower priority items such as central services, examination expenses, premises and meals costs, and increasing expenditure on teaching services and particularly on the provision of new forms of educational technology and staff support.

The committee remains sensitive to the charge that this new budget approach only makes allowance for objectives and programmes which are quantifiable, and underestimates or ignores activities which are not easy to quantify and which deal mainly with intangible human relations. Last year the committee made a special study of this aspect and in fact invited the county inspectors to evaluate it. Their report shows that effective human relationships in this school, as in most, remain as much the product of accident as of design, and we note with pride their satisfaction that there is no evidence that this type of activity has suffered under the new budget approach. In contrast, the committee notes with pleasure the persistent trend for pupils and adults to enrol for additional classes and for increased use of the school premises out of school hours, which suggest that the general budget strategy is the correct one. (For budget estimates see Table 13:1.)

## *Disadvantages*

The school budget approach does have substantial inherent disadvantages, and it is important that these are faced. It is ideal in a world where conditions do not alter, where prices remain static and numbers constant. Special care is needed to ensure that the system can respond to external changes as well as it can to changes within the school itself.

*Inflation*

An autonomous budget will only work if grants from the LEA are adjusted realistically for inflation. There is, however, already a tendency for LEAs not to make proper allowance for inflation, as discussed in Chapter 10. This tendency may be enhanced with an autonomous budget because the local authority may feel less responsible for an institution which is expected to run itself than for one for which it has to provide directly. Failure to adjust to inflation may be the result of failure to appreciate the true position, or it may

**Table 13:1** Budget estimates for Holyrood School, financial year 1989/90

| | ESTIMATED INCOME | TOTAL ESTIMATED EXPENDITURE | ESTIMATED EXPENDITURE BY EDUCATIONAL PROGRAMMES: *1 Basic communications skills* | *2 Information handling and individualized learning* | *3 Core knowledge areas* | *4 Additional knowledge areas* | *5 Physical, leisure, arts and design skills* | *6 Vocational and educational guidance* | *7 Social, moral and political education* | *8 Community educational service* | COMPARATIVE EXPENDITURE 1979/80 *(rounded off)* |
|---|---|---|---|---|---|---|---|---|---|---|---|
| LEA CENTRAL SERVICES | | | | | | | | | | | |
| Central administration and inspection | 25,000* | 25,000 | | | | | | | | | 25,000 |
| Information resources (computer assisted learning, library and museum services) | 2,600* | 3,000 | | | | | | | | | 1,600 |
| In-service training for teachers | 5,300* | 4,500 | | | | | | | | | 3,300 |
| Education and resources centres | 3,000* | 2,500 | | | | | | | | | 3,000 |
| Social worker (schools) | 3,000* | 2,000 | | | | | | | | | 3,000 |
| Sub-total, above items | | 37,000 | 5,100 | 6,000 | 5,700 | 6,400 | 7,400 | 300 | 6,100 | | 35,900 |
| Residential centres | 300* | 600 | | | | | | | 600 | | 300 |
| Educational Psychological Service | 1,300* | 900 | | | | | | 900 | | | 1,300 |

| | | | | | | | | | | |
|---|---|---|---|---|---|---|---|---|---|---|
| Careers Service | 8,000* | 7,000 | | | | | | 7,000 | | 8,000 |
| (Note: LEA administrative service for premises and grounds, meals, transport and community education, with loan charges, are shown under the section below. Grants for these total £111,600) | | | | | | | | | | |
| Total, LEA central services | 48,500 | 45,500 | | | | | | | | 45,500 |
| TEACHING COSTS | | | | | | | | | | |
| Salaries, teaching | | | | | | | | | | |
| (establishment) | 420,000* | 422,000 | | | | | | | | 420,000 |
| (supply) | 8,500* | 7,500 | 66,000 | 27,500 | 69,000 | 78,000 | 109,000 | 4,000 | 76,000 | 8,500 |
| Salaries, non-teaching support | 48,000* | 55,000 | 3,500 | 16,000 | 10,500 | 11,500 | 8,000 | 500 | 5,000 | 48,000 |
| Books, stationery, materials, equipment, furniture | 40,000* | 56,000 | 6,000 | 10,000 | 7,500 | 9,000 | 13,000 | 500 | 10,000 | 40,000 |
| Examination fees | 5,500* | 4,800 | | | | | | | | |
| Postage and telephone | 2,700* | 3,200 | 1,200 | 2,000 | 1,300 | 1,400 | 1,600 | 300 | 1,400 | 2,700 |
| Travelling, advertisement and interview expenses | 1,500* | 1,200 | | | | | | | | 1,500 |
| Income from sale of materials | 5,500 | | | | | | | | | 5,500 |
| Income from examination fees | 1,000 | | | | | | | | | 800 |
| Donations from Parents Association | 3,000 | | | | | | | | | 3,000 |
| Purchases by parents of books and equipment | 1,000 | | | | | | | | | 1,000 |
| Purchases by pupils of additional courses | 3,000 | | | | | | | | | |
| Total, teaching costs | 539,700 | 549,700 | | | | | | | | 531,000 |

**Table 13:1** Budget estimates for Holyrood School, financial year 1989/90

| | ESTIMATED INCOME | TOTAL ESTIMATED EXPENDITURE | ESTIMATED EXPENDITURE BY EDUCATIONAL PROGRAMMES | | | | | | | | COMPARATIVE EXPENDITURE 1979/80 *(rounded off)* |
|---|---|---|---|---|---|---|---|---|---|---|---|
| | | | *1 Basic communications skills* | *2 Information handling and individualized learning* | *3 Core knowledge areas* | *4 Additional knowledge areas* | *5 Physical, leisure, arts and design skills* | *6 Vocational and educational guidance* | *7 Social, moral and political education* | *8 Community educational service* | |
| PREMISES AND GROUNDS COSTS | | | | | | | | | | | |
| LEA administration, premises and grounds | 1,800* | 1,800 | | | | | | | | | 1,800 |
| Salaries (caretaking, cleaning, grounds, clerical) | 41,000* | 42,500 | | | | | | | | | 41,000 |
| Rates | 20,500* | 20,500 | | | | | | | | | 20,500 |
| LEA debt charges | 102,700* | 95,700 | | | | | | | | | 102,700 |
| Maintenance, premises | 25,000* | 25,000 | 28,000 | 24,500 | 34,000 | 39,000 | 45,000 | 1,400 | 34,000 | | 25,000 |
| Heating and lighting | 14,400* | 16,400 | | | | | | | | | 14,400 |
| Water | 1,500* | 1,500 | | | | | | | | | 1,500 |
| Cleaning materials and equipment | 2,500* | 2,500 | | | | | | | | | 2,500 |
| Maintenance, grounds | 1,600* | 1,600 | | | | | 1,600 | | | | 1,600 |
| Swimming-pool (repairs, electricity, chemicals) | 1,100* | 1,100 | | | | | 1,100 | | | | 1,100 |
| Modifications to premises | | 1,000 | | 1,000 | | | | | | | |
| Total, premises and ground costs | 212,100 | 209,600 | | | | | | | | | 212,100 |

(In the printed table, a brace groups the programme figures 28,000 … 34,000 against the items from "Salaries" through "Cleaning materials and equipment".)

| | | | | | | | | | | |
|---|---|---|---|---|---|---|---|---|---|---|
| ASSISTANCE TO PUPILS | | | | | | | | | | |
| Free meals served at paying rate | 4,500* | 3,500 | | | | | | | | 4,500 |
| Uniform grants | 900* | 900 | | | | | | | | 900 |
| Maintenance grants | 2,100* | 2,100 | | | | | | | | 2,100 |
| Total, assistance to pupils | 7,500 | 6,500 | 900 | 1,000 | 1,000 | 1,100 | 1,300 | 100 | 1,100 | 7,500 |
| SCHOOL TRANSPORT | | | | | | | | | | |
| LEA central administration | 2,400* | 2,400 | | | | | | | | 2,400 |
| School buses, other vehicles, season tickets | 35,300* | 35,300 | | | | | | | | 35,300 |
| Total, school transport | 37,700 | 37,700 | 5,200 | 6,200 | 5,800 | 6,500 | 7,500 | 300 | 6,200 | 37,700 |
| SCHOOL CATERING SERVICE | | | | | | | | | | |
| LEA central administration | 2,700* | 2,700 | | | | | | | | 2,700 |
| Food | 12,100* | 9,600 | | | | | | | | 12,100 |
| Salaries, supervisors | 2,300* | 1,700 | | | | | | | | 2,300 |
| ditto kitchen staff | 16,000* | 14,000 | | | | | | | | 16,000 |
| ditto clerical support | 1,000* | 900 | | | | | | | | 1,000 |
| Premises | 3,100* | 3,100 | | | | | | | | 3,100 |
| Equipment | 500* | | | | | | | | | 500 |
| Total expenditure, gross | 37,700* | 32,000 | | | | | | | | 37,700 |
| Less income received, pupils (offset against grants) | −8,000* | −6,800 | | | | | | | | −8,000 |
| Net expenditure | 29,700* | 25,200 | | | | | | | | |
| Net income, vending machines | 2,000 | | | | | | | | | |
| Total, school catering service | 31,700 | 25,200 | 3,400 | 4,100 | 3,900 | 4,500 | 5,000 | 200 | 4,100 | 29,700 |

**Table 13:1** Budget estimates for Holyrood School, financial year 1989/90

| | ESTIMATED INCOME | TOTAL ESTIMATED EXPENDITURE | ESTIMATED EXPENDITURE BY EDUCATIONAL PROGRAMMES: *1 Basic communications skills* | *2 Information handling and individualized learning* | *3 Core knowledge areas* | *4 Additional knowledge areas* | *5 Physical, leisure, arts and design skills* | *6 Vocational and educational guidance* | *7 Social, moral and political education* | *8 Community educational service* | COMPARATIVE EXPENDITURE 1979/80 *(rounded off)* |
|---|---|---|---|---|---|---|---|---|---|---|---|
| COMMUNITY EDUCATION | | | | | | | | | | | |
| LEA central administration | 2,000* | 2,000 | | | | | | | | | 2,000 |
| Salaries, tutors | 4,600* | 5,600 | | | | | | | | | 4,600 |
| ditto clerical | 900* | 1,000 | | | | | | | | | 900 |
| ditto caretaking | 600* | 800 | | | | | | | | | 600 |
| Postage, telephone, printing | 300* | 600 | | | | | | | | | 300 |
| Total expenditure, gross | 8,400* | 10,000 | | | | | | | | | 8,400 |
| Less fees target for classes | −3,900* | | | | | | | | | | −3,900 |
| Total expenditure, net | 4,500* | | | | | | | | | | 4,500 |
| Fees from classes above target | 2,000 | | | | | | | | | | |
| Fees received for use of information and individualised learning systems | 500 | | | | | | | | | | |
| Net total, community education | 7,000 | 10,000 | | | | | | | | 10,000 | 4,500 |
| Full cost totals | 884,200 | 884,200 | 119,300 | 98,300 | 138,700 | 157,400 | 200,500 | 15,500 | 144,500 | 10,000 | |
| Total student hours | | | 150,000 | 180,000 | 170,000 | 190,000 | 220,000 | 10,000 | 180,000 | N/A | |
| Average cost per student hour (£) | | | 0·80 | 0·55 | 0·82 | 0·83 | 0·91 | 1·55 | 0·80 | | |

* = Grant from LEA

be mismanagement. More seriously, it may be a deliberate attempt to achieve a concealed reduction in expenditure. The problem does need to be faced squarely. There is a risk that some LEAs could use autonomous budgets to implement unpopular cuts which it would not be prepared to impose centrally. For example, a worsening pupil–teacher ratio might be politically unacceptable in certain authorities as an overt act of policy, but could be covertly implemented by not allowing sufficiently for wage drift.

*Incorrect adjustment for changes in numbers*
If an LEA is fully responsible for a school, it feels under strong obligation to make reasonable adjustment for either falling or rising rolls. If the school management is responsible for the school, the LEA may not be so sympathetic.

*Failure to adjust for changing needs*
In the last thirty years there have been considerable changes in schools' functions, and such changes have often been encouraged by LEAs. Enthusiastic officers have often spearheaded the introduction of innovations and have persuaded elected members that these shall be paid for. If officers see themselves more in a caretaking capacity, they may not have the same enthusiasm.

*Insufficient allowance for a difficult catchment area*
The new approach throws more emphasis upon local fund-raising and upon additional resources contributed locally. Obviously some catchment areas are more likely to respond than others.

*Insufficient allowance for variations in the starting base*
Earlier chapters in the book argue that there are substantial variations between comparable schools. Unless the local authority deliberately builds in a weighting to attempt to redress this, the whole budget system might simply perpetuate existing inequalities (as in fact it does now!).

*The risk of inefficient local management*
Complete devolvement to schools brings the risk that the school may have staff or governors who manage the finances unimaginatively or even incompetently, so that over a period the school suffers. Centralized administration leaves much less scope for local initiative and enterprise but may create a more even service.

## Safeguards

*School prices index*
A national system to measure inflation increments, rather like the

retail price index, would offset the problems of masked inflation raised earlier.

*The safeguard of a mixed centralized/devolved financial system*

As long as some schools within a local authority still operate on the traditional system of being managed at the centre, and others are on the autonomous system, the latter can be safeguarded. For as long as the two systems exist side by side, direct comparisons can be made. Equally it would be possible for a school which felt it was suffering under one system to opt for the other.

*Special mechanisms*

Special financial mechanisms can be devised to safeguard schools with devolved budgets. Examples would be an earmarking system which earmarks certain grants for specific purposes, for example, in-service education. In general the system is not a good one, because it destroys local choice of priorities, but it may be useful for particular aspects. Another mechanism is 'valving', where expenditure can flow in one direction but not in the other. A good example here would be heating charges which can be valved, so that the school pays charges to a certain limit. If a severe winter occurs and the limit is exceeded, then the financial flow from the school is checked, and replaced by LEA contingency funds.

*Special treatment of teachers' salary costs*

Since these are by far the largest element of the budget they are particularly sensitive to variation. Although in the sample budget above they have been shown as a cash figure, in fact it would make more sense for the authority to continue to allocate this in kind – so many full-time, part-time teaching posts and so many special responsibility points. If virement of salaries and responsibility allowances were possible it would still allow schools considerable flexibility.

## *The changing role of the LEA*

With autonomous budgets the role of the LEA would change considerably. It would tend to disappear, like Alice's Cheshire cat. However, the LEA would still be important. It would retain the following functions:

A central administrative function, though greatly reduced;
Responsibility for specialized centralized services, very much as now
Obtaining of financial resources and their allocation, albeit on a formula basis
An increased advisory service, giving advice to schools, staffs and governors on a wider range of affairs

Coordination of practice throughout the county, circulation of best practice
Countywide monitoring of practice and performance.

While the LEA will have shed much of its direct management function, it will have enhanced its advisory and coordinating functions.

## *Conclusion*

Some readers will have found this chapter preposterous. The idea of schools functioning on an autonomous financial basis may seem far-fetched. Yet to many independent schools and technical colleges the idea will be commonplace and of course it is common to many commercial organizations. It certainly is not as preposterous as the present situation, in which only familiarity dulls our sense of disbelief - namely that educational finance should be allocated without local management and with the users kept largely in ignorance. Some readers will argue that the process is too complicated and time-consuming. I would reply, not one hundredth as time-consuming as the school timetable - and we take that for granted! Other readers may be defensive because they feel ill-equipped to cope with this sort of development. But there is no mystique about the management of school finance. It mainly needs professional application. After all, school teachers have dipped into many other disciplines in the past few years to enhance their skills, so why not into finance and accountancy? But the reader's judgement will probably finally rest upon his or her assessment of the sort of world into which schools are heading. If they are going to go trundling on much as they are, then perhaps the foregoing is a quite unnecessary complication. If, on the other hand, one reads the current world as a time of almost revolutionary technological, economic and social change, then it seems likely that this change will be reflected in ways as yet unclear in the role of the school, and that in this transformation the utmost financial flexibility and local autonomy will be an asset rather than a liability.

# 14 Action!

Most of us are naturally resistant to other people's suggestions. So a list of recommendations for action is a sure pass to the graveyard of Unimplemented Good Ideas.

Yet it is the prevailing proposition of this book that the study of school costs and school finance has been woefully neglected. For too long it has been regarded as of little account, as an unseemly occupation or an irritating distraction. I would suggest that we have great leeway to make up – in theory, in practice and above all in attitude. And if a properly professional handling of school costs at all levels could steer us through our present sea of troubles, if new approaches will be essential for the educational structures that are already beginning to form in the silicon-chip era, then the education service must take the study of its costs seriously. So the list of recommendations below for action from the highest educational citadel to the lowest chalk-seam is breathtaking effrontery. Perhaps that is needed.

## *1 Action by the Department of Education and Science*

*Develop a specialist service for school-centred finance*

The DES already has an excellent financial section, but it is very much geared to the macro level. It does make annual studies of mean unit costs, but it does not delve deeply into the detailed aspects explored in this book. An influential specialist unit is needed like the Further Education Unit for development of curriculum or the Assessment of Performance Unit. It should lead to a branch of the inspectorate specializing in school costs and finance, and so mounting DES courses which are at present so notably lacking in this area.

*Make financial information more readily available*

The DES holds a great deal of current financial information, some of which is of considerable interest to people involved in school finance studies. Some is published, but much is unpublished although readily made available to inquirers. A list of the information which is available should be published annually.

*Publish an annual school price index*

The discussions in Chapter 10 have illustrated the damage which inflation creates on school capitation and other allowances. A very high priority therefore is the establishment of an objective and nationally reputable index. Some authorities already compile their own, and do it very creditably, but the variations in the inflation increments given by authorities are enormous. Publication of an annual index, broken down by categories of expenditure, which could then be readjusted for quantities if necessary, would be of very considerable value. It would also save the same process being repeated in a hundred authorities, and it would be of value outside the maintained sector. (See also 4 below.)

*Survey the financial practices of LEAs, and recommend and publicize good practice*

The machinery for doing this already exists - surveys by HM Inspectorate, circulars from and returns to the DES. It could be done easily and cheaply, and would bring quick benefits.

*Overhaul Schools' Regulations*

It has already been suggested that a reform of these is well overdue. Schools' Regulations should be thoroughly reviewed to allow institutions the greatest flexibility of action. Particular areas for change are the regulations relating to school year and school day referred to in Chapter 12, and also the unnecessary difficulties created by the distinction between Schools' and Further Education Regulations.

*Explore modular courses*

The DES should explore the possibility of creating a modular structure to the secondary-school curriculum as envisaged in Chapter 12. This would obviously need to be related to the present study of the curriculum and of the examination system.

*Examine the four-term year*

There has been desultory discussion of the four-term year on previous occasions, but never a really searching review. The apparent advantages of the system in terms of efficiency in the education service requires that this should be taken seriously.

## 2 Action by the Schools Council - and its successors

*Acknowledge that school costs and school finance are a proper and important area for development* (surprisingly they are largely ignored in the Schools Council Programme One-Purpose and Planning in Schools).

*Sponsor studies and investigations within LEAs and disseminate findings.* Suitable areas could be:

Development of financial management skills for heads, bursars and senior staff
Role of the school governors in school financial management
Good and bad practice
Possibilities for financial devolution to schools and local financial autonomy.

## *3 Action by colleges and schools of education and departments of educational management*

*Encourage research into educational costs and finance*
The present situation is bedevilled by the fact that there is very little research, a scanty published literature, and no respectable theoretical framework. Research in these areas has been very thin indeed. A trickle of research theses is now beginning to appear from educational administrators on diploma courses. Assignments from teachers in this area are very few. I would hope that this book would at least provide some spur and assistance to researchers in a very neglected field. Particularly promising areas would be: functional unit costs; costs of individual schools, particularly primary schools; financial practices operated by the LEAs; financial practices operated by schools; output measurements; programme budgeting; and the use of school time. But there are many many others. There is also a need for academic centres to establish library sections on school finance. Not only is the present literature very thin, it is also hard to come by. The contrast with the USA is unfavourable, where there exists the American Education Finance Association, the *Journal of Education Finance* and the *Economics and Education Review*.

There is also need for the establishment of a sound theoretical framework. Chapter 1 indicated that there is no consensus at present on the use of elementary terms in school finance such as prime and subsidiary costs, fixed and variable costs; the handling of debt charges; the way in which costs are classified; the virtues and vices of full cost accounting. It is, however, essential that such theory is closely related to the actual situation and needs of schools and LEAs.

*Provide courses on the management of school finance*
At present these are virtually non-existent. Once some of the theoretical work has been done, there is no reason why short courses on educational finance should not develop in the way that educational management courses have grown. However, it will be important that the membership of such courses remain balanced. The ideal mix would be drawn from treasurers, educational admin-

istrators, advisers, heads, bursars, and heads of departments. It is through their interaction that ideas will develop and attitudes change.

*Include educational finance within courses on educational management*
At present, most prospectuses of educational management courses totally or almost totally ignore mention of school costs. Rectification is long overdue.

## *4 Action by LEAs as a group and/or by CIPFA*

*Improve national statistics*
The present CIPFA statistics are often criticized but they are certainly the best we have. They are also improving every year. This process needs to continue. In particular more detailed information would be useful. The more headings under which the data can be broken down, the easier it is for authorities to compare their performance with others. However, this can only be done if the categories are very clearly described, so that the statistics are genuinely comparable. Recent cuts for financial reasons in published education statistics by the DES look likely to be counter productive.

*Create a standard analyis for school costs*
At present each LEA analyses its costs slightly differently, and so comparisons of school costs across borders are difficult, particularly in relation to detailed costs. Moreover there is no general agreement on how an analysis of a school's costs should be set out, and what should be included or excluded. CIPFA has already produced a manual of guidance on a Financial Information System for institutions of higher and further education, and a counterpart is clearly needed for secondary schools. This is becoming particularly urgent with the growth of LEA computerized financial information systems.

Naturally I would hope that any standard analysis would contain many of the features for which I have argued and which are shown in the analysis in Chapter 2. In particular I would stress the importance of a 'full cost' analysis as discussed at the beginning of Chapter 2 and of the inclusion of debt charges. It will be essential that any standard analysis is closely related to possible use at school as well as at LEA level.

*Produce a reputable school price index*
The reasons for a good national index have already been clearly stated, and it will be necessary for CIPFA or LEAs as a whole to produce this if the DES does not take it on as suggested above.

*Improve exchanges of information*
There does not seem to be the flourishing LEA information network on financial practices that exists on say, the curriculum or educational practices. It is therefore of high priority that this should be built up through conferences, courses, working parties, and journals.

## 5 Action by individual LEAs

*Improve comparative financial information*
LEAs already produce detailed financial information for their own budgets, but these are produced on a line item basis, and are compacted for the sake of simplicity. For comparisons, however, detail is needed. The more these aggregated headings can be broken down into sub-items, the easier comparison becomes. For example, separating supply teachers' salaries from establishment teachers' salaries immediately produces useful cost information. The cost audit form given in Appendix C indicates some of these sub-items. Many LEAs could make a useful start by publishing information which is already used internally within their department but is not known to schools or outsiders. A good example has been the information on reapportionment of community education costs in Leicestershire quoted on page 65.

*Improve financial practices*
Chapter 8 listed a range of good practice which ought to be automatic in all authorities: such items as schools being able to carry capitation balances forward; easy virement; non-compartmented allowances; direct crediting of income; freedom to order when and where schools like; bank accounts. Yet many medieval practices persist. Each LEA should review its own practice with an open mind. Perhaps LEAs should also introduce more training in accountancy principles for education staff.

*Encourage cost reduction*
Despite the economies of recent years there is still scope for a reduction in costs if this is thought out systematically. So, a systematic campaign at all levels in the education service, along the line of the CIPFA suggestions discussed in Chapter 10, will still be of benefit. In particular, there should be dissemination of good housekeeping practices and introduction of fuel economy schemes which give schools financial incentives.

*Establish schools as local cost centres*
The sequence suggested in Chapter 9 would benefit all authorities and could be adopted step by step when the time is appropriate.

(a) Annual cost print-outs
(b) Annual cost audits
(c) Cost comparisons
(d) Devolvement of select budget headings to schools
(e) Cost reapportionment of central costs to the users.

*Establish financial flexibility for the future*

(a) Autonomous school budgets. Obviously, these will not come overnight, but the need for them needs to be accepted and pilot schemes established.
(b) Recharging. This follows quite naturally out of the 'full cost' accounting approach to cost analysis. Again it should be introduced on a limited basis, and gradually extended.
(c) Other aspects such as possible sources of additional finance, the introduction of mini-vouchers and the decentralization of accounting systems all need to be explored.
(d) Encouragement of experiments in the better use of school time. Once the DES Regulations have been overhauled, LEAs should change their own to allow much more flexibility in the number of days in the school year and the length and pattern of school days to suit local conditions, providing of course that the total quantity of education remains the same as at present.

## *6 Action by schools*

*Take school costs seriously*
Schools need to understand how their total costs are made up. Only then can they control and manage them. The era when 'theirs was not to reason why' is fast receding. This means that heads and senior staff will have to take their cost structure as seriously as their timetable structure. Initially this will need personal research and training in new skills.

*Improve management of capitation*
Some schools need to review their system for allocating capitation, and possibly move towards a formula. Schools which carry forward large balances should immediately check the practice. The idea of a five-yearly extended resources review should be considered.

*Extend good housekeeping practices*
Practices such as fuel economy, care with stationery and cleaning materials, etc., careful checking of inventories, reducing wear and tear – all these matter. Whenever possible schools should claim a share in the saving.

*Encourage the spread of the autonomous budget approach*
Far-sighted heads will see the ultimate advantage of this, and also the safeguards as long as any scheme is of a pilot character and the ability to revert to the original scheme is still retained.

*Explore more flexible use of time*
There are a thousand and one possible variations on the school day. Schools should be adventurous in looking at variations, and particularly those which offer more timetable flexibility – an alternative to seat-time.

And what about you, gentle reader? What action will you take? Will you close this book and just say 'Interesting . . .' – that most damning of English put-downs. Or will you actually *do* something to make our use of school finance more effective? Because, if you do not, your time in reading this book and mine in writing it will have been quite wasted.

# Appendix A

## *Basis for some figures in Table 2:1**

| | | |
|---|---|---|
| A: | Holyrood pupils 11 to 18, September 1979 | 1,088 |
| B: | Somerset school pupils 11 to 18, September 1979 | 32,876 |
| C: | Somerset secondary schools net expenditure, 1979 excluding:<br>(12) payments to other local education authorities<br>(13) fees for non-maintained schools<br>(14) recharges, libraries and museums<br>(19) debt charges<br>(20) revenue contributions to capital outlay | £17,160,240 |
| D: | Somerset primary school net expenditure, excluding items as in C | £13,178,100 |
| E: | Total LEA expenditure | £62,669,540 |
| F: | Somerset further education colleges net expenditure, less debt charges and RCCO | £5,433,471 |

(a) Administration and inspection net expenditure $\times \frac{A}{B} \times \frac{C}{E}$

(b) Recharge to secondary schools for libraries and museums $\times \frac{A}{B}$

(c) County centres little used because of school's own centre

(d) Educational Psychological Service net expenditure $\times \frac{A}{B} \times \frac{1}{3}$ (Psychological Service estimate for its secondary services)

(e) Careers Advisory Service, net expenditure $\times \frac{A}{B} \times \frac{C}{C+F}$

(f) Resources and Education Centres and INSET expenditure $\times \frac{A}{B} \times \frac{C}{C+D}$

* *Source:* Chairman's Sub-committee, Somerset Education and Community Services Committee, Estimates 1979/80 (actual expenditures).

(g) Secondary school debt charges and RCCO $\times \dfrac{\text{Holyrood rates}}{\text{Somerset secondary school rates}}$

(h) Guestimate of community education administrative costs

(i) Estimate of percentage of services of social worker (schools) supplied by Social Services Department, not recharged, with on-costs and support costs.

(j) Budget for teacher vacancies $\times \dfrac{A}{B} \times \dfrac{1}{2}$ (estimated secondary share)

(k) Recharge of administration $\times \dfrac{A}{B} \times \dfrac{1}{2}$ (secondary share of meals)

(l) Recharge of administration $\times \dfrac{A}{B} \times \dfrac{C}{C + D + F}$

(m) Employees, recharge for highways, and RCCO $\times \dfrac{A}{B} \times \dfrac{C}{C + D}$

(n) Total grants $\times \dfrac{A}{B}$

(p) Guestimate

This basis for reapportionment is somewhat crude, and undoubtedly could be improved by research.

# Appendix B

## *Weighting for sixth-form students*

Since teachers' salaries are such a large element and since sixth forms are more generously staffed and count more heavily towards unit totals, there is clearly an argument for weighting unit costs for sixth-formers. Otherwise a school with a sixth form will have higher average per pupil costs, so making it difficult to compare the costs for its main school pupils with other schools. Hough (1981) discussed this at length (pages 126–8) and suggested that an overall weighting of 1·6:1 is appropriate for sixth form: main school pupils, reflecting the calculation of the rate support grant. Currently, however, grant assessment for Grant Related Expenditure treats pupils over 16 as 1·77 more costly than those under 16.

The effect of Hough's weighting can be seen dramatically in my Table 3:4, which compares the costs of one independent and one maintained school. As the former had a large sixth form, 32 per cent of its total roll, and the latter a relatively small one, only 8 per cent, the distortion from sixth-form pupils is quite considerable. So, overall unit costs per pupil alter as follows:

| | Unweighted | Weighted |
|---|---|---|
| Independent school | £864·5 | £726·4 |
| Maintained school | £800·5 | £763·9 |

However, the issue is complicated. If we look at the unit costs for particular items, the weighting as used in Table 3:4 may not be appropriate. Obviously sixth-formers increase the average per pupil cost of teachers' salaries. They are solely responsible for maintenance allowances, considerably increase examination expenditure, and partially increase capitation. However, they decrease the average pupil cost of meals, free meals and uniform grants (younger pupils tend to be more keen on school meals, more compelled to wear uniform). Their effect on other items is small or difficult to gauge.

In practice, too, the effect of sixth-formers is not often dramatic. In Hough's Table 6:2, for example, total costs per pupil for sub-groups of schools were altered by weighting, but not so that the general picture was significantly different. The effect was rather to soften the extremes. In Table 3:4 the actual effect of the weighting is to reduce the unweighted costs per pupil by 16 per cent for the independent school and 5 per cent for the maintained school.

Finally, the unweighted costs that schools incur are their real costs and should not be lost sight of. Perhaps the best answer is to use unweighted costs, as in Table 2:1, but to insert as additions weighted per pupil costs for five items only: teachers' salaries, capitation expenditure, examination expenses, total assistance to pupils and total costs.

# Appendix C

## *A possible form for a school cost audit*

........................................................................ School    ANNUAL COST AUDIT: Financial Year 19........–19........

| | *THE CURRENT YEAR* | | | | *CHANGE SINCE LAST YEAR* | |
|---|---|---|---|---|---|---|
| | *This school net cost* | *This school % of total costs* | *This school cost per pupil* | *Cost per pupil, average of similar schools* | *% +/– this school per pupil* | *% +/– average of similar schools per pupil* |
| 1 LEA SERVICES NOT REALLOCATED IN OTHER SECTIONS BELOW | | | | | | |
| This school's appropriate proportion of: | | | | | | |
| A 1·1 Administrative and advisory services | | | | | | |
| A 1·2 Training of teachers (centres, courses, etc.) | | | | | | |
| A 1·3 Careers Advisory Service | | | | | | |
| A 1·4 Educational Psychological Service | | | | | | |
| A 1·5 Residential centres | | | | | | |
| A 1·6 Educational Museum Service | | | | | | |
| A 1·7 County Library (recharge) | | | | | | |
| 1·8 Total LEA Services | | | | | | |
| 2 TOTAL DEBT CHARGES (notional) | | | | | | |

| | *THE CURRENT YEAR* | | | | *CHANGE SINCE LAST YEAR* | |
|---|---|---|---|---|---|---|
| | *This school net cost* | *This school % of total costs* | *This school cost per pupil* | *Cost per pupil, average of similar schools* | *% +/− this school per pupil* | *% +/− average of similar schools per pupil* |
| 3 TEACHING COSTS | | | | | | |
| 3·1 Salaries, teaching establishment, with employers' contributions | | | * | * | | |
| 3·2 Salaries, supply teachers, with employers' contributions | | | | | | |
| 3·3 Interview expenses, teachers | | | * | * | | |
| 3·4 Advertisement expenses, teachers | | | * | * | | |
| 3·5 Non-teaching salaries and on-costs (all non-teaching, excluding caretaking and cleaning, grounds, meals and transport) | | | | | | |
| 3·6 Expenditure from capitation on books, stationery, equipment and materials, and from other county allowances (replacement of equipment, curriculum development, other special grants for equipment, materials, books, stationery, etc.) and virement into capitation: | | | | | | |
| (a) gross | | | | | | |
| deduct (b) income received from sales of materials | | | | | | |
| deduct (c) ditto payments for visits etc. | | | | | | |
| deduct (d) ditto to avoid VAT | | | | | | |
| deduct (e) ditto from virement | | | | | | |
| deduct (f) payments made for self-help redecorations and improvements (see 4·3(b)) | | | | | | |
| deduct (g) payments made for swimming-pool | | | | | | |
| deduct (h) all other income, excluding earmarked LEA grants | | | | | | |
| (i) net expenditure (take deductions (b-h) from (a)) | | | * | * | | |

3·7 Examination fees
(a) GCE A Level
(b) GCE O and CSE
(c) others
(d) total fees
Less (e) fees collected
= (f) net cost
3·8 Linked courses: transport
3·9 Postage
3·10 Telephone rental
ditto charges
3·11 Travelling expenses, INSET
3·12 ditto other
3·13 TOTAL, Teaching costs, net

4 PREMISES
4·1 Caretaking and cleaning salaries and employers' contributions (excluding payments for community education)
4·2 Maintenance to premises:
Area Building Surveyor and School
4·3 Maintenance, school
(a) Electric light bulbs and tubes
(b) Self-help activities
4·4 Heating and lighting:
(a) electricity
(b) oil
(c) gas
(d) solid fuel
(e) total heat and light
4·5 Water
4·6 Cleaning materials
4·7 Cleaning equipment
4·8 Protective clothing
4·9 Rates
4·10 TOTAL, Premises

| | | *THE CURRENT YEAR* | | | | *CHANGE SINCE LAST YEAR* | |
|---|---|---|---|---|---|---|---|
| | | *This school net cost* | *This school % of total costs* | *This school cost per pupil* | *Cost per pupil, average of similar schools* | *% +/– this school per pupil* | *% +/– average of similar schools per pupil* |
| | 5 GROUNDS | | | | | | |
| | 5·1 School groundsmen's salaries and employers' contributions | | | | | | |
| | 5·2 Expenditure made by school (fuel, materials, repairs, etc.) | | | | | | |
| | 5·3 County grounds services: | | | | | | |
| A | (a) appropriate proportion of group scheme | | | | | | |
| A | (b) appropriate proportion of county repairs to equipment | | | | | | |
| | (c) county supplied materials | | | | | | |
| | (d) county maintenance of fences, paths, etc. | | | | | | |
| | 5·4 Swimming-pool costs: | | | | | | |
| | (a) school pool | | | | | | |
| | (b) visiting other pools | | | | | | |
| | 5·5 TOTAL, Grounds | | | | | | |
| | 6 ASSISTANCE TO PUPILS | | | | | | |
| | 6·1 Uniform grants | | | | | | |
| | 6·2 Maintenance grants | | | * | * | | |
| | 6·3 Free meals (........meals × ........p) | | | | | | |
| | 6·4 TOTAL, Assistance to pupils | | | * | * | | |

7 SCHOOL MEALS

7·1 Food

7·2 Salaries and employers' contributions

7·3 Maintenance and repair of equipment

7·4 Cleaning equipment and materials

7·5 Protective clothing

A 7·6 County administration appropriate share

7·7 Free meals to teachers, supervisors, other staff

7·8 Summary

(a) total gross cost 7·1–7·6 above

less (b) income received

less (c) income lost for free meals to pupils, 6·3 above

less (d) income lost for adult free meals 7·7 above

= (e) Total net cost of meals for paying pupils

7·9 TOTAL, school meals, net costs (7·7 + 7·8e)

8 SCHOOL TRANSPORT

8·1 Coaches: daily costs of each route to be attached (appropriate proportion if shared with other schools)

8·2 County vehicles, full estimated cost

8·3 Season tickets

8·4 Salaries, transport (e.g. supervision)

8·5 County administration, recharge from county surveyor, appropriate proportion

8·6 TOTAL, transport costs

9 TOTAL SCHOOL COSTS (sum of totals above)

| | *THE CURRENT YEAR* | | | | *CHANGE SINCE LAST YEAR* | |
|---|---|---|---|---|---|---|
| | *This school net cost* | *This school % of total costs* | *This school cost per pupil* | *Cost per pupil, average of similar schools* | *% +/− this school per pupil* | *% +/− average of similar schools per pupil* |
| 10 COMMUNITY EDUCATION AND USE | | | | | | |
| 10·1 Community or similar tutor salaries with employers' contributions | | | | | | |
| 10·2 Caretaking, supervisory and cleaning salaries: with employers' contributions | | | | | | |
| 10·3 Clerical salaries: with employers' contributions | | | | | | |
| 10·4 Equipment and materials | | | | | | |
| 10·5 Postage | | | | | | |
| 10·6 Publicity and printing | | | | | | |
| 10·7 Telephone | | | | | | |
| 10·8 Electricity – estimated cost | | | | | | |
| 10·9 Oil/gas/solid fuel – estimated cost | | | | | | |
| 10·10 Other | | | | | | |
| Summary: | | | | | | |
| (a) total gross cost, 10·1–10.9 above | | | | | | |
| less (b) fees | | | | | | |
| less (c) letting charges | | | | | | |
| less (d) other income | | | | | | |
| = (e) total net cost | | | | | | |

*Note:* A = School's 'appropriate' share of LEA costs – to be supplied by LEA
* Each sixth-form pupil should be weighted as 1·6 main school pupil

# Select Bibliography

## *Bibliographies*

J. R. Hough in *A Study of School Costs* (NFER-Nelson, Windsor, 1981) makes a most useful survey (Chapter 2) of the existing literature on school costs, both English and North American. He summarizes some of the important arguments of the main studies. He also gives a full bibliography.

M. Blaug (ed.), *Economics of Education, an Annotated Bibliography* 3rd edn., (Pergamon, Oxford, 1979) provides a standard bibliography.

## *General works on costing and school costs*

P. H. Coombs and J. Hallak, *Managing Educational Costs* (Oxford University Press, New York, 1972) is a good book to begin with. It takes a 'systems', cost-benefit approach, and exposes some key principles in a broad context. It draws widely on UNESCO experience (much of the overseas detail can be skipped). It is readable, but does not deal with the details of financial management.

R. A. Anthony and R. E. Herzlinger, *Management Control in Non-profit-making Organizations* (Richard Irwin, Illinois, 1975). This provides a very comprehensive review of the problems of accounting in such organizations. It is a little dull, and is based on US experience, but it is very thorough and balanced.

C. T. Horngren, *Cost Accounting: a Managerial Emphasis* (Prentice-Hall International, Englewood Cliffs, NJ, 4th edn., 1977). A good standard work. Clear and detailed exposition of the main current theory and practice. Geared to commercial organizations, but much of it relevant to schools. The detailed synopsis helps selection of chapters.

J. Fielden, 'Educational costing for troubled times', Proceedings of the Eighth Annual Conference of the British Educational Administration Society (Sheffield City Polytechnic Department of Educational Management, 1980a). A short, lucid paper on the value of costing in education, with some useful check-list questions for planning any cost exercise. Good for sceptics and initiates.

C. E. Cumming, *Studies in Educational Costs* (Scottish Academic Press, Edinburgh, 1971). The pioneering work in school costs. If only it had been taken up seriously ten years ago! The statistics are now a little dated, and the Scottish background creates some difficulties - but it is still an essential starting-point.

J. R. Hough, *A Study of School Costs*, is a thorough and scholarly examination of mainly secondary-school costs in four LEAs. Again, indispensable.

## References


Anthony, R. A. and Herzlinger R. E. *Management Control in Non-profit-making Organizations*. Richard Irwin, Illinois, 1975. See above.

Arthur Young McClelland Moores & Co. 'Costing educational provision for the 16-19 age group'. HMSO, 1982. But see criticism by P. Newsam in the *Guardian*, 2 March 1982.

Atkinson, B. and Butel J. H. 'Counting costs in LEAs', *Education* (6 November 1981).

Bartman, N. and Carden T: 'Falling rolls and building costs', *Education* (16 October 1981).

Briault, E. and Smith F. *Falling Rolls in Secondary Schools*, Part 1. NFER Publishing, Windsor, 1980.

Byrne, E. *Planning and Educational Inequality.* NFER Publishing, Windsor, 1974.

Byrne, E., Williamson, B. and Fletcher B. *The Poverty of Education*. Martin Robertson, Oxford, 1975.

Cambridgeshire. *Local financial management: a pilot scheme*, 1982.

Chartered Institute of Public Finance and Accountancy. *Education Statistics (Actuals)* and *Education Estimates Statistics*. CIPFA, annually.

*Cost Reduction in Public Authorities*. CIPFA, 1979.

*Financial Information System for Institutions of Higher and Further Education in the Maintained Sector: Manual of Guidance*. CIPFA, 1980.

Coles, O. B. 'Cost and access implications of rural primary school provision', *Educational Research*, vol. 23, no. 1 (November 1980).

Coombs, P. H. and Hallak, J. *Managing Educational Costs*. Oxford University Press, New York, 1972. See above.

Council for Educational Technology. *Microelectronics: Their Implications for Education and Training.* CET, 1978.

*Report of the National Development Programme in Computer Assisted Learning*. CET, 1977.

Coutts, I. 'Cuts and costs', *County Councils' Gazette* (September 1979).

Cumming, C. E. *Studies in Educational Costs* Scottish Academic Press, Edinburgh, 1971. See above.

Day, B. E. 'How capitation allowances can keep pace with inflation', *Education* (25 September 1981).

Department of Education and Science. *Report of the Working Party on Teachers and the Schools Meals Service*. DES, 1968.

*Teacher Education and Training*. James Report. HMSO, 1972.

*Primary Education in England.* A Survey by HM Inspector of Schools. HMSO, 1978.

*Aspects of Secondary Education in England.* A Survey by HM Inspectors of Schools. HMSO, 1979.

*Education for 16-19 year olds*. MacFarlane Report, DES, 1980.

*Education Statistics for the United Kingdom*. HMSO, annually.

*Handbook of Unit Costs*. DES, annually.

Educational Publishers Council. 'Guide to Schoolbook Spending in the Home Counties', 1980.
Fielden, J. 'Educational costing for troubled times'. Proceedings of the Eighth Annual Conference of the British Education Administration Society, Sheffield City Polytechnic, 1980a. See above.
'How costing helps the slimming pill go down', *Education* (20 June 1980b).
Fielden, J. and Pearson, P. K. *Costing Educational Practice*. Council for Educational Technology, 1978.
Furno, O., Collins, G. and Brain G. *Planning Programming Budgeting Systems*. 1972.
Glennerster, H. and Wilson, G. *Paying for Private Schools*. Allen Lane, 1970.
Harling, Paul. 'Effective Resource Managment in Primary Schools' *Educational Administration 9/3*. BEMAS, Spring 1981.
Hinds, T. M. 'The rising costs of falling rolls'. Proceedings of the Eighth Annual Conference of the British Educational Administration Society, Sheffield City Polytechnic, 1980.
Horngren, C. T. *Cost Accounting: a Managerial Emphasis*. Prentice-Hall International, Englewood Cliffs, NJ, 4th edn., 1977. See above.
Hough, J. R. *A Study of School Costs*. NFER-Nelson, Windsor, 1981. See above.
Howick, C. with Hassani, H. 'Education spending: primary', *Centre for Environmental Studies Review*, no. 5 (1979).
Howick, C. with Hassani, H. 'Education spending: secondary', *Centre for Environmental Studies Review*, no. 8 (1980).
Inner London Education Authority. 'Allocation of Resources and the Alternative Use of Resources (AUR) scheme', 1980/81.
Ilett, K. G. 'The cost of selected secondary schools in Walsall'. M.Ed. dissertation, University of Manchester, 1981. Unpublished.
Kalton, G. *The Public Schools: a Factual Survey*. Longman, 1966.
Kent County Council. *Education Vouchers in Kent – a feasibility study*. Kent County Council Education Department, 1978. Library edition contains technical report, including finance and costs.
Knight, B. A. A. *The Cost of Running a School*. Scottish Centre for Studies in School Administration, 1977.
LAFIS Project. *A Guide to LAFIS*. Obtainable from ICL, Computer House, 322 Euston Road, London NW1 3BD.
National Union of Teachers. *CIPFA 1980/81 Unit Cost Estimates*. NUT Research Unit, 1980.
*Pupil–Teacher Ratios (January 1980)*. NUT Research Unit, 1980.
*A Guide to the Rate Support Grant, 1981/82*. NUT Research Unit, 1981.
Neuman, J. L. 'Making overhead cuts that last', *Harvard Business Review* (1975).
OECD. *Educational Financing and Policy Goals for Primary Schools – General Report*. OECD, 1979. There are also country reports, in three volumes.
Pearson, P. K. *Costs of Education in the United Kingdom*. Council for Educational Technology, 1977.
Plowden Committee. Report on Primary Education. HMSO, 1967.
Research Corporation of the Association of School Business Officials of US and Canada. *Planning Programming Budgeting Evaluation Systems Handbook*. Research Corporation of the Association of School Business Officials, 1974.

Roberts, J. K. 'Secondary school costs'. MBA dissertation, 1980. Unpublished. Copies held in Brunel University Library and at the Administrative Staff College, Henley-on-Thames.

Rutter, M., et al. *Fifteen Thousand Hours*. Open Books, 1979.

Secondary Heads Association. *Big and Beautiful*. SHA, 1979.

Thomas, H. R. 'Cost-effectiveness analysis as a method of monitoring A-level performances within institutions'. *Educational Administration 9/2*. BEMAS, May 1981.

Vaizey, J. and Sheahan, J. *Resources for Education*. Allen & Unwin, 1968.

## *Addendum*

Readers should note that there is a growing US literature relating to school finance, particularly in *Economics of Education Review* and the *Journal of Education Finance*. There are also a number of publications from specialist agencies such as:

Institute for Research on Educational Finance and Governance, Stanford University, California.

Education Finance Center, Education Commission of the States, 1860 Lincoln Street, Denver, Colorado.

Center for the Study of Educational Finance, Department of Educational Adminstration, College of Education, Illinois State University, Normal, Illinois.

# Index